LEADING FROM WITHIN

A Guide To Maximizing
Your Effectiveness
Through Meditation

By
Steven M. Cohen

Published by Meditation4Leadership 2019

ISBN: 978-0-9996337-0-0

Library of Congress Control Number: 2019904948

Printed in the United States by BookBaby.

Book jacket design by Julie Forlepa.

Illustrations by Dawn Vernon.

Logo designed by Melissa Epstein.

TABLE OF CONTENTS

I. WHY CONSIDER MEDITATION

We are in the midst of a turning point in human history. The Information Age has shifted the focus of business and society from production to knowledge.[1] As with every meaningful change we face, this one offers both challenges and opportunities. Every decision we make, in life and in business, is impacted by the onslaught of information now available with a simple touch of a finger on a computer or cell phone. Our effectiveness is based in large part on how we process and utilize this wealth of information. How do we sort through that abundance of information so that we can most successfully navigate challenges while leveraging all possible opportunities?

The answer may be internal rather than external. Yes, a wealth of data and advice is available to us from many sources, including books, media, and the Internet. The ability to process information requires an understanding of a critical difference: the difference between factual knowledge and wisdom. Wisdom is described differently across cultures, religions and societies, but no matter how we characterize this type of insight and perspective, there is growing empirical evidence that greater access to this wisdom directly translates to improved workplace performance.[2] How can we access and use this wisdom to lead our lives more successfully and lead others more effectively?

We each have so much potential. So many of the organizations in which we work or volunteer have the potential to make a greater impact than they do. Leadership is the process of maximizing your impact and the impact of others to achieve a mission. We can all be leaders.

The primary culprit holding us back from achieving our optimal performance is usually ourselves. Too often, we miss opportunities right in front of us because we are not sufficiently aware. Too often, our reaction to a person or situation is impacted by our prior personal history. Too often, we view an event, situation, or opportunity through a distorted lens, leading us to an emotion-based reaction that is ineffective or insufficient. Too often, we create physical and emotional stress for ourselves based upon this distorted view. This self-imposed stress inhibits our health, our joy and our effectiveness. Too often, our fears hold us back from taking the actions necessary to achieve our goals. We disconnect rather than stay connected to the situation and the people that can best assist us.

How can you avoid becoming your own worst enemy by being more aware and, in the process, improve your focus, creativity and perspective, reducing stress, addressing your fears, enhancing your relationships, and increasing your interpersonal and intra-personal effectiveness? How can your personal growth facilitate meaningful change in the organizations in which you work and volunteer?

Millions of people around the globe have discovered that the answer to these questions is the same: meditation. At its core, meditation is a practice that assists us in being more "present," more aware in each moment of what is going on around us and inside us. This awareness facilitates our ability to make better decisions, take better actions and be happier doing so. Meditation practices are centuries-old and incorporated into every religion and culture, sometimes simply as a "moment of silence." More recently, the benefits of meditation have been studied and supported by leading neurologists who have demonstrated that regular meditation practice actually changes brain structure, verifying scientifically-reported cognitive and psychological benefits that go beyond just relaxation.[3] All it takes to realize these benefits is for you to learn which techniques work best for you, and 10 minutes a day of practice.

The insight and perspective that comes from a daily meditation practice can help you become a better leader, in whatever way pertains to your life—as a leader of a business, a community organization, a work team, a household, or as a leader of your own personal growth. An examination of the top leaders and leadership theories developed over the last five decades highlights the critical importance of contemplative qualities that can be developed or enhanced through practice.

This book presents 13 personal traits that are central to effective leadership. Each chapter explains the importance of a leadership trait; describes how that quality is emphasized in leadership theory and practice by a renowned organizational leader, management professor or author; and offers meditative techniques and guided meditations that will help you access and develop that trait and apply it to the organizations in which you have a leadership role.

The 13 traits are integrated into Four Pillars, Awareness, Connection, Perspective and Potential, each of which is enhanced by meditation practice to provide a foundation for increasing effectiveness. These pillars can ground us as we proceed through our lifelong journey. When we stray or fail or feel lost, we can sense which of these pillars requires reinforcement and set our intention during meditation practice to focus on that pillar. What we practice in our meditation impacts how we live our life.

This book offers you the tools to develop your own meditation practice based upon which types of meditation and preparatory contemplative techniques work best for you at this time. At the same time, this book profiles lessons from recognized leaders and leadership authors to assist you in better recognizing the traits where you are strong and those where there is opportunity for growth using a different technique. Hopefully, your experience will help you appreciate the value that regular meditation practice can have on your health, your relationships, and your effectiveness as you practice and integrate the wisdom you gain from your meditation practice into your life.

What Can a Daily Meditation Practice Do for You?

The various meditation practices profiled in this book were chosen to facilitate your ability to:

- become more aware and perceive things closer to how they really are
- access your capacity for creativity, insight and wisdom by quieting the everyday chatter inside your head
- diffuse stress and experience more moments of calm, balance and joy
- connect to your emotions and embrace your feelings, reducing the impact of suppressed feelings in future situations
- expand your sense of who you are, beyond fears and self-judgment, by helping you recognize these fears and judgments
- learn how to respond effectively instead of react emotionally
- broaden your perspective and facilitate problem-solving after considering issues from different viewpoints
- apply the focused effort, perseverance and resilience lessons from your ongoing meditation practice to all aspects of your life
- increase your performance to make a greater positive impact on the organizations where you work and volunteer
- transform your world view from one of isolation and chaos to one of connection, clarity and potential

Explore what daily meditation can do for you.

Meditation and Science: Proof of Positive Impact

Sometimes an idea we know to be true comes to us, but it takes a while to be able to demonstrate objectively the same result scientifically. Science is now catching up to what centuries of meditators have experienced. In

1999, the National Institutes of Health created the National Center for Complementary and Integrative Health to further evidence-based study of meditation and other complementary health practices. More information about meditation and access to evidence-based publications is available at https://nccih.nih.gov/health/meditation.

The positive outcomes of meditation and other mindfulness practices have been documented with increasing frequency in the scientific literature over the past few decades. A December 2018 search of the National Library of Medicine database of scientific articles using the term "meditation" yielded a total of more than 5,000 articles published between 1950 and 2018 (www.pubmed.gov). Some examples of study findings are presented below.

An analysis combining the results of 115 studies that involved 8,683 individuals with various conditions found that, compared to treatment as usual, meditation and mindfulness practices were associated with moderate or significant improvements in a wide variety of medical issues. The conditions included depression, anxiety, stress, and physical functioning, as well as patient reports of quality of life.[4] *Scientific American* published an article entitled "Mind of the Meditator,"[5] noting the effects that three common types of meditation (focused attention, mindfulness and lovingkindness) have on the brain. According to *Scientific American*, research results from 47 clinical trials with 3,515 participants have found that people who practice meditation have quicker reactions to stimuli and are less likely to fall victim to different types of stress. Stress produces the worst symptoms where your body is most vulnerable. Mindfulness meditation, in particular, was shown to help people suffering from anxiety or depression and to promote healthier sleep patterns. Still other recent scientific studies show that meditation and/or mindfulness-based interventions lead to measurable improvements in depression,[6, 7] depression and anxiety in patients with chronic pain,[8] stress,[9] high blood pressure,[10,11] heart failure,[12] insomnia,[13] memory and mild cognitive impairment in people at risk for Alzheimer's disease,[14] pain and quality of life in patients with chronic low back pain,[15] menopausal symptoms[16] and mental health[17] in breast cancer survivors, symptoms of borderline personality disorder,[18] symptoms of psychosis/schizophrenia,[19 20] consumption and craving in individuals with substance use disorders,[21] and binge eating.[22]

A study investigating the effect of meditation on the aging process showed that long-term meditators have significantly younger brain aging compared to the control group.[23] This may be due to evidence that focus and concentration meditations stimulate growth in neural structures and promote increased connectivity and efficiency within neural networks or simply due to the benefits of lower chronic stress.[24] Other studies have shown a cumulative reduction in physician payments of over 25% in meditators with chronic illness versus non-meditators.[25]

You may even be able to grow more tissue in essential areas of the brain through practicing meditation. The affected areas are partially responsible for functions such as attention, processing sensory information, and internal bodily sensations.[26] If your inner voice is telling you that you simply do not have time to grow brain tissue, then it might be comforting for you to know that several studies indicate that changes associated with meditation can be seen in the brain in just a matter of weeks.[27] Some of these studies have been criticized for their lack of sound scientific method, but the weight of the scientific conclusions regarding the benefits of a daily meditation practice are overwhelming. More research is needed and is being performed every day.

The way I think about it, meditation is for your mind similar to how physical exercise is for your body. In physical exercise, you do not tell your muscles to get stronger, but your muscles are strengthened automatically by the activity. Similarly, meditation practice results automatically in the benefits further described in this book. You don't have to fully understand why. You can simply practice and experience it for yourself.

Some Thoughts on Meditation

Experienced . . . or Not

Are you new to meditation, or have you tried it "unsuccessfully" in the past? Many times, we are deterred from learning something new by the language used or the teaching setting. This is definitely the case for many people who try to learn about meditation. Traditionally, meditation has been taught in religious settings, yoga studios, and spiritual retreat centers, generally using the language of that setting. In contrast, this book integrates the language of business and leadership (much of which is universal across cultures) with various meditative practices in order to make these practices more accessible to people who are comfortable with that language.

Alternatively, have you practiced meditation for many years? If so, and if you learned meditation practice in a religious setting or yoga studio or elsewhere, you may have only been taught "quiet mind" objectless meditation or meditation through prayer (which is valuable spiritually). This book can help you identify additional techniques and a "practical" application for the lessons from the meditation techniques you already practice. Furthermore, by expanding your practice and integrating it with your daily experiences, your meditation practice can become more meaningful and help you become more successful and effective, both personally and professionally.

Your Way is the Right Way

A critical point to keep in mind—particularly if learning meditation practice makes you nervous or uncomfortable—is that there is no right or wrong way to meditate. Meditation is not about sitting cross-legged in the traditional lotus position for hours; rather, meditation allows for a wide variety of different techniques and positions you can easily integrate into your daily life, even if only for 10 minutes per day. While some people practice one meditation technique exclusively, others prefer variety. Different techniques work differently for different people at different times in their lives, depending upon their needs at that moment. For example, some people who want to improve the effectiveness of their relationships may achieve success through a lovingkindness practice, while others limited by inner turmoil may be released by an emotional mindfulness or a gratitude practice; still others may find that the traditional silent mind-focused practice helps them achieve higher levels of consciousness and wisdom that positively impact their perspective. The point is that benefits from meditation arise from 1% theory and 99% practice.[28] This book will help you learn the 1% theory and expose you to approximately 50 different meditation practice variations. The rest is up to you.

You Can Do It

Many people find the biggest resistance to meditation is their mind telling them, "I can't meditate." Meditation is a state of consciousness that you get into rather than an action, verb or something else that you can "do."

I use the term meditation to refer to a broad variety of focus and concentration practices that allow you to focus on your physical, emotional, mental, and spiritual state. Successful use of these techniques can result in greater levels of relaxation, capacity for love, compassion, problem solving, and a deeper spiritual connection with something greater than yourself. The practice of the concentration technique is the tool that will help your consciousness achieve a meditative state.

Meditation, then, is simply a practice in which an individual's inner self trains his or her mind to focus on something (object meditations) or nothingness (objectless meditation) that induces a different state of consciousness from the day-to-day mind chatter consciousness. In this meditative state of consciousness, where the everyday chatter is quiet, your inner self can witness the insights that fill the void. According to Buddhist teachings, when practiced regularly in an isolated setting, this meditative state can evolve into "enlightenment." Our goal, however, is to use meditation practice to live our everyday lives more effectively.

I once discussed meditation with a successful CEO who indicated that he "couldn't meditate," but wished he could. After I assured him that everyone can meditate, he responded that he "can't sit still." He told me that every morning he wakes up around sunrise for an hour-long run without listening to any music. "Why running?" I asked him, to which he responded that it was primarily for his physical health and to obtain daily exercise before his busy day. "Why no music?" I then asked, to which he simply replied he liked to clear his head while he runs. He then noted that many of his best ideas come during his morning run.

Although a simple routine such as a morning run did not appear to be a traditional form of meditation to this type-A CEO, he was, in effect, meditating (experiencing a different level of consciousness during his morning run) but was unaware that he was doing so. Different people respond to different types of meditation practices, which is why this book provides a sample of different practices. There is no pressure to do them all; you can choose the meditation practice that is comfortable for you at any given time.

I will note that quieting the mind is not easy. I have heard the mind analogized to a two-year-old, always trying to get your attention and willing to go to drastic extremes to do so. A two-year-old acts better once he or she learns that you, the adult, are in control (mostly), and that his or her actions have limits. You and your "two-year-old"-like mind will live a more peaceful existence together once your inner self establishes awareness and then control (to some extent), and you have established this new relationship with your mind during daily meditation. You never actually control your mind, but you can teach yourself to observe and process information and thoughts differently, and without judgment.

The irony is that if there were a hypothetical spectrum of people ranked from most likely to least likely meditators, the least likely meditators are the ones who would benefit the most from meditation. So, if you are the kind of person whose immediate reaction to meditation is that you can't do it, that your brain works too fast and your constant multi-tasking is simply how your mind works, you're exactly like I was - the kind of person who most needs meditation.

No Judgment

As leaders, we fall into the habit of constantly judging ourselves and others. Try not to judge your meditations or label your practice for the day as a success or failure. In fact, thinking about succeeding only gets in the way. Ironically, a meditative state of consciousness only comes when you have released yourself from the struggle to meditate.

With the same open mind, try not to judge whether you can integrate the meditation and leadership techniques in this book until you try them. There is no way to know upfront what will work best for you. There is no predetermined timeline for how long it will take for you to see the benefits of meditation manifesting in your life. Accept that you will perceive some meditation sessions to be more impactful than others—and that this is not an indication of either success or failure. In fact, you may not even feel or understand the impact of a meditation session for weeks or months, as meditation tends to build upon itself with eventual revelations ("ah ha" moments) coming seemingly out of nowhere.

A Word about "God"

Meditation is not limited to any religion, and in fact, is consistent with all religions. All major world religions have a mystical tradition, and most religions and tribal practices include some sort of meditative or contemplative practice as part of their rituals. Many people do practice meditation as a way to deepen their relationship with God (however they define "God"), and find that meditation strengthens their belief in something greater than themselves. I count myself among those who have used meditation to enhance my understanding of, relationship with, and oneness with, that which I choose to label "God."

However, meditation is also highly relevant for those who don't believe in God or any particular religion. An affinity for a particular religion—or any belief in a higher power, for that matter—is not a prerequisite for success with meditation. Your inner voice will deliver the wisdom without need to assign credit to the source. There is much we as humans don't know or fully understand. The acceptance that "what is, is" that develops through meditation practice allows us to move beyond our understanding (or lack of understanding) and follow our intuition regardless of our belief system or the source of that wisdom.

Using These Materials

You may choose to read this book and practice the meditation techniques, or your own variations of them, on your own. Alternatively, you may choose to read this book with a partner and take turns guiding each other through the meditation techniques. You also may choose to listen to the meditations that are available as audio podcasts online (www. meditation4leadership.org). You may use this book as a stepping stone that encourages you to attend a local meditation class or a workshop at a yoga studio or retreat center; such opportunities will provide tools and experiences that will help you explore and evolve your meditation practice. You may even create a quiet meditation space at home or at work. You may want to try all of these methods and determine what works best for you.

This book is also intended to introduce or reintroduce you to acknowledged leadership experts—a range of professors, professional writers, well-known CEOs, and even a basketball coach—and to share with you their lessons that have made an impression on me. For those authors whose message resonates with you, I encourage you to purchase and read their books in their entirety. The excerpts I have included are not book summaries but quotes and commentary to make a specific point about a specific profiled leadership principle and how the leader's work impacted my journey; in some cases, these excerpts are used differently from the author's original context. In an ideal scenario, you will read this book and say to yourself, "I knew everything or almost everything he said; I just don't always practice it." The primary purpose of this book is to provide you with tools to practice universal leadership traits (and maybe receive a few incremental insights along the way to fine-tune your own leadership style).

It is in the link between meditation techniques and universal leadership traits where I hope you find a unique approach to these teachings. However, I expect that the most valuable learning will come not through my insight but through your personal practice of these meditation techniques.

Please note the following "technical" tips before you begin your practice:

It is not possible to read and effectively meditate at the same time. Please read the meditation several times; once you feel that you understand the technique, put the book down and practice.

Put the electronics away (and preferably out of the room) during your daily meditation. Cell phones make us available 24/7 and foster the constant chatter in our mind and our lives. Meditation provides a break from that chatter.

Find the meditative position that is most comfortable for you: lying down, sitting on a comfortable chair, or using a traditional cross-legged sitting posture. The key is to relax your body so that you are not distracted by physical discomfort. Meditation "habits," such as body position and time of day, facilitate moving into a meditative state more quickly as you practice more regularly.

Keep practicing. When you inevitably miss a day, start again the following day. During meditation, practice observing. During the rest of the day, notice if you spend more time observing "what is" instead of being distracted by "what was" or "what could have been."

Can I Really Become More Effective At Work by Meditating?

Absolutely. I understand this may seem like a leap. It may be more intuitive for you that meditation can lower stress and the byproducts from stress. That in and of itself is a great result and worth the time meditating. However, the benefit is so much more.

Ultimately, learning to meditate is about becoming the best that you can be. It is about connecting to your inner wisdom, being more aware in the present moment, and, in doing so, connecting better with others. The byproducts of meditation include unleashed creativity, better relationships, more clear decision making, and greater recognition of opportunities. When you become a more effective person, you contribute more to the people around you and the businesses and organizations in which you work or volunteer. Those organizations then become more effective in serving their stakeholders and achieving their missions.

This monumental impact is possible for each and every one of us—all arising from only 10 minutes a day.

* * *

Let's start with a simple exercise.

Notice whether you are in a comfortable position. If so, great. If not, adjust to be comfortable. Notice how you are feeling physically, what part of your body is least comfortable (for me, often shoulders or lower back) and simply focus your breath into that area of your body, possibly deepening your breath as you do so. Notice how you are feeling emotionally. Are you calm or are you feeling stressed? Do you feel a bit anxious or uncomfortable or scared? Whatever it is, or if you are not aware of any feelings at this time, just notice that. Notice what is going through your mind—notice the thoughts—and observe the difference between your thoughts and your inner self doing the noticing. Contemplate without self-judgment why you are reading this book. What are your hopes and goals in doing so? There are no right or wrong answers. Just become aware of your observations. Greater awareness is a reason why you meditate.

II. ABOUT THE AUTHOR

As I neared my 40th birthday, I was a hard-working young partner practicing corporate law at a large international law firm—working on mergers and acquisitions and managing financing transactions for clients ranging from start-up technology companies and the venture capital firms that finance them to middle-market public companies. I graduated from the University of Pennsylvania Wharton School, with concentrations in organizational behavior and finance, and New York University Law School. By my late 30s, I had built a successful legal practice. I cared deeply about the success of my clients and took a lot of pride in my work. I worked long hours and was highly stressed, with a typical "type A" achievement-oriented personality. I had—and still have—a beautiful wife and three wonderful daughters. However, I spent a lot of my time at work wishing I were home with my family or on vacation, and a lot of my time at home contemplating problems at work.

Physically, my body was aging rapidly. I had stopped exercising regularly—who has the time? Since my early 20s, I had suffered from periodic back spasms, initially once a year and progressing to monthly, which became increasingly debilitating. Interestingly, the back pain wasn't always in the same spot, but seemed to rotate. When I awoke each morning, the question on my mind wasn't whether I would be in pain, but where and how much. I was often hunched over like an 80-year-old man instead of standing straight and tall like a vibrant 39-year-old in the prime of his life. I had seen several doctors who recommended surgery or at least regular physical therapy. I believed that I had a physical back problem, but would later realize that it was a life problem manifesting as back pain.

A client who had become familiar with my periodic days off due to debilitating pain gave me a book[29] that presented an interesting theory: back pain is often a manifestation of the mind to stop the sufferer from doing something. The book suggested waking up each morning and repeating a saying or mantra—something to the effect of "my back won't hurt, my back won't hurt, my back won't hurt." At the time, that sounded ridiculous, but it did get me thinking about alternatives to traditional medical solutions to my back problem.

Around this time, a friend had started practicing a form of "hot yoga" called Bikram yoga, which involves practicing 26 postures in a room heated to 105 degrees at 40% humidity (with bottles of water nearby). I had never practiced yoga—it seemed so boring—but this was a challenge. At first, it was the hardest exercise I could ever remember doing. At that time, my ego was still in control of my mind; I tried to go farther and farther with each pose and willed myself to go on during each class, not taking the care or time to distinguish between discomfort and harmful pain. As a result, I injured myself once again. I had learned a few lessons, but my ego kept pushing me to the breaking point.

Over the next five years, I tried different forms of yoga, which still seemed to me to be mostly about stretching and building core strength to minimize back pain. However, over time, some of the yoga theory presented by the teachers started sinking in, and I began to enjoy rather than dread the few minutes of meditation at the beginning or end of the class. My chronic back pain subsided into the background.

The real turning point for me was another, much more severe injury. After several years of practicing different styles of yoga, my back was definitely feeling better physically. I was still working hard, trying to do it all. I had always loved tennis and started playing in a recreational tennis league. I was getting better, although not nearly as good a tennis player at 44 as I was at 14. Then, two weeks after my 45th birthday, playing doubles in a game with one of my closest friends—SNAP. I thought someone threw a tennis ball that hit the back of my calf; I turned around but couldn't see the ball. I was confused and then just went down. I had ruptured my

Achilles tendon. Three days later, I had surgery, followed by 10 weeks of wearing a boot, walking on crutches, and using a scooter—and a lot of free time.

At first, I was concerned about the pain and logistics of the surgery. I couldn't drive to the office. I started worrying about all that I planned but could no longer do (or do in the same way) during the recovery period. Stress began to build.

My injury was terrible, but my recovery was the break I needed. Looking back, it was a positive turning point in my life. For 10 weeks, no driving, no racing to work, no running errands—just quiet time. I decided to try to take advantage of the break in routine and started reading *The Yoga Sutras*, an amazing compilation of 196 aphorisms (or lessons) compiled by Patanjali, an Indian author and sage, around the year 400. I then started reading about Buddhism, as well as taking in a few spiritual books such as *The Alchemist* by Paulo Coehlo and *The Celestine Prophecies* by James Redfield.

I also had plenty of time to think and what I would later call "meditate." I was one of those people who swore that "I can't meditate"—the chatter kept going in my mind, moving from one thought to the next. But with practice, things changed.

The next key step in my journey was taking an "Introduction to Kabbalah" class. Kabbalah is the mystical religious interpretation of the Old Testament (Torah); its origin resides in Judaism, but it was later layered with Christian and New Age interpretations as well. I was born Jewish and, while the meditation techniques of yoga and Buddhism appeal to me, the language used in describing them was a significant barrier for me. Kabbalah broke down those barriers, bringing to me these same meditative techniques in a language and religious tradition with which

I was comfortable. For the next few years, my Thursday evenings were devoted to meditation and group Kabbalah study.

Over time, I developed a regular 10-20 minute meditation practice in the morning and learned meditation techniques to keep me centered throughout the day. When things get tough, I sometimes lose my meditation practice without realizing it. The key for me now is simply to be aware and acknowledge it. Once I do (or a spouse, child, friend or teacher reminds me), I return to meditation, and within days, seem to be able to find the perspective to deal with whatever life throws my way. I have come to realize that it is not the events of our lives that tend to make us happy or sad or joyous or angry, but rather our reaction to those events. I have fortunately not been faced with a personal tragedy that seems virtually impossible to overcome, but everyone's life has challenges that can be overwhelming. Once we recognize that these challenges are part of life—and accept that what will be, will be—we can use the perspective gained through meditation and greater mindfulness in our daily lives to be more effective. We can have greater appreciation and gratitude for positive experiences. We can demonstrate forgiveness and compassion during difficult experiences. We can each gain wisdom from our inner voice.

That inner voice—the voice I access through meditation practice—guided me to delve deeper into my studies, take more seminars, and teach the various meditation techniques I have learned from others. It also prompted me to translate those teachings for people who may not want to walk into a yoga studio or may not respond to the language of the Zen Buddhist or the Kabbalist. These people, like me, seek guidance from the inner wisdom that permits them to be the best leaders and best people they can be; you may respond better to a more "practical" viewpoint that uses more accessible secular language that can help the value of meditation resonate for you.

Over the years of my professional and personal journey, I have come to the realization that there is no such thing as great people. There are just people—people are who they are. Effective leaders are not perfect, and not all of their decisions have positive outcomes; perfection is not a realistic goal. I embrace the Army slogan that each of us should "be the best that you can be." However, don't be too hard on yourself as long as you are still trying. As you read this book, there may be times, particularly in the first few chapters, when you may want to quit or when you find something about the book not to your liking. I strongly encourage you to work through that discomfort to build the foundation of your meditation practice with a variety of techniques. Consider that if you take a break from your meditation practice, that may be just your mind playing tricks on you to deter you from change (your mind has been perfecting its ability to be in charge all of your life). You may need more tools in your tool box, so be sufficiently aware that it is happening and return to your practice. If you can work through that resistance, meditation can help you to be the best that you can be and to fulfill your life goals and mission. It has certainly continued to help me achieve mine, both personally and professionally, but not without struggle and perseverance.

I have accepted that I am who I am. I am not perfect and make mistakes despite my good intentions. I am a counselor and advisor. I am an excellent lawyer whose annual practice has grown significantly since (and, in part, because of) my awakening to meditation, a middle manager who went from managing a local office practice area to managing both the entire office and our global emerging business and technology practice area, an active board participant in community non-profit organizations that try to make the world a better place, and a husband, father, son and friend who is significantly more attentive now than in the past. I am certainly not a guru. I am a regular guy.

Daily meditation helps me on many personal levels, from simple stress reduction and alleviation of stress-induced back pain, to freedom from emotional suffering (practicing forgiveness and letting go), to allowing me to create a space to be able to listen to inner wisdom and to others. It has helped me to be a better advisor, a more effective leader and a more well-rounded person. Meditation facilitates achieving my potential to be the best that I can be. I hope that it can help you as well.

III. 13 TRAITS OF EFFECTIVE LEADERS AND THE FOUR PILLARS

Leadership cannot really be taught; it can only be learned.

Harold Geneen, CEO,
International Telephone and Telegraph (ITT)

We can all be leaders. Some of us may be CEOs; some may be middle managers in charge of a division or function or office; some may work in a staff position by day but lead a church or community group in the evenings; and some may lead or co-lead a household. We are all part of larger teams and communities where our thoughts, words and actions impact others. Those we impact then impact others with whom they have relationships.

Before defining leadership, let's acknowledge the difference between being an effective leader and an effective manager. I was speaking with Matt Miller, a successful CEO, who noted that he considers himself an effective leader. He also noted, however, that he is not an effective manager and pairs himself with a COO who is one. Matt further noted that a good manager is well organized, very detail oriented and able to implement and coordinate a team. Matt puts together an administrative team with all of the skills and experience to successfully run an organization, but not all in one person. This is very self-aware of Matt. He asked me: "Does meditation make you a better leader or a better manager?" My answer is both, but this book is focused on assisting everyone, including managers, to be better leaders.

The 13 Traits

Leadership is a nebulous term. You know it when you see it, but different people exhibit it differently. We are all a different combination of traits, and we all express them differently as we try to lead. However, I have observed that effective leaders seem to excel in some or all of the following 13 traits:

1. **Self-Awareness**
2. **Focus**
3. **Creativity**
4. **Communication skills**
5. **Relationships**
6. **Attunement**
7. **Team orientation**
8. **Insight**
9. **Balance**
10. **Influence**
11. **Vision**
12. **Grit**
13. **Growth mindset**

The 13 leadership traits are interrelated, and some build upon others. For example, all effective leaders seem to have the ability to find clarity amidst the chaos that helps them identify and implement what is centrally important to the organization. This clarity comes from a combination of self-awareness and insight. Effective leaders cultivate influence in organizations of motivated people using communication skills, relationship-building skills, attunement to others, and a team orientation. They connect well with others. Effective leaders create disciplined organizations that are focused, balanced, and innovative. Effective leaders create opportunities rather than simply manage what exists, and are willing to change and facilitate organizational growth. Effective leaders have vision, but vision alone is not enough. Effective leaders demonstrate grit—which I define as a combination of passion, persistence, resilience and effort—when times are tough or uncomfortable. Effective leaders are willing to adapt, continue to grow personally and professionally and strive to achieve their potential.

These leadership traits are not expressed the same way in every leader. Every person brings his or her own personality to the job. Each of us evolves over time as we incorporate the lessons from our life; hopefully, we improve as leaders over time and with practice. Most of these traits are exhibited to various degrees on a spectrum, rather than as all or nothing. Some will seem natural, while others will make you uncomfortable, require more practice, and feel like hard work. That is ok. We each do the best we can and learn to express each trait as best we can in ways that are consistent with our own personality. That is how we each evolve into the most effective leader we can be.

Each of the next 13 chapters of this book is devoted to one of the 13 leadership traits and how meditation can help you develop that trait. These leadership traits are applicable to varying degrees at all levels of an organization. These leadership traits do not instantly appear in someone who is given the title of manager or CEO, but are nurtured and developed with practice throughout a lifetime. These 13 traits are integrated into 4 foundational pillars. The 13 traits are the "why" certain leaders are more effective and the meditation techniques are "how" you will build those skills and solidify the foundation expressed in the Four Pillars through practice.

Your first reaction, like mine, might be, "Why 13?" In fact, the use of the number 13 might make you uncomfortable; it makes me uncomfortable for superstitious reasons. Some of my initial readers begged me to pare it back to 12 (or even 10 as a round number), or suggested identifying a 14th trait. Being more comfortable with the uncomfortable is something effective leaders learn to do; running away or avoiding difficult issues is easier, but doesn't get them resolved.

According to a National Geographic article titled *Friday the 13th: Superstitions Rooted in the Bible and More,*[30] the origin of superstition around the number 13 is unclear. The early Romans thought 13 was a sign of death. According to Norse mythology, 13 people at a table was a very unlucky scenario; apparently in Norse lore, at a banquet table of 12 gods in Valhalla, intruder number 13 (the god Loki) upset the balance and caused the death of one of the participants. The people at the Last Supper included Jesus Christ and the 12 Apostles; Judas was the 13th to sit down at the table. Friday the 13th as an unlucky day is a relatively modern (and Western) superstition that traces back to the 19th century. Many hotels and tall buildings in the United States (up to 80%, according to the article) skip the number 13 (or stop at 12 stories) because a 13th floor causes general discomfort. There is even a disorder called triskaidekaphaphobia, which is a severe fear of the number 13.

With this information, I asked myself, should I (i) cut or add a trait to reduce discomfort, or (ii) proceed as planned through the discomfort? Ultimately, I decided to maintain the integrity of the number of traits I find most important. Shedding light on the discomfort and meditating on the reasons for the discomfort can help us as leaders work through our discomfort and effect real and difficult change. This sounds easy, but few people do it regularly. It is much easier to avoid discomfort or tuck it away, perhaps planning to return to it another day (which may or may not actually happen).

The Four Pillars

The 13 leadership traits and the lessons learned through meditation can be integrated and grouped into four core categories—what I refer to as the Four Pillars from meditation:

- Awareness
- Connection
- Perspective
- Potential

We learn to focus on the present moment, observe our thoughts and feelings without judgment and to access our inner wisdom through meditation. That ability to be more present is incorporated into our everyday life, facilitating increased awareness. This awareness increases our capacity for connection and perspective. Acting with greater awareness, connection and perspective facilitates our ability to be more effective and achieve our potential. Each of the 13 traits, and the Four Pillars themselves, can be built and reinforced through daily meditation. Once established, these pillars provide us with a strong foundation to express the 13 traits and thus become more effective in everything we do.

13 Leadership Traits Within Four Pillars Enhanced by Meditation

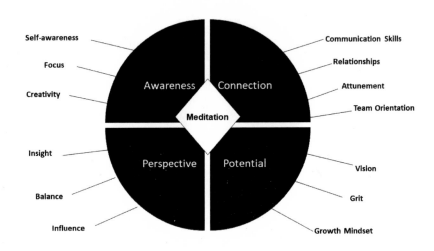

One of the difficulties we have learning from "self-help" books is that while the message often sounds "right" at the time we read it, it fades over time. You may practice some of the self-help techniques for a short period of time, and it may even be helpful, but your mind then distracts you with the "next thing."

Daily meditation is how you will be able to integrate, and utilize, not just the leadership lessons from this book, but everything else you learn and experience for the rest of your life. You will learn to be more aware of what you want to change, learn to access and follow your instincts, and be able to act upon the resulting wisdom for yourself and as a leader. You will also hopefully be less hard on yourself when mistakes, failures, or setbacks inevitably occur. You will still excel as you always have, probably even more so, and also be less stressed and more effective in handling what life has to offer you.

As Daniel Goleman and Richard Davidson concluded in their book, *Altered Traits: Science Reveals How Meditation Changes Your Mind, Brain and Body,* "Beyond the pleasant states meditation can produce, the real payoffs are the lasting *traits* that can result. An altered trait—a new characteristic that arises from a meditation practice — endures apart from the meditation itself. Altered traits shape how we behave in our daily lives, not just during or immediately after we meditate."[31]

Practice. Return to practice. No matter how long the break, return again to practice. You can't control the benefits, let the benefits emerge and observe them.

The techniques profiled will also assist in all types of organizations, including businesses, non-profit organizations, community organizations, government institutions, and families. We often take our family for granted, but really, a family is simply another organization of people; we are leaders of our nuclear family organization and often middle managers in our extended family organization. I have taught this material to diverse groups and always marvel when a CEO will choose to apply these techniques to both their work lives and to their family relationship dynamics. Applying the wisdom derived from meditation to your family and personal life, as well as to your business and community, is holistic and can help you be successful in all facets of your life.

Please keep in mind that many variables impact whether an organization will succeed, even with a leader who exhibits all 13 traits. A myriad of factors impact whether a decision will lead to a positive outcome, even when one makes that decision with solid factual knowledge and wisdom. Employing all of the leadership best practices summarized in this book will not guarantee that every decision will be productive or every organization in which you are involved will be successful—but it *will* increase the likelihood that more decisions will turn out successful and that the organizations in which you are involved will thrive. Suboptimal results will simply provide more opportunities for further growth in some other way.

One of the frustrating aspects of engaging in self-improvement is the following possibility: what happens if you try your hardest to develop these 13 traits and seek to develop them for your organization, but no one else follows and you think that no progress is being made? Let that concern go. It just holds you back. Fear of failure is natural. Some failure is positive—it demonstrates taking risks. Additionally, some outcomes may feel like "failure," but in fact, they are just clearing the path for a different solution to take hold. Keep in mind that risks also sometimes lead to rewards. You don't need to become an ideal leader as described in this, or any, book. Your goal should be to continue to evolve into the best version of you, and both you and the world will benefit.

BUILDING THE PILLAR OF AWARENESS

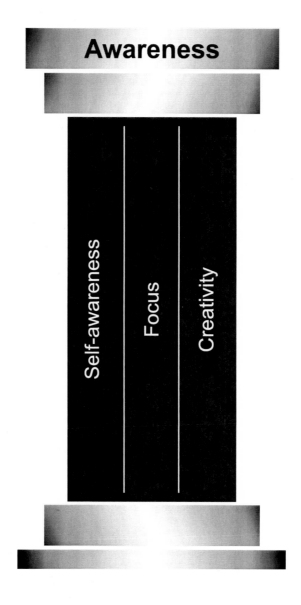

IV. DEVELOPING SELF-AWARENESS— TO GO FROM GOOD TO GREAT

Self-awareness is probably the most important thing towards being a champion.

Billie Jean King

"Good is the enemy of Great" is the first line of Jim Collins' seminal leadership book *From Good to Great: Why Some Companies Make The Leap… and Others Do Not.* You may be thinking that you are doing things well enough, that life is proceeding okay. Why do I need meditation? Because meditation is the tool that can help you go from good to great.

Five Levels of Leadership

The one leadership trait that "turns the light on" and enables us to be more effective with respect to all of the other leadership traits is self-awareness. Without self-awareness, we simply keep doing the same thing repeatedly. A survey of 75 members of the Stanford Graduate School of Business Advisory Council rated self-awareness as the *most* important competency for leaders to develop.[32] Furthermore, many MBA programs recognize the key role self-awareness plays in leadership success. Harvard Business School lists self-awareness as one of the key attributes of prospective candidates.[33] Many colleges are now creating programs that focus on self-awareness as the first step in leadership development. Leaders who foster self-awareness are able to successfully adopt or develop tools for leveraging their strengths and confronting their weaknesses. This helps them earn credibility and cultivate relationships. They remain open to new ideas, inquiry, and constructive criticism. That is because awareness comes without judgment. It is the ability to observe things as they are. A self-aware person can choose to put himself or herself in a position and organization with a better chance to succeed.

Author and leadership expert Jim Collins first made me aware that we are all leaders. Collins set forth a framework to help us understand different types of leadership within an organization. His framework categorizes leadership into five levels, which are described in the box below. This framework is valuable because it will help you: (i) understand the skills and traits required for each level; (ii) develop an awareness of what level is best for your current skills and traits and (iii) better understand what you would need to develop to thrive at a higher level.

This self-awareness has multiple benefits. First, there is nothing wrong with being at any level as long as you are at a level that is consistent with your skills, traits and experience. If you are promoted to a level that is beyond your skills and traits, significant frustration can result for you and the organization or it can be an opportunity for personal growth. If you are in a frustrating place currently, maybe you will recognize the traits associated with your level and, with this new awareness, work to improve in those traits required to succeed. Alternatively, maybe you will realize that your skills and traits are not conducive to that level and understand why you are no longer succeeding when previously you were. Either way, only good comes from greater self-awareness.

Collins' Five Levels of Executive Capabilities[34]

Level 1: An individual who is knowledgeable and generally has good work habits; an "implementer"

Level 2: An individual who contributes individual capabilities to group objectives and works effectively with the group; a "team player"

Level 3: An individual who competently manages people and resources toward the effective and efficient pursuit of the group's objectives; a "middle manager"

Level 4: An individual who has the ability to catalyze commitment to a clearly communicated and compelling vision, thus leading to higher performance standards; a "senior manager"

Level 5: An individual who builds enduring greatness through a paradoxical blend of personal humility and professional will, and possesses clarity of purpose, integrity, and perspective in implementation; an "effective executive"

A Level 1 leader leads by example. The ability to work well with others is what differentiates a Level 2 leader from a Level 1 leader. The Level 2 leader mindset changes from self-fulfilling to group-oriented in order to achieve a goal.

Going a step further, a Level 3 leader has the ability to be sensitive to group dynamics and is thus able to manage the group toward common goals. A Level 4 leader has broad vision and is thus able to set organizational goals and address internal and external challenges. Level 4 leaders often prepare budgets and business goal implementation plans. The challenges that inevitably arise may require adjustment of these budgets and business plans to maximize the effectiveness of the result. Level 3 and 4 leaders complete tasks through effective management of others, and are often evaluated based upon the performance of a group.

Level 5 leaders realize that there is something greater than themselves and their organizations. They view the organization and their role in it as small parts of a greater whole. Their perspective is not focused solely within the organization, but also on how the organization fits within the greater society. The professional success of a Level 5 leader derives from a clear understanding of the organization's role within the greater whole and successful implementation of the organization's goals and mission within this greater context.

According to Collins, five attributes typify the effective Level 5 leader:[35]

- Self-confidence, especially in setting up others for success
- Humility and modesty
- An unwavering resolve
- A workmanlike diligence
- An ability to give credit to others for successes and take full responsibility for poor results

Organizations run by Level 5 leaders tend to be more successful. Of the 1,435 Fortune 500 companies Collins studied in the years 1965—1995, few had great Level 5 leadership. Only 11 of the Fortune 500 companies studied met all of his "good-to-great" criteria. All 11 of these companies had Level 5 leadership at the pivotal time of business transition to become great, and they achieved an average cumulative stock return of at least three times higher than the market average over a 15-year period.[36]

Awareness of each employee's appropriate leadership level is critical for personal and organizational success. Collins posits that effective organizational vision, strategy, and tactics are not possible without the right people on the team in the right positions. Collins observed that Level 5 leaders get the right people on the bus at each position in the organization (and the wrong people off the bus) and then figure out how to drive it.[37] This requires awareness on the part of the organization's leaders, who keep organizational goals in mind during the determination and implementation of strategy. It also requires self-awareness by most of us in the organization who are not CEOs that we are each valuable and contribute meaningfully to the organization regardless of level or position.

One of the most self-aware leaders I have read is Sheryl Sandberg. Sandberg has an impressive professional resume from being a consultant at McKinsey to being an early Google executive to becoming COO of Facebook. Her book, *Lean In, Women, Work And The Will to Lead*[38] describes with self-awareness her strengths and clarity in decision making and how she was treated differently as a female executive (for the most part non-judgmentally, simply with awareness of the differences). I learned so much, not just about what I think was her intended primary theme of differences between men and women in the workplace, but universal leadership improvement through greater self-awareness of differences among colleagues.

For example, Sandberg notes that Ken Chenault, then CEO of American Express, would openly point out in meetings when he observed people interrupting a woman speaker.[39] Apparently, he observed that both men and women were more likely to interrupt a female speaker and to give credit during a brainstorming session to a man for coming up with a new idea that arose from group discussion. As an aware leader, he sought to correct this bad cultural habit, which both helped foster Amex as a female-friendly place to work and facilitated innovation at Amex by ensuring that a diversity of ideas are fully discussed. Sandberg also noted how difficult it is for female leaders to come across as both competent and well-liked.[40] A woman who exhibits the same traits as a man might be "too aggressive," "not a team player," and a "bit political" or "difficult."

If the woman is perceived as nice, she may be perceived as less competent or "a lightweight" for lacking "presence."

I have tried very hard as a manager over the past few years to become more conscious of these social patterns and look past these stereotypes, with mixed success. To move forward, it will take both male and female managers to be more aware of these social patterns and to call people on them, as well as greater self-awareness by both female and male workers when they witness these patterns in action. Often, once aware, a subtly different behavior can make all the difference in others' reactions. For example, a female team member could simply point out: "May I finish my thought?" before allowing the conversation to move on or confirming an idea she shared at a meeting by email. At our law firm, we undergo periodic diversity training to help make us aware of various common workplace biases and barriers, with the result that identified biases can be remedied and diversity is valued in our law firm culture. We are all aware that women and minorities still face greater barriers in the workplace than white men; there is no choice but to forge ahead by identifying bias when we become aware of it and seeking to intentionally counter bias once identified, even where the original bias arose unintentionally.

Self-awareness is not just about identifying ourselves as part of various groups and better understanding group biases. It is also better understanding how we evaluate and process information, how we communicate, and how others react to us, and then altering behaviors when necessary or advantageous. Another business book that focuses on self-awareness is Selana Rezvani's *The Next Generation of Future Leaders: What You Need to Lead but Won't Learn in Business School*.[41] While focused on female leaders, the book points out universal ways in which we are insufficiently self-aware in the workplace and tools and techniques for increasing self-awareness. Rezvani encourages using self-assessments to better understand your unique personality traits, preferences and interests[42] Self-assessments can provide insights to identify where you best fit in the Collins leadership pyramid, good industry fits, dominant personality traits and preferred communications and learning styles. Self-assessments can also put clear language to vague concepts to help you better identify the dominant traits and preferred style of others and to adjust accordingly your communication with the other person based upon how they are most likely to best receive your message based on your perception of their dominant traits and style. Rezvani specifically lists 16 different self-assessments categorized by focus area for personality or psychology type, interest and Career, skills, and values.[43]

With greater self-awareness, you can also better understand your role in your organization. This may lead to a conclusion that you are on the right track, or it could lead to a greater understanding of why you aren't getting promoted, or perhaps why you didn't get the compensation you perceive you deserved. Your performance may actually be excellent but your expectations (particularly with respect to timing of advancement) exceed reality within that organization. Once you achieve greater self-awareness, you may then choose to simply be more comfortable with where you are or the compensation you did receive. There is nothing wrong with being content where you are. You may, however, desire near term advancement. You may contemplate how you can adapt to better meet the organization's expectations. Maybe that can occur by increasing your skills or by changing your behavior towards others or simply by creating a stronger and more positive presence. It starts with non-judgmental observation.

Marilyn Hailperin, Chief Operating Officer of Meditation4Leadership, described leaders who "lean-in" as always thinking first about the best interests of the organization and how the leader can add value to the organization and his or her colleagues without need for credit or title. She contrasted that with people who "lean out" and use rules and blame to create divisions, often with the perception that the person doing so is in the right (and by definition others are in the wrong), frequently resulting in unsuccessful relationships. I am not sure this is how Sandberg meant to use of the term "lean in" but I found it a self-aware group dynamic observation.

Organizational leaders can look internally at how the organization functions and create and evolve their corporate culture and business strategy with greater leadership awareness. For example, suppose an organization's leadership team sets a strategy goal to reinforce a collaborative culture that fosters teamwork. Executives look at how things are done in the organization and see some teamwork, and also observe some work silos not collaborating with others. Once self-aware, the leadership team can implement changes such as (i) including internal business cross-referrals as a factor in compensation, (ii) publicly acknowledging examples of intergroup collaboration, (iii) implementing technology to make collaboration or shared work product easier and (iv) instituting the dreaded "team building activities." These can be relatively easy to implement once you are organizationally self-aware of the issue.

Awareness also includes awareness of the context or marketplace in which you conduct business including how others view your organization and the competitive landscape in which the organization operates. This external awareness also includes observing the actions and reactions of the people around you, including customers, and adjusting your behavior and your organization's behavior based on that additional input.

Collins notes that external awareness helps great leaders decide what to do, and what to stop doing. Collins tells the story of one "good-to-great" company: Kimberly Clark.[44] Its leader, Darwin Smith, understood that the path to long term growth lay in the consumer business, where the company had demonstrated a best-in-world capacity in building the Kleenex brand. On the other hand, at that time, the vast majority of

Kimberly Clark's resources and revenues lay in traditional coated paper mills, turning out paper for magazines and writing pads in addition to tissues. This was the core business of the company for 100 years. Most leaders would have stayed the course and continued down the same historically successful path. As a more aware leader, Smith looked at all of the potential strategic alternatives for the future, and determined that Kimberly Clark's best shot at maximizing its value was to sell its long-standing paper manufacturing business to focus on higher-growth, higher-margin consumer products. Instead of trying to do everything as a vertically integrated organization, Smith decided to stop doing something (manufacturing the paper). Twenty-five years later, Kimberly Clark emerged as the number-one consumer products company in the world, surpassing Procter and Gamble.

No matter how acute your awareness becomes, note that being an effective leader does not mean you can make your organization perfect. There are no perfect organizations and no perfect people, even if we are satisfied with our achievements for a moment in time. An effective leader like Kimberly Clark's Darwin Smith does not just continue on the current path but maintains a vigilant awareness of organizational strengths and weaknesses, market opportunities, employee strengths and weaknesses, and new challenges as they arise. Leaders can make better decisions from that place of both personal and organizational self-awareness.

How Does Self-Awareness Relate to Meditation?

Meditation and self-awareness are inextricably linked. Meditation can be described as a practice of awareness: a practice of being in the present moment and observing instead of thinking. Once we are more aware in the present moment, we find that we can observe and process information we didn't realize was right in front of us.

Just as we sometimes don't know what we don't know, we are too often unaware of that of which we are unaware. Have you ever been in a park and someone says, "Listen to the birds chirping?" Suddenly, you hear the birds . . . . and can't stop hearing the birds. The birds were there chirping all along; before, you didn't process those sounds, but after becoming aware, you did.

I am sure everyone has been in a situation where someone was talking and your mind seemed somewhere else (sometimes called "day dreaming"). When you notice you weren't listening, you come back to listening to the conversation. You can try to catch up but rarely completely. Your mind will always stray; greater awareness helps you bring it back sooner so you miss less. Being more aware and present more of the time can allow us to observe more from our surroundings and more about our self. But how do we become more aware?

Meditation allows you to quiet the distracting chatter of your mind. In that state of quiet mind, what flows to the foreground of your mind can be observed without judgment to provide you with greater insight and perspective on work tasks, relationships, problems in need of solutions, and keeping the bigger picture in mind while living your life.

An outcome of meditation is to bring the mind out of its normal thought patterns to a different state of consciousness. What some describe as quietness, stillness or silence is not actually completely quiet, still or silent at all. It is a different pattern of activity (or level of consciousness) that allows us to observe what is available behind the surface—beyond the chatter and multi-tasking of the mind.

Meditation is not just about being more aware of your thoughts. At its core, meditation is using a set of techniques to practice being in the present moment, which makes us more aware of what actually *is*. It is truly amazing what you can notice that you didn't before—whether it is the beauty of nature or your spouse, or that fear, shame and self-doubt are a major influence on your behavior (or inability to take action), or that that there are some things you can do to add value to your work place or the world. Overall, regular meditation can provide you with greater awareness on both life and leadership while renewing your body, heart, mind, and soul.

The practice of meditation is a method to break the spell of continuous thought, and in doing so, to achieve awareness. However, in the beginning you are unlikely to understand just how transformative this shift in attention can be. You may spend most of your time trying to meditate without assurance that it has been successful. The first sign of progress is noticing the difference between when you are distracted and when you are focused during your meditation—just noticing. As you proceed with daily practice, you will discover tools, such as returning to focus on your breath, to bring you back once you notice your distraction. Over time, you will get a real sense of awareness of the difference in your mind between a meditative state and your ordinary thought patterns. It is hard to describe, but easy to observe once you separate your "self" consciousness from your thoughts, begin to observe your thoughts as a witness during your meditation practice, and witness the insights that flow through the wider lens of your "self" consciousness. That is when the wisdom comes.

Meditation also avoids the self-induced stress we often create for ourselves from the "story" we tell ourselves around what is being observed. Instead, the focus, when mindful, is fully on the present moment. During meditation practice, we are not changing the past or sitting with fear of the future. We are observing the present.

This leads to the realization that accepting "what is" in the present moment is accepting that what happened in the past is merely history and what may happen is merely the future. These are key realizations that can assist you in being more effective, calm, and content.

Ultimately, meditation facilitates becoming more aware of awareness itself. You will have your own experiences while more aware and draw your own conclusions about the benefits to you from your meditation practice.

It is not too big a leap to conclude that a leadership team with greater awareness of "what is" will be able to make better decisions for an organization. As Collins noted in a forward to *Lead Yourself First, Inspiring Leadership Through Solitude* by Raymond Kethledge and Michael Erwin, "Solitude can play a catalytic role in gaining clarity about what must be done and summon a fierce resolve to carry [it] through."[45]

Meditation is not easy, at least not in the beginning. Your mind will resist the process of trying to be quieted, expressing judgmental thoughts regarding the merits of meditation until otherwise convinced. Robert Wright tells a story in his book, *Why Buddhism is True, The Science and Philosophy of Meditation and Enlightenment*, when during his first meditation retreat he had a chance to discuss his meditation issues with his teacher:[46]

> *Teacher: So you know your mind keeps wandering?*
>
> *Robert: Yes*
>
> *Teacher: That's good.*
>
> *Robert: It's good that my mind keeps wandering?*
>
> *Teacher: No, it's good that you notice that your mind keeps wandering.*
>
> *Robert: But it happens, like, all the time.*
>
> *Teacher: That's even better. It means you're noticing a lot.*

Self-awareness is the first step toward self-improvement. If all you do is notice more, you will have achieved significant gain from meditation.

Mindfulness and Awareness

A buzzword in meditation today in the United States is "mindfulness." Mindfulness-based stress reduction (MBSR) is a mindfulness-based program developed by Jon Kabat-Zinn at the University of Massachusetts Medical Center to assist people with pain and a range of conditions and life issues that are difficult to treat in a hospital setting.[47] It uses a combination of mindfulness meditation, body awareness, and yoga to help people become more mindful, with many beneficial effects including stress reduction, relaxation, pain relief, sleep improvement and illness reduction.[48]

As Eckhart Tolle notes in his seminal book, *The Power of Now*,[49] the reality of your life is always "now": as a matter of conscious experience, our life is a series of "nows." The past has already happened and the future has not yet arrived. The basic theory of mindfulness is that because we forget this fundamental truth, we spend much of our lives burdened by the past and planning for the future, which creates suffering. We manage to avoid being happy while struggling to be happy, we avoid being productive by spending all our work time trying to produce, and we create more suffering by continually grasping for more—thinking about how to do more and produce more. We sometimes fail to appreciate colleagues until they have left the organization.

A remedy to these problems is to foster greater mindfulness. There is nothing scary about mindfulness. It is simply a state of clear, nonjudgmental and undistracted attention to the contents of what is being observed, whether pleasant or unpleasant. As Jon Kabat-Zinn has put it, "Mindfulness is paying attention in a particular way: on purpose, in the present moment and non-judgmentally."[50] With mindfulness, the meditator simply notes without reactivity whatever comes into mind, such as thoughts or sensory impressions like sounds or mental pictures, and let's them go.[51] The key is to observe without judgment and let go. The clarity of observation through mindfulness fosters greater clarity of thought in your daily life and resulting clarity of action with greater self-awareness.

Mindfulness and Awareness Meditation Practices

We are going to start with a few physical mindfulness meditation practices that can help build self-awareness. These focus meditations put something that is normally in the background, such as walking, into the foreground of our consciousness. Notice the difference. You may then wonder, what else don't I notice?

i. Walking Meditation

How often do you walk somewhere and never think twice about it? It is interesting to realize how many things we do every day without awareness.

Start to walk.

Focus on each physical movement as you walk: the lifting of the left leg, the striking of the left heel to the ground, the rolling through the left arch to the toes while the right leg starts to lift. The striking of the right heel, rolling through the right arch to the toes. The repetition of this movement.

Walk around a room or your house or the office for a few minutes. Every time you walk, pay attention to your walking.

You don't have to change the way you are walking or the pace of your walk, just notice it and try to keep noticing it for as long as your mind will let you.

Then, walk a little slower (or even very slowly) and then a little faster. Lift your legs a little higher when you walk. Playfully alter your gait to see how many ways you can walk differently. This walking meditation starts to teach us how we can lead our mind instead of allowing our mind to lead us (subconsciously).

This is also one of my favorite meditations to use to return to awareness during the work day. Everyone needs bathroom breaks. Consider making your bathroom break an aware walking meditation to snap you out of your routine consciousness. You may choose to return to your routine or may realize something you "forgot" to do or become aware of a relationship that requires attention and fit that in before returning to your routine.

ii. Body Scan Observation Meditation

A body scan observation meditation is one of the simplest and most powerful methods for putting us in touch with our bodies and becoming more aware of ourselves. I like to practice this meditation while lying in bed before I go to sleep, but it can be done anytime, anywhere, and in any position.

Start at one end of your body—for example, the left pinkie toe. Focus on (meaning, simply observe) your left pinkie toe, then each of the middle toes on your left foot, and then your left big toe. You may choose to wiggle the area to bring it into focus.

Move your focus down your foot to your left heel, then to your left ankle. Circle your ankle; maybe you will hear a joint click, maybe not. Move to your left calf—is it a little tight today? Up to your left knee—your knees hold so much weight and only generally get attention when they cry out in pain. Move your focus up your leg through your left thigh to your left hip. Most people have some tightness in their hips, particularly as they age.

For this exercise, continue up the left side of the body before moving to your other side.

Move your attention up your left side of your torso. Do you feel a little tightness in your lower or middle back? Notice how your front feels where your stomach and other organs are, up through your heart to your breast. Can you actually feel or hear your heart functioning?

Move your focus to the fingers on your left hand, one at a time: your pinkie finger, ring finger, middle finger, pointer finger and thumb. You can wiggle each one if you like. Make an affirmative decision and apply it consistently to each finger.

Notice your left hand and left wrist. If it feels good, rotate your wrist and/or massage your left hand gently with your right hand.

Move your attention to your left elbow and shoulder; maybe rotate your shoulder clockwise and then counter-clockwise. How is your neck feeling today? Would it feel good to gently move your neck to the left and then to the right? Would it feel good to gently rotate your neck?

Now move your attention up to your mouth and then jaw. It is amazing how much tension we hold in our jaw. Open your mouth wide and let out an Ahhhhh!

Wiggle your nose. Then blink your eyes. Focus on your forehead, and see if you can feel that place in the middle of the forehead (sometimes called the "third eye" because of its perceived connection to the spiritual world). Take a few deep breaths and then return your focus down to your eyes, then nose, then mouth. Move your jaw around again. Does it feel different?

Move your neck to the left gently and then to the right; maybe rotate your neck.

Move your attention to your right shoulder; rotate your shoulder clockwise and then counter-clockwise.

Turn your attention down your right arm to your right elbow and then wrist. Maybe shake your wrist or make circles with your wrist. Notice your right hand and massage it with your left hand if you did that for the other side. Focus on your thumb, pointer finger, middle finger, ring finger and pinkie finger in turn.

Move your focus to your right side of your torso from your breast down to your abdomen. Observe your lower back on the right side. Does it feel the same, or different, from the lower back on the left side?

Focus on your right hip, down your thigh to your right knee and then right calf and right ankle. Consider making gentle circles with your right ankle. Go through your right foot—your heel, arch, front foot, pinkie toe, middle toes and finally the big toe.

Now that you have scanned your body with focus and attention, how do you feel? Have you noticed any part of your body that may need greater attention in the future? Have you been caring for your body and exercising your body? Have you been giving your body the nourishment it deserves? This is your only body. You need to take good care of it to be able to move your way through life and accomplish your goals.

Consider how this body scan didn't really require much time. About 10 minutes. Doesn't your body deserve this much time every now and then?

iii. Five Senses Awareness Meditation

There are many ways to practice awareness or greater mindfulness. One approach is to focus on each of the five senses we use to gather information from our surroundings. Focus on what you see, what you hear, what you smell, what you taste and what you feel.

You can do so with your eyes open or closed (or some of each).

Take a few deep breaths to center yourself. You can focus on the pace of your breath, either maintaining your natural breath pace or deepening your breath. You can focus on the feel of your breath, in through your nose, out through your mouth, and then change to in through your mouth and out through your nose. How do those feel different?

Observe the saliva in your mouth. What is the subtlety of the taste? Is your mouth moist or dry? Do you notice a thirst for hydration that you hadn't previously?

Look at your surroundings. Observe what you see slowly and perhaps notice something you have never noticed before, even though it has always been there.

Next, focus on your position. Feel your feet against the floor or your back against the seat. Notice the pressure, the temperature of the room, any stiffness in your body, and any place where you are not comfortable.

Notice what you smell. Every place smells different—not always good or bad, but different. Bring yourself to a place in your mind where you remember the smell—like the ocean or the mountains or even a garbage dump. Smells can cement an experience in our minds. What do you smell currently?

Notice what you hear. Maybe cars out on the street, the humming of an electrical appliance or the ticking of an old-fashioned clock. You hadn't previously heard the background noise but suddenly it is all you can hear.

Consider being more mindful during a meal and really taste every bite of that meal. Be more mindful as you walk from your car to your office, or drive to or from work, or stand in the shower as you feel the individual beads of water hit and fall off your skin. You can do this any time you have a few moments to practice mindfulness. Practice being more mindful with your senses aware rather than just when sitting with your eyes closed.

iv. Integrating the Meditation Technique and Leadership Principle—Doing and Stop Doing Meditation

Sometimes I start meditation practice with an intention to just focus on my breath, sometimes I set a specific intention and sometimes I go in with no intention.

For this practice, choose an organization in which you are involved. You may be involved in multiple organizations—professional, community and family—and serve different level roles in different organizations. Choose just one to focus on for this exercise today. Consider your role in your focus organization. You may want to use Collins' pyramid level system if that resonated with you. Be aware of what is —maybe you are sometimes at one level and sometimes at another. This exercise is about being aware, putting a label on it to better understand it and then considering within the scope of that role how you can add meaningful value to your focus organization.

Close your eyes or lower your gaze. Focus on your breath.

With awareness of your role or level in the organization, ask yourself:

What are the organization's expectations of me?

Pause

What can I do to add more value to the organization?

Pause

What should I stop doing?

Pause

What stops me from taking action?

Pause

Pause a minute or so between questions and observe the thoughts that fill your mind repeating each question a few times before moving on.

As you end this meditation, consider the last time you stepped back from acting and asked yourself, "How can I add more value?" Have you ever asked yourself what you should stop doing? It seems so simple, but it is easy to forget. We often find ourselves continuing in our routines, adding to them until we find ourselves overwhelmed. Encourage yourself to consider your routine and, where warranted, break from it—become more self-aware, and your path will come to you.

V. MAINTAINING FOCUS—IN SEARCH OF SILENCE

The successful warrior is the average man with laser-like focus.
Bruce Lee

You want to become a better leader and a better person. You are willing to try meditation (what could be the harm?). Being more aware sounds logical. How do you actually go about quieting the chatter in your mind—searching for silence amid the thoughts that seem to stream one after another, without end, every waking moment?

Most people who do not have a regular meditation practice think, "I can't meditate—I don't think I can take a break from the chatter inside my mind." This chatter is what the ancient yogis called "monkey mind." However, everyone can meditate. It is just a question of training, practice and understanding that achieving a meditative state is a process, not a goal.

The process for uncovering calm, quiet mind takes practice. It is like learning a language or an instrument. Don't be fooled by those who say there is only one right way (theirs). Most teachers teach what has worked best for themselves. Some may lack the exposure and experience with other methods or the sensitivity to realize that each person is different and at a different place in his or her life at this moment. You can explore the many meditation techniques and discover which work best for you.

Self-awareness is not sufficient, though. Being aware that I need to lose weight has never been enough to prompt me to drop a few pounds. It requires focus as well as discipline to retain that focus and return to that focus. Effective dieters are able to retain focus on an eating plan and have the discipline to mostly stay on it, while realizing that they are not perfect and will sometimes just lose focus and eat what they want to. When that happens, they wake up the next morning and refocus on the plan.

Effective leaders are not only aware of what needs to occur strategically, but are able to focus their organization to make it happen. Effective leaders seem to be able to retain a similar focus themselves and, when they become aware of having lost focus, to regain that focus, both for themselves and their organizations.

Meditation practice develops focus. A meditation practice session requires focus so that you can get started and awareness when you have lost focus to return to focus. Effective meditators also seem to have the focus and discipline to practice meditation every day—and get the results when they do so. That doesn't mean they won't miss a day or find a particular meditation session to be frustrating or not meaningful. Rather, it means that they continue to practice and when they are practicing, they try to stay focused during that practice. Periods of quiet mind are the result.

Many of the great leadership books and business school professors have sought to create "one size fits all" business success methodologies. However, each organization has different issues and must implement different techniques and strategies based on its own unique circumstances and stakeholders. Many business and leadership books that teach organizational behavior methodologies specifically teach what to focus on.

Retaining focus for employees, trustees and volunteers of a non-profit organization is as important as for a for-profit organization. A for-profit organization generally has a numerical bottom line, which produces clear short-term performance targets and long-term growth performance metrics. Although a non-profit may have some similar numerical targets as for-profit businesses, its focus is more on satisfying its mission than financial metrics. Effective non-profit leaders are often able to develop specific mission-related performance targets that measure effectiveness both internally and to donors and to keep all of the organization's stakeholders on a clear, focused path. Other non-profits are by nature reactive, such as a disaster relief agency, and must have systems in place to manage volunteers and limited staff when called upon and raise money at the exact same time as the crisis is occurring. Although most of the leadership skills and leadership examples in this book are applied to for-profit business examples, the core skills and traits are equally applicable to non-profit and other types of community, governmental and even family organizations.

A success methodology does not have to be new to be useful. The seminal management book in the early 1980s was *In Search of Excellence* by Tom Peters and Robert Waterman.[52] This work was important not just for its conclusions (which differed from much of the conventional wisdom taught at business schools at the time) but for the methodology the authors used to develop their landmark insights. Peters and Waterman increased our awareness of the areas where successful business organizations focus. Peters also continued to focus on and evolve these theories 25 years after the book was published, based on his further research and empirical evidence; I find the examples in some of the later Peters articles to be even better lessons than those in the original book.

The Value of Focus

Peters and Waterman studied 43 of the top-performing Fortune 500 companies, tracking performance and interviewing the CEOs and others within these organizations. They identified the top performers over extended time periods and then identified eight themes among the top performers:[53]

1. **A bias for action:** Active decision-making; a culture of doing something after due consideration rather than running through cycles of analyses and committee reports.
2. **Stay close to the customer:** Learning from the people served by the business and adapting to meet their needs.

3. **Autonomy and entrepreneurship:** Fostering innovation and nurturing "champions" by breaking the larger entity into coordinated smaller groups that encourage practical risk taking.

4. **Productivity through people:** Treating all employees as valued assets and creating incentives or rewards so that they shift from self-focus to focus on the organization and share in the company's success.

5. **Hands-on, value-driven:** Clearly communicating management philosophy and company values throughout the organization; these values and philosophies guide every-day practices, with leaders in the organization serving as role models.

6. **Stick to the knitting:** Focusing on the business that the company knows best, expanding logically from that core business and the organization's core strengths.

7. **Simple form, lean staff:** Maintaining minimal headquarters staff, few administrative layers, and simple organizational reporting structures.

8. **Simultaneous loose/tight properties:** Providing autonomy to employees in implementing basic job activities within the confines of the company's core values.

These basic tenets of effective organizational behavior seem to be as true today as they were 30 years ago. Focusing on these themes can enhance the leadership of an organization or a division or group within that organization, whether it is for profit (start-up or large organization), non-profit, or governmental. The guiding Peters and Waterman principle is that by maintaining focus on these eight themes, any organization can be more successful.

What Peters and Waterman were able to do is to step back and observe. They separated themselves from the leading organizational management theorists at the time, such as Peter Drucker in business and Robert McNamara in the military, who posited that successful organizations put processes in place that assign employees distinct tasks and then monitor performance "by the numbers." Peters and Waterman observed that many large, seemingly successful U.S. companies had turned into heavily systemized organizations of bean counters and assembly line workers. They were temporarily successful, but not innovative. Peters and Waterman theorized correctly that these types of companies maximize profits in the short-term, but as times change and markets evolve, they often get left behind, sometimes completely. An example of this is Smith Corona, which maintained its focus on typewriters and mechanical calculators for years after the home computer was introduced into the marketplace; eventually, the company entered into bankruptcy and was reinvented as a thermal label and ribbon manufacturer.

A main lesson from *In Search of Excellence* is that it is not all about the numbers and control from the top. Rather, positive long-term profits and other quantitative indicators are the result of "excellence" in managing people and ideas in pursuit of a core vision. A focus on qualitative indicators of leadership (sometimes called "soft traits"), in addition to the quantitative indicators, is what leads to long-term success, including high profits.

An example noted by Peters is Xerox. Xerox hired employees with MBAs and IQs of 180 or higher who spent much of their time and energy arguing about theoretical economic principles rather than striving to enhance product performance or focusing on their customers' needs. Meanwhile, the company manufactured poor-quality (albeit the first) copiers. Xerox tried to manage financial performance more than product innovation, which only works for so long.[54] Eventually, Xerox lost primacy in the copier business to more customer-focused manufacturers, such as Canon, which was chosen in 2015 by Fortune magazine as one of America's most admired companies. This basic story repeated itself in many industry segments, such as automobiles, where, again, many of the Japanese brands that focused on customer desires in terms of quality, features, and affordable pricing thrived over historically dominant American companies.

Two of the most effective business people I have had the pleasure to work with are Barry Siadat and Jamshid Keynejad, the founders of the private equity firm SK Capital Partners. Barry and Jamshid made their fortunes through a combination of effort, focus and perspective. It was their rare focus that caught my attention. I observed success after success that came from the SK Capital Partners team, who notice during due diligence where efficiencies can be created (which all business buyers attempt to do). They have an above-average ability to actually implement those efficiencies, focusing not just on cutting costs, but on creating real process efficiencies and revenue generation efficiencies. Barry would even spend time in a manufacturing facility following the product creation process from beginning to end, focusing on how each detail in the process could be improved or how a particular machine could be better engineered. Jamshid focuses on the accounting and financial metrics; no detail is too small to escape his consideration for how performance can be improved. They exhibit focus, focus, focus and with awareness and perspective I have not seen matched in my career (and passed down that "focus on focus" to the other professionals in the organization).

Effective leaders learn to balance short-term performance demands with a focus on long-term mission related initiatives that are ultimately in the best interest of the organization and its stakeholders. That is the trick for effective leaders at all levels of an organization and all types of organizations. How do we continue to innovate in our organization while at the same time maximizing performance? This applies to each of us personally as well. We must strive to maintain focus on both short-term required tasks, which often take up most of our time, and still find enough time to focus on longer-term development tasks that are important for our own careers and our personal lives.

Using Meditation to Develop the Ability to Focus

We can develop our ability to focus, and to consciously shift focus, through meditation practice. That which we practice in meditation, we exhibit in our lives.

The common starting point for developing the ability to focus through meditation is to focus on our breath. Our breath is our life force: we can go at least a week without eating, days without drinking, but only a few minutes without breathing.

At a basic level, the breath brings oxygen to the body. The level of oxygen needed varies according to circumstances; for example, physical exertion increases the body's need for oxygen, and thus we breathe harder and faster to supply it.

At a higher level, the breath is the bridge from the body to the mind and from the outside world to the inside. Our mental and emotional states also affect our breathing. When we feel agitated or stressed, our heart rate increases and our breaths become shorter, thus reflecting the increased need for oxygen. When we are more relaxed, our need for oxygen is lower; our heart rate slows and our breathing becomes deeper and more relaxed.

Yet, for the most part, breathing just happens. As an autonomic nervous system function, breathing is automatic rather than intentional, occurring below the level of consciousness. We are not aware of it. We are not focused on it.

The focus on your breath at the beginning and end of most meditation exercises is a transition for your mind. One key aspect of meditation that is applicable to leadership is that meditation develops our ability to focus on the foreground (our conscious) and the background (our subconscious) and to become aware of the difference. Breathing typically resides in the background. During a breathing meditation, we move breath from the background to the foreground in order to focus on it; we focus on the breath in such a concentrated fashion that almost everything else (including the chatter of our day-to-day thoughts) fades into the background. Quiet mind can be observed for moments in time. New thoughts and insights often come forward to fill the void in the foreground where the day-to-day thoughts once were. These new insights provide us with greater perspective from which we can make better decisions. A refocus on the breath can often return us to the state of quiet mind.

Another key aspect of meditation is the ability to use meditation techniques to keep us centered or in balance. Balance often equates to the ability to achieve focus, calm, and perspective. When we are centered, we are able to be more aware and "see things as they really are." However, balance is illusory: once we are in balance, we seem to tip over again. Here is a common analogy: our mind is like a boat. We may at times be able to keep it securely anchored, but inevitably the currents shift and the boat drifts. Each time it drifts too far, the anchor chains tighten and the boat is brought back. It may then drift again until it reaches a point of stillness, which is temporary until the next wave.

We all come in and out of balance. However, all of us are generally at our best when at or close to balance.

Similarly, we come in and out of focus in our attention, both personally and organizationally. It would be an unreasonable expectation for someone to remain constantly focused on his or her goal, or for an institution to plow forward with a singular and constant focus. In fact, doing so might not even lead to goal achievement, as there would be no awareness or willingness to evolve or change.

In meditation, the mind naturally drifts back and forth, but a focus on the breath or on your walking or other meditation technique can be a beneficial source of refocus . . . the reminder that brings us back. The benefit is not as much in the initial focus but in the practice of greater awareness when you lose focus and the intentional return to focus.

The focus battle thus becomes whether you are able to return to focus and place your wandering mind in the background, or your wandering mind continues to break your focus and control your thoughts. The single biggest insight for me as a meditator was the moment I realized that my conscious mind/ego didn't want to be quieted. It was accustomed to controlling my thought patterns and didn't want to lose control. It would use every trick at its disposal, such as unleashing fear and anger and judgmental shame, when I tried to quiet its regular thinking pattern for even a few moments.

One of my mind's tricks for keeping control was its tendency to chastise me for "mistakes" during meditation. If I was trying to meditate and quiet my mind and a thought came into my head (as it naturally will), instead of just letting it go and continuing in meditation, my mind would start screaming at me inside my head, admonishing me for having failed and trying to convince me that meditation isn't worthwhile and I couldn't do it. It wasn't until I recognized the difference between that conscious thought process and the thoughts that come through when the conscious mind was quieted that I was able to realize the wisdom that can come from meditation. As I became aware of the resistance, I was also able to address it with self-compassion and refocus on the practice. Awareness and lack of self-judgment take the power away from the mind and I can return attention to the observer self behind the mind.

In the beginning of your meditation practice, the difference between ordinary thought and meditative experience may not be clear. It takes time to recognize the difference, just as it does to develop any new skill.

Your insight will come in time as you practice and become more aware of this difference.

Our battle with our mind is not one that most of us win all the time. In fact, the only way to win is to let go of the battle. That takes practice.

Mindfulness Meditation to Enhance Focus

Sometimes people think of meditation as doing nothing. However, the heightened levels of consciousness from a meditative state don't "just happen." This requires focused awareness or mindfulness. It requires practice.

This brings us back to the affirmative practice of mindfulness: the practice of being aware of and paying attention to the present moment throughout the day. By practicing mindfulness, we can begin to see and be aware of each image, idea, sight, sound, and sensation as it appears and changes, and observe them more purely. With practice, mindfulness becomes a well-formed habit of focused attention; the difference between doing something with mindful attention and ordinary habit will become increasingly clear. Eventually, you can affirmatively decide at various moments during the day to become more aware of the present, to look around either externally or internally, and to really see or hear or feel or touch what you observe. Those more mindful observations will be more real, more accurate and more insightful.

There is nothing passive about mindfulness. One might say that it even expresses a specific kind of passion—a passion for discerning what is subjectively real to the individual in every moment. Being mindful is not a matter of thinking more clearly about experience; it is the act of experiencing more clearly, including experiencing the arising of thoughts themselves. Mindfulness is a focused awareness of whatever is appearing in one's mind or body—thoughts, sensations, and moods—without grasping at the pleasant or recoiling from the unpleasant. One of the great strengths of this meditation technique is that it does not require us to adopt any specific cultural or religious beliefs. It does not require us to act differently at work than outside work. It simply demands that we pay close attention to the flow of experience in each moment.

The challenge of mindfulness (or any meditation technique) is distraction by uncontrolled thoughts. As noted, our mind uses this technique to distract. Even now, your mind may be asking you, "What is wrong with that?" The problem is not the thoughts themselves, but the tendency to cling to certain reoccurring thoughts and create a state of thinking without knowing that you are engaging in repetitive thought patterns that don't serve your future growth.

During meditation, there is not the absence of thoughts but the absence of clinging to those thoughts—a key difference. We observe our thoughts as they pass through our mind, we may even let them unfold a bit, but after noticing them, we let them go and move on through. We then witness what next fills the void in that present moment. It is not a question of if, but of when, the next something will appear, which may be a shape or a light or a vague concept or a different thought subject.

It is when you are in that state of being present and mindful in your everyday life that you are able to see the faults in the everyday processes in your life and in the business processes of your organization. The "fix" can be so obvious that you can't believe that you or no one else has thought of it or implemented it. It wasn't "fixed" because, although the people involved acknowledged the problem existed, they weren't paying present attention to finding solutions. Once you are aware and focus on these organizational processes with a focus on improvement, you are able to see desirable innovations and communicate them clearly and without defensiveness or other emotion. This is how mindfulness can help you be a better worker, leader and person while innovating your organization and the world.

Take some time each day to simply pay attention to the present moment. What do you see when looking with focused attention? What do you hear when listening to your colleagues and customers? View what you see and hear with awareness of the details. Be open to "ah ha moments" suggesting change.

Focus Meditation Practices

i. Breathing Exercise—Focus on Breath

Here is a meditation practice that involves a basic focus on your breath.

Observe yourself breathing.

The inhale, the pause, the exhale, the pause.

At this point, there is no need to change the pace of your breath; just notice it.

On the first day, try to spend 25 breaths focusing on your breath.

Really focus on the inhale, notice the pause, the exhale, notice the pause.

If a thought comes through your mind, notice it and let it go. Try to maintain your focus on your breath.

If you find your mind wandering and you lose focus on your breath (and you will), start over again and try to go 25 breaths focusing on your breath.

This is easier said than done.

Don't spend more than five minutes on this exercise on the first day. As previously noted, meditation is a "practice," not a "perfect." Try to resist getting frustrated at what you may perceive as a lack of success; this is truly just part of the learning process. Partake in the practice for the sake of practice.

On the next day, try to do this for a longer period of time, or try the next exercise.

ii. Breathing Exercise—Four-Part Breath

Many people (particularly Type A personalities) try to begin with this exercise because the first exercise was "easy." If this is what you think, ask yourself why. Why do you find it important to rush? Why do you prefer to control and challenge the directions? No judgment—just be aware of your answer. Spend about five minutes repeating these questions yourself.

Why do I find it important to rush?

Why do I prefer to control and challenge the directions?

Try letting the answers come to you instead of affirmatively thinking of them. The answers may tell you something about your leadership style and the extent to which you "listen" as opposed to "hear." Then, return to this second meditation tomorrow.

When you are ready to continue:

Focus on your breath.

The inhale, the pause, the exhale, the pause.

No need yet to change the pace of your breath; just notice it.

After a minute or so, try to even out your breath so that each of the four parts takes the same amount of time:

The inhale (perhaps count 1, 2, 3 as you inhale)

The pause (perhaps count 1, 2, 3 as you pause)

The exhale (perhaps count 1, 2, 3 as you exhale)

The pause (perhaps count 1, 2, 3 as you pause)

If a thought comes through your mind, notice it and let it go. Try to keep your focus on your breath.

If you find your mind wandering and you lose focus on your breath, start over again. Try to go two straight minutes focusing on your breath.

Deepen the breath after a few breaths, deepen the pause—then shorten the breath, shorten the pause for another few breaths.

Practice for about 50 breaths, each one with intention and awareness.

iii. Breathing Mindfulness Meditation

Start by taking a moment to be aware of your breath as it moves through your body.

Lower your gaze or close your eyes.

Take a few deep breaths. Inhale through your nose, exhale through your mouth.

Listen to the sound of your breath.

Feel your breath as it passes through your nostrils on the inhale.

Feel your nostrils expand. Is there a sensation in your nose that you recognize when you are mindful of it? Perhaps it is always there but in the background?

Hold the air in your lungs. Expand the lungs a little on one breath and a lot on another breath, then a little again. How does that feel different?

Feel the breath through your throat as you exhale. Make a little "ha" sound as you push the air through your throat.

Inhale through your nose and, in the next breath, inhale through your mouth. How does that feel different?

Play with your breath a little bit—meditation, like life, doesn't always have to be serious. Play with your breath and notice that you are doing so.

Notice whether you are holding any tension anywhere in your body. Set your intention to send the breath to that place of tension. With your exhale, let out a "ha" sound and try to relax that place of tension. Inhale towards the tension, then exhale.

Now come back to normal breathing. Notice how that feels, how that sounds—does it feel or sound different? How strange it is that you do this breathing involuntarily thousands of times a day without noticing.

Maybe it feels a bit different when you are aware of it. How many other things would be different if you were more aware of them?

iv. Counting Focus Meditation

Sometimes focusing on the breath just isn't sufficient. You need something to focus your mind and your breath is not sufficiently interesting. In this instance, consider a counting focus meditation. This works on the same principle as "counting sheep" when you are trying to fall asleep. In doing so, your focus on counting sheep distracts your mind from whatever activity was keeping your mind active and awake; eventually, you get bored with the sheep and fall asleep. This meditation, however, is more difficult and requires more focus than simply counting sheep.

Count in your head (or out loud) with each breath, starting with 50 and counting down by twos until 40, then counting down by ones until 30, then counting down by twos until 20, then counting down by ones until 10, and finally counting down by twos until zero.

It sounds easy, but is actually surprisingly difficult. Your focus needs to be solely on breathing and counting; if your mind starts to wander, stop, pause, and start again at 50.

Breathe in
50
Breathe out

Breathe in
48
Breathe out

Breathe in
46
Breathe out

Breathe in
44
Breathe out

Breathe in
42
Breathe out

Breathe in
40
Breathe out

Breathe in
39
Breathe out

Breathe in
38
Breathe out

Breathe in
37
Breathe out

Keep going. Not as easy as it sounds, is it?

Consider observing when you have lost complete focus on the number and the breath. When that happens return to 50. This is one of my favorite practices. It took me over a year to get to zero the first time without interrupted thought.

v. Integrating the Meditation Technique and Leadership Principle—A Focus on Excellence Meditation

Focus is very important in being an effective leader. Practicing focus in meditation has the wonderful ancillary impact of assisting us in focusing in our work and personal life. However, we often spend so much time focusing on our weaknesses and need for improvement (which is also fine for another day), we fail to be aware of and appreciate our strengths and what we do every day with excellence. We lose focus on how we can add more value through our current excellence. Today, you will focus on your excellence.

Now that you have your intention set for this meditation, start by focusing on your breath. The inhale, the pause, the exhale, the pause. You don't need to change your breath.

Close your eyes or lower your gaze to avoid distractions.

Focus again on your breath.

Ask yourself, "What is my strongest positive trait?"

What do I do with excellence?

Wait 5 breaths.

Although you likely have many, try to settle on one trait for today.

Once chosen, keep your focus on that attribute.

After 5 breaths, say the attribute again. This generally initiates a new thought stream.

Replay how you use that attribute to add value.

Pause when your thought stream runs out. Refocus on your breath.

Contemplate how you can use your attribute of excellence in a different manner in the future to achieve new value to achieve greater impact.

If you find your mind wandering during the meditation, return to your focus on your breath for a few breaths; then start again with a focus on your attribute of excellence.

As you practice, hopefully you will experience the "ah ha" moments, those moments of wisdom and insight that provide clarity. These moments typically aren't brilliant in and of themselves, but can provide perspective on things you don't tend to acknowledge when you focus on the normal chatter and tasks of your life. But don't judge or be too hard on yourself if nothing comes to you yet. It will come.

VI. NURTURING CREATIVITY—AN APPLE (AND 10 MINUTES OF MEDITATION) A DAY

Three apples have changed the world.
One seduced Eve, the second awakened Newton,
and the third was in the hands of Jobs.
Spread by social networking (origin unknown)

Once you are more aware and begin to quiet your mind on a daily basis, what fills the void of the day-to-day chatter of your "to do" list is your creativity and wisdom.

Creativity works differently and is nurtured differently in different people. I have seen creativity manifest in some people as manic spurts of being "in the zone" followed by periods of no new ideas. Other people have an ability to "think outside the box" on a regular basis. Not everyone has the same style or methods.

For me, a regular meditation practice every morning facilitates my creativity throughout the day. Whether new ideas arise during the practice or at some other time during the day, meditation facilitates the flow of new ideas that are somehow different from the regular chatter of my thoughts.

Self-awareness and focus are not enough. If we are self-aware and we focus, we may still keep doing the same things over again—we are simply more aware that we are doing so, and may be doing them a bit better and with greater attention to detail. An effective leader prompts an organization to do things better. Doing things better requires creativity to think differently about how things have always been done—in other words, innovation. The pillar of Awareness is achieved when our increased self-awareness and focus during meditation unleashes the creativity and wisdom previously harbored behind your everyday thoughts. Once unleashed, you can then observe and become aware of additional information leading to the ability to change behavior, and to achieve personal growth and innovation.

It would be inconceivable not to profile Steve Jobs, one of the great innovators of our time and co-founder and leader of Apple Computers, in a book about leadership and meditation. Jobs was able to conceptualize the personal computer when the originators only saw business uses. Jobs was able to comprehend that people would want to carry all of their music around with them on a small portable device (which seems so obvious now). Jobs was able to grasp the power of combining a computer, a music device, a telephone and Internet access together into something that literally changed how the world communicates. Jobs also spent time learning about, studying and practicing meditation.

In his book, *Steve Jobs,* renowned biographer Walter Isaacson has given us insight to Jobs' life through exclusive interviews with friends, colleagues, family members, competitors, and Jobs himself before his passing. Jobs, a self-described control freak and perfectionist, uncharacteristically allowed Isaacson to have complete discretion over what went into the final book. Thanks to Isaacson, we have the opportunity to look inside the mind of one of the greatest and most creative leaders of our time; we can also learn how Jobs' meditation training and spirituality played a crucial role in his leadership.[55]

The Story of Jobs

Jobs demonstrated how the combination of vision, creativity, and focus leads to innovation. This is the central reason why Jobs' Apple products became market leaders. Jobs became aware of an unmet need, conceptualized a product, and spent every ounce of energy developing and perfecting that product. He put his people on tight time schedules and felt that "waiting until the right time" was too late. He then stayed with the product development post-launch, listened to customer feedback, and introduced new and better versions. These are the patterns of an effective innovative leader.

How did he get there?

A devotee of meditation since his college years, in 1974 Jobs started working as a technician for Atari, which, at the time, only had about fifty employees and the best video display of the early computers. Atari's founder, Nolan Bushnell, saw past Jobs' hippie looks (and what others found to be eccentric behavior), noting that Jobs was technically proficient but more philosophical than his colleagues at Atari.

Jobs informed the Atari CEO that he wanted to quit his job at Atari in order to travel to India to find his guru. The CEO countered, telling Jobs he would pay for the India trip if Jobs first went to Germany to solve a technical discrepancy for Atari that no one else had been able to solve. "Say hi to your guru for me," were his parting words for Jobs on his way to Germany. [56]

Jobs didn't need long in Germany to resolve the technical problem. He then made it to New Delhi, but immediately fell ill. He eventually mustered enough strength to travel to a village in the Himalayas to find the guru he sought, Neem Karoli Baba. Unfortunately, by the time Jobs arrived, Neem Karoli Baba was no longer living (or, as his students pointed out, he was "no longer alive, at least in the same incarnation").[57] Jobs returned to New Delhi to experience more of India. "By this point, Jobs was no longer trying to find a guru who could impart wisdom," writes Isaacson, "but instead was seeking enlightenment through ascetic experience, deprivation, and simplicity." [58] He sought meditation and related practices that taught focus, discipline and perspective.

Most of us spend some time disappointed that our own road is not linear. We assume that things must have just "worked out" for those who are successful. As part of learning awareness and leadership development, it becomes apparent that different people have different life stories. None is better or worse than others. Inevitably, all include positive and negative experiences. Some of our most positive lessons and growth come from experiences that initially appear to be negative, such as being assigned an overwhelming work project or being fired from a job that wasn't really a good fit . . . or even traveling across the world to find that your "guru" is no longer alive, when you were sure that this guru would provide you with all the answers you were seeking.

Upon his return to America, Jobs began working again with his high school friend Steve Wozniak and a few others in a garage, creating what eventually would become the first Apple computer. While pursuing technological innovation, however, Jobs did not stop his search for enlightenment. In the mornings and evenings, he would study meditation techniques, and in between he would drop in to audit physics or engineering courses at Stanford.

Jobs was advised by his Zen teacher in California not to go to Japan or India to find a new guru. "He said there was nothing over there that isn't here," recalled Jobs. "I learned the truth of the Zen saying that if you are willing to travel around the world to meet a teacher, one will appear next door."[59] Jobs used Zen meditation techniques to tune out distractions. He began to realize that intuitive understanding and higher consciousness were more significant than abstract thinking and intellectual logical analysis. Eventually, he encouraged Apple's employees to practice meditation to boost their creativity and overall awareness.

Part of Jobs' strength as a leader was his charisma and strong leadership presence. "Jobs came to believe that he could impart that feeling of passion and confidence to others and thus push them to do things they hadn't thought possible," writes Isaacson. "[Jobs was] masterful at cajoling, stroking, persuading, flattering, and intimidating people . . . There were some upsides to Jobs' demanding and wounding behavior. People who were not crushed were only made stronger. They did better work, out of both fear and an eagerness to please."[60]

For example, Isaacson retells the following story. "One day Jobs came into the cubicle of Larry Kenyon, an engineer who was working on the Macintosh operating system, and complained that it was taking too long to boot up. Kenyon started to explain, but Jobs cut him off. 'If it could save a person's life, would you find a way to shave ten seconds off the boot time?' he asked. Kenyon allowed that he probably could. Jobs went to a whiteboard and showed that if there were five million people using the Mac, and it took ten additional seconds to turn it on every day, that added up to three hundred million or so hours per year that people would save, which was the equivalent of at least one hundred lifetimes saved per year. 'Larry was suitably impressed, and a few weeks later he came back and it booted up twenty-eight seconds faster,' Atkinson [a Mac designer] recalled. Steve had a way of motivating by looking at the bigger picture.'"[61] This story shows how creatively reframing a challenge can help it resonate with people and motivate them toward innovation.

Jobs infused Apple employees with an abiding passion to create groundbreaking products and a belief that they could accomplish what seemed impossible. As Isaacson observes, they didn't just make what we already had better; Apple created products that we didn't even know we needed— and once we became aware of them, we couldn't live without them.

Leadership Lessons from Jobs

A key benefit of meditation, and what one can learn from combining a regular meditation practice with the study of leadership and management principles, is how to develop this creativity and turn it into innovation—how to take facts and data and turn them into solutions. Sometimes these solutions are right before our eyes; it is just a question of being aware enough and focused enough to see them. Sometimes, they are behind our eyes; we need to open up the space in front of us by having the awareness to conceptualize the solution within the empty space of a meditative state of consciousness. Then, once we are aware of the solution, we can use our conscious mind to think through the creative solution logically to implement it.

In contrast to the Peters' and Waterman's "business school" attributes of excellence which stress staying focused on key organizational themes, Jobs' leadership attributes focus on creating solutions; they stem from the ability to direct one's creativity toward a practical purpose. Isaacson published lessons he learned from Jobs in the April 2012 issue of the *Harvard Business Review*.[62] Below are 10 lessons extracted from Isaacson's list and published by Forbes magazine to highlight how Jobs' spirituality combined with intensity allowed him to "Think Different".[63]

1. **Simplify**—Apple achieved a Zen-like simplicity in the minimalist design of Apple products. According to Apple's first brochure, "Simplicity is the ultimate sophistication." Jobs was able to look at products and processes with a fresh view toward simplifying. For example, Jobs surprised his colleagues when he decreed that the iPod would not have an off-on switch. It became true of most Apple devices. The software could be created to turn off the device when not in use for a period of time and thus there was no need for one. How many processes in your life or organization could be simplified?

2. **Control the experience**—Apple's "closed and proprietary system" made the company and its add-on software products more attractive to consumers and set them apart from competitors. Control can be positive, but too much control can be limiting. Apple later published code so that everyone and not just Apple could make iPhone and iPad apps, a key decision

that fostered the widespread development of useful apps versus what was then a more closed BlackBerry system. We each balance our desire to control our environment with the awareness that full control is not really possible, and always seeking control can be limiting.

3. **Innovate**—Jobs believed that it is not enough to continue to do what has already been done. Apple sought to provide different and better solutions. We each have the potential to continue to grow. All organizations, products and services that do not innovate will ultimately become obsolete — it is only a question of time.

4. **Ignore reality**—Jobs' "reality distortion field" proved to be efficient even when others doubted him. According to Apple software designer Bud Tribble: "In his presence, reality is malleable. He can convince anyone of practically anything. It wears off when he's not around, but it makes it hard to have realistic schedules." This may seem contrary to a meditation practice that fosters greater awareness of reality. However, reality is always changing. The difference is being limited by current reality and opening up to the possibility of what can be a new, expanded reality.

5. **Have confidence**—Debi Coleman, who joined the Mac team in 1982, said, "'I had learned that you had to stand up for what you believe, which Steve respected. I started getting promoted by him after that.' Eventually she rose to become head of manufacturing." Standing up to be heard is an important part of being a leader. You simply have to pick your moments and be willing to listen to the response.

6. **Rethink designs** —Jobs would look at each component and require the design team to go back and make improvements. He purportedly said that design is not just how a product looks and feels, but how it works. It requires that you maintain discipline during innovation and focus on the details.

7. **Team with winners**—Jobs believed his "rough treatment" ensured that only the best and brightest worked at Apple. Jobs noted, "It's too easy, as a team grows, to put up with a few B players, and then they attract more B players and soon you will

have some C players. The Macintosh experience taught me that A players like to work only with other A players, which means you can't indulge B players."

8. **Collaborate**—Jobs believed in holding spontaneous meetings and using the experience and ideas of everyone in the group to reach the best result. "Collaboration" is the big leadership and corporate culture buzzword today. Formalizing collaboration in your corporate culture fosters effective collaboration actually occurring.

9. **Vision and details**—Jobs noted, "Some CEOs are great visionaries while others know that God is in the details." Great organizations have both a clearly articulated vision with broad organizational buy-in and a continuous focus on implementation consistent with enhancing that vision.

10. **Rebel**—As stated in the "Think Different" advertisements that Jobs helped create, "While some see them as the crazy ones, we see genius. Because the people who are crazy enough to think they can change the world are the ones who do." Know that you can change the world.

Few of us could be (or perhaps even want to be) Steve Jobs. But the awareness and focus that comes from being fully in the present moment—something that Jobs practiced through meditation—undoubtedly contributed to the creativity that allowed him to create visionary new products and innovative business models, and to become the leader of one of the greatest companies of our lifetime. Challenge yourself to "think different" to break out of personal and organizational patterns that may assist you in achieving moderate success but limit your ability for greatness. Meditation is how we learn to "think different."

Using Creativity to Foster Innovation

At our law firm, we had an "innovation challenge." Teams voluntarily formed groups of up to 6 employees (not just lawyers) to develop an innovative idea. There were few rules (other than an unrealistically short word limit to articulate the group's innovative idea). Each group could only propose its best single idea and a committee would choose the single best idea from all of the submissions. The winning idea would be implemented, and the winning team members would be awarded an attractive travel prize. Naturally, many great ideas were produced and more than one was implemented.

In addition to a great personal experience with my diverse group, which included four lawyers in different practice areas, a secretary staff leader and a billing staff member, the process improved morale and created an atmosphere where staff now know that new ideas from anyone will be considered. We all can be leaders, and participation in innovation is a morale-boosting experience.

As part of the process, we received a syllabus of books about innovation. I was surprised by how different the approaches to innovation are. My favorite is by Wharton Professor Adam Grant, who I also had the opportunity to hear speak at a venture capital conference where I saw why he was Wharton's top-ranked teacher for four consecutive years. In his book *Originals—How Non-Conformists Move the World*,[64] Grant articulates how originality and innovation can be launched, nurtured and sustained.

Grant points out that originality starts with creativity: generating a concept that is both novel and useful.[65] "Originals" are people who take the initiative to make their vision a reality. Grant points out that Originals have the same fears and doubts as the rest of us, but what sets them apart is that they push through these fears and doubts and take action anyway.

To be an innovation leader, thinking of the idea is not enough. I know a tremendous number of creative and visionary people and would-be entrepreneurs who think of lots of interesting ideas and are not able to implement any of them. That happens to most of us to varying degrees; often, we hear about someone else who built a company or created a new product or service offering and think, "I thought of that and should have done something."

In the world of infinite possibilities that visionaries live in, one important trait for actually accomplishing goals is not just the ability to conceptualize new ideas, but the ability to focus (whether self-focus or channeling the focus of others) on the implementation of those new ideas.

Practices to Foster Creativity

Creativity generally cannot be forced. You can't simply say to yourself, "I am now going to take 15 minutes and be creative and innovative and solve all of the problems I face. Start the clock—GO!" Creativity has to be nurtured. The scope of creativity that exists within each of us is amazing. All we have to do is open the space, let our creative ideas float to the front of our consciousness, and then be aware enough to recognize them and focused enough to retain and implement them.

The way in which we open space during meditation is to focus on something other than our day-to-day thoughts. As Albert Einstein said: "No problem can be solved with the same level of consciousness that created it." The thoughts that pass by and can be observed during meditation are different. If we allow ourselves in the safety of our own meditative consciousness to remove limits we place on ourselves and our thoughts in our day-to-day consciousness, new thought patterns emerge, so called "out-of-the-box" thoughts. You don't have to judge them as they arise, simply observe them and you can later add the additional analytic input during your conscious analysis. I find that this combination of meditative observation and later conscious analysis is my best source for creativity, innovation and growth. The innovation is not usually groundbreaking like a Steve Jobs invention but a marginal improvement or new way to communicate an idea or a reminder of something I knew but was not implementing. Becoming more aware of a series of incremental improvements can make each of us more effective.

We begin again with self-awareness to get started and choose a technique to unleash our inner creativity. There is a focus on the activity to take our mind out of its day-to-day chatter to create moments of stillness. Stillness can be where creativity, the solutions to problems and innovative ideas, can be found.

Open the space for innovation by trying the meditative practices below.

i. Practice the Arts

Sometimes creative thinking can be fostered through other creative activities. Pick an art medium and practice it daily for a while during your allotted meditation time.

For example, you could buy a basic paint set and paint for 10 minutes a day. Don't worry about how technically good it is. Just paint and let happen whatever happens without judgment. No one else even has to see it. Adult coloring books have become a quick, easy and popular way to achieve creativity without the need for artistic talent. You can decide to stay within the lines or decide to color outside the lines. Try a page each way and notice whether one way makes you uncomfortable.

You could also try singing daily, or African drumming, or daily prayer. For this purpose, it doesn't matter what you are singing, playing or praying, or how well you are doing it. The key is that you are focused on the song, musical beat or prayer, and that you are wholly present for the experience. Many people sing in the shower, where they feel less likely to be overheard. Many people pray alone in their bedroom in the morning or before going to sleep.

Another common practice is to keep a journal. You can write whatever comes to your mind. Some people like to write about what is going on in their lives and some people write creative fiction. Consider starting a short story about whatever flows through your mind.

My daughters very effectively use art and music not simply to de-stress, but to educate and entertain themselves and others with their talent and creations. This fostering of creativity can be a meditation in and of itself by distracting you from your day-to-day thoughts and life, thus allowing space for new and innovative thoughts. It can also sometimes result in meaningful insights that wouldn't come to you through other mediums.

ii. Creating Your Space Meditation

Escape, whether physical on vacation or metaphysical in meditation, can create space for new and different ideas that are harder to generate in the midst of everyday life.

Consider a "happy place" where you visualize being free from life's pressures and can really escape your day-to-day world. For me, that is a lake surrounded by mountains, but it could be a meadow or a beach, a deserted island or your childhood bedroom. The lake metaphor is used below, but feel free to substitute your own location.

Close your eyes and take a few deep breaths to center yourself. Deep breath in, pause, deep breath out, pause. Deep breath in, pause, deep breath out, pause.

Imagine yourself looking out on a lake surrounded by mountains. Take a few deep breaths from your nose to smell the fresh air. Feel the temperature and a subtle breeze.

You see a wooden boat and get inside. Pick up the paddles and start paddling to the middle of the lake. Steady paddling—back and forth, back and forth. The water moves gently with each stroke.

Be aware of the feeling in your arms and shoulders as you continue to paddle. Be aware of any other sensations in your body.

In the middle of the lake, you arrive at an island. You feel very comfortable. You are upbeat and excited as you get out of the boat and walk forward toward the middle of this island.

This will be your new work space. It may look like your existing work space or quite different. Picture what your ideal work space would look like for you. Would it be inside or outside? Would it be light or dark? Would it feel warm or would it feel cool? Would it be in your current organization or someplace else? Try to observe what your imagination is creating.

After a few moments, consider how this is different from your current work space. Note the differences and move on.

Set an intention for your work. What do you wish to accomplish? What value would you like to be creating?

Reflect on the differences from your current career.

Consider a few concrete ideas to hold on to about the differences between your imagined work environment and your actual work environment. What changes can you make to more closely align the two? How can you innovate your personal work space to increase your productivity?

After a few moments, focus again on your breath and begin to allow your consciousness to return. If you desire to do so, write down your ideas.

iii. Take a Yoga Class

At its core, the practice of yoga is meditation in motion. Yoga practice brings your focus to physical postures to quiet the everyday chatter of your mind. More than 36 million Americans participated in at least one yoga class during 2016.[66]

The word yoga derives from the word "yoke," which implies yoking the body to the mind and also to the soul.[67] There are many forms of traditional yoga, including karma yoga (pursuit of action devoted to the divine), jnana yoga (pursuit of the path to wisdom), bhakti yoga (devotio ich's classes start with guided postures (like a normal class), and then, when you are in a state of greater awareness of your body (at least that day at that time), he gives you the freedom to follow your own inner guidance to complete your yoga practice (and thus his style has become known as "freedom yoga"). Erich observes: "Moving into stillness in order to experience your true nature is the primary theme of yoga simply because everything about you—every thought, feeling and emotion, as well as every aspect of your behavior—is predicated on the way you feel about yourself. The way you feel about yourself determines how you think, what you do, and how you interact with the world."[69]

At its core, yoga is the practice of postures without attachment to results. It doesn't matter how far the person next to you can go or what you could do on a different day. You are taught to go to your edge, and not beyond, in each moment. I think of the difference between yoga and stretching as moving with awareness and intention versus simple physical movement—awareness not just of body but of both breath and body moving in sync with intention to stay in that awareness. My favorite vinyasa yoga teachers are able to help me integrate the timing of the postures with the timing of my breath in a flow of movement. While it may not look difficult, it is not easy. What I find to be the "magic" of yoga is what is unleashed into my consciousness after I have become focused in the flow. That is when ordinary thoughts move to the background and creative ones can be observed. That is where virtually all of the innovative concepts in this book originate. I observed them during practice and then wrote them down.

Most styles of yoga practice are designed to provide the practitioner with a different experience each session, depending on that person's needs at that time on that day (even within a class of others with different needs). We all get "stuck"—whether in our thoughts, our emotions, or our bodies—and that "stuckness" inhibits our creativity. Yoga certainly helps to get physically unstuck—many practitioners (including myself) report vast improvements in back pain and other ailments—but it also works to relieve energetic blockages and mental and emotional blockages, which can positively unleash creativity.

Stephen Cope was one of my first yoga teachers. When I was 40, my wife and I went to the Kripalu Institute to take a one-week seminar on yoga basics. During that week, while learning the postures and listening to teachings from a variety of the Kripalu staff, I read Cope's book, entitled *The Wisdom of Yoga: A Seeker's Guide to Extraordinary Living*.[70]

Cope taps into the rich wisdom and tradition of yoga beyond the stretching movements (or asanas) and demonstrates its relevance to our daily lives as a tool to deal with suffering and achieve contentment. While an initial lesson of yoga may be awareness, a continuing practice can encompass your own personal evolution and development. Here is an excerpt from Stephen Cope on the use of yoga as part of our quest for wisdom:

"I first discovered yoga more than twenty years ago. Like most Americans, I came to it initially as a form of physical exercise. It didn't take me long to appreciate the enormous benefits of yoga postures and breathing exercises, and I found myself drawn into a regular practice that steadily increased my energy, stamina, concentration, resilience, and enjoyment of life. In the early years of my practice, however, I didn't appreciate that these physical practices are only one facet of a vast and extremely sophisticated wisdom tradition. I didn't realize that the yoga postures I was doing at my health club are part of a three-thousand-year-old science of extraordinary living that concerns itself with every aspect of human functioning—mental, physical, and spiritual.

As I discovered the larger wisdom tradition of yoga, I was intrigued: The practitioners of this science of extraordinary living have lived and thrived on the Indian subcontinent for at least the last three millennia. They have concerned themselves with a series of perennial questions—questions that are as challenging today as they were when scantily clad yogis first gathered in the forests and mountains of India: What is an optimal human life? What would it be like to function at the maximum potential of our minds and bodies?

For at least three thousand years, yogis have carried out experiments to investigate these questions. Their bold investigations have led to remarkable discoveries about human perception, attention, cognition, motivation, sensory integration, memory, intuition, and volition. These early yogis found that very few human beings live anywhere near the optimal range of human functioning. At the same time, they demonstrated that almost any of us could do so, with much less effort than we imagine. **Surprisingly extraordinary living does not require more native genius than most of us already have** (emphasis added)."[71]

It would take me at least five years of yoga practice and returning to Kripalu for another Cope teaching to appreciate what he was communicating: yoga is not just stretching that helps my back; instead, yoga is a philosophy of living that helps one live a better life with less suffering.

If you don't practice yoga (or haven't in a while), consider finding a beginner yoga class in your area and give it a try. If you don't like one yoga style, keep trying until you find the style and teacher that is right for you. If you do practice yoga, try to make your practice more regular. As we learn more about leadership and meditation, you may find your yoga practice to be a meditation in motion, and a lot more meaningful.

iv. Integrating the Meditation Technique and Leadership Principle—Process Innovation Meditation

To again quote Apple's first brochure, "Simplicity is the ultimate sophistication." Many of the most innovative ideas are, in fact, simple once they are recognized. Meditation is a tool to assist us in making these recognitions, which we sometimes call awareness.

This next exercise incorporates many of the ten lessons inspired by Jobs along with our meditation lesson of being aware of our observations.

Close your eyes or lower your gaze. Focus on your breath, the inhale, the pause, the exhale, the pause. You don't need to change your breath.

Try mindful breathing. Focus first on the physical feeling of your breath as the air enters your nostrils, goes down through your throat, sits in your lungs and then moves its way back up your chest to your throat and out your nose. Try breathing in and out through your mouth and notice whether that feels different.

Now listen to your breath as your breathe in and breathe out. Do you hear any other noises?

Breathe in and notice whether there is any smell in the air that you are breathing. Does the air feel clear? Do you feel any temperature, either a bit of warmth or some coolness in the air as the air moves through you?

Now consider a complex business process within your organization—something that people do every day and that is important to your organization or simply time-consuming. Bring that business process into your awareness.

Slowly go through each step of that business process over the next few minutes. Repeat this a few times.

The first time, slowly run through each step of this business process—not just your role, but the role of each person during each step of the process, from input to resolution to output.

The second time, imagine the emotion each person feels at each step of the process. Is there frustration? Is there gratification? Is there sometimes anger? Is there sometimes satisfaction? Try to experience what each participant may be feeling.

The third time consider whether there might be untapped efficiencies in the process. Is there a simpler way a step could be completed? Don't focus yet on why the step is inefficient or the details of how it could be improved; rather, be aware of what can be done in an ideal setting. What would be the simplest way to get from input to output?

Now consider what holds back this change. Why might others think you can't make a change? What will impede the change, even though it is simpler and may be innovative and increase efficiency? Often, overcoming what holds us back is simply a question of recognizing it and addressing that obstacle with the same level of intention as the problem itself. Now that you are aware, how can you overcome what holds back a better outcome?

If you have come up with a change, go through the process again step-by-step with the obstacles to change lifted, this change implemented, and notice not just the logistics but how the participants feel while going through the process. Is it different? Did you come up with any additional ideas for fine-tuning the better process, now that the obstacles to change have been removed?

Consider writing down some of your observations from this meditation exercise.

Building the Pillar of Awareness

Meditation is a practice of using concentration and focus techniques to be more aware in the present moment more of the time. Simple practices such as a focus on the breath or focus on walking or any of your senses take your mind out of its day-to-day pattern. This gives you the opportunity to observe what fills the void, both externally and internally. Over time, you will experience moments of stillness or quiet mind.

While more aware, you will see situations more clearly and with greater context. You may notice changes or trends in the marketplace that significantly impact your business, customer dissatisfaction before they stop ordering, morale of a valued employee before he or she departs without warning, how fear or self-doubt influence your behavior (or inability to take action) or innovative creative ideas that add value to your workplace or the world. You may become more aware of your thoughts and actions within the context of a greater purpose.

Observing without judgment facilitates your ability to see things as they really are. As will be set forth in the following chapters, being more aware also helps you see people more as they really are, facilitates decision making with more clear perspective and helps you spot opportunities you didn't previously realize even exist.

BUILDING THE PILLAR OF CONNECTION

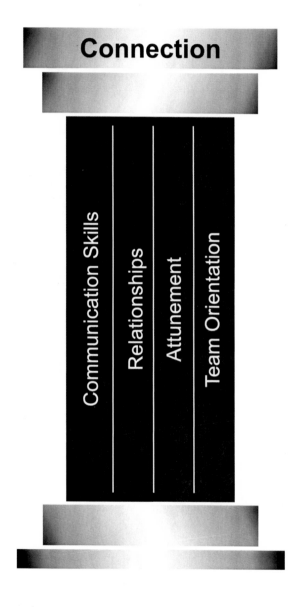

VII. HOW TO COMMUNICATE WELL
(AND INFLUENCE PEOPLE)

The art of effective listening is essential to clear communication and
clear communication is necessary to management success.

James Cash (JC) Penney, Entrepreneur

One of the keys to successful leadership is the ability to communicate effectively with other people. Interacting with someone else—someone who brings his or her own personality and personal life experience (much of which you won't know) to the relationship—in a manner that works for both of you is what effective leaders seem instinctively to be able to do. Successful interpersonal interactions are heavily dependent upon communication skills. Communication skills are a key differentiating factor between an effective and an ineffective person.

The communication inflection point for me was realizing that effective communication is greatly assisted by emotional awareness and the ability to control the emotional response. In my life it has rarely been the better decision to react emotionally instead of waiting to formulate a thoughtful response.

In prior chapters, we practiced meditation to make us more aware, enable us to focus and regain focus, and help us open up space for creativity; we used practices that make us more mindful by focusing our attention on our body, our breath, and our surroundings, and by engaging in a mindful physical activity such as yoga or an art project. At this point, we are still focused primarily on our self and our own actions. Meditation can also make us more aware emotionally, sometimes also known as "emotional mindfulness." Our emotions impact not just ourselves but our interactions with others.

Once we are more aware of an emotion, we can experience it and then release that emotion, rather than keep it pent up inside. We can change our actions and reactions (which shape our communications with others), so that we can ultimately forgive both ourselves and others. We can avoid carrying old negativity around as "emotional baggage" that serves as a barrier to our relationships with others and develop effective communication skills that are not weighed down by the challenges from our past. Our actions influence others' reactions. This means that meditation can positively affect not just your own actions, but the actions of others, creating a scalable leadership impact.

When in a neutral emotional state and paying focused attention during a conversation, it is easier to hear what is being said and to observe subtle information about what is not being said. This can lead to asking questions that you wouldn't have asked if you hadn't been truly listening and gaining further insight from the answers. It all starts from your own state of awareness.

Awareness of your emotions can have as great a result as awareness of your thoughts and actions on your effectiveness, both in the workplace and at home. Communication built upon emotional mindfulness is less about changing the substance of what you say than adapting how you say it (if you even choose to say something at all). How you say something when reacting to someone is often more important to that person than what you actually say. In fact, other people will be much more likely to react positively to *what* you say if they respond positively to *how* you say it.

When we are unaware of the past's impact on our present, we are more likely to deal with difficult emotional situations by compartmentalizing our emotions, tucking them somewhere in our minds and bodies, rather than fully dealing with our emotional response to those situations. As a result, what often limits our effectiveness is not an event or situation itself, but the emotional baggage that impacts our reaction to the event or situation based on some lingering (conscious or unconscious) emotional residue from our past. Thus, instead of seeing the situation and the participants as they are, you see them through the misleading lens of a past reaction. What others see is your anger, impatience and disapproval.

The way in which you communicate with others, and the way you react to how others communicate with you, is dictated by your past experiences, how you deal with them, and your current awareness. By recognizing the link between communication and reaction to communication, you will become more aware of the emotional component of your and others' reactions, better understand how past emotional situations impact you and others, and adjust your communication style so that you are more likely to be an influential leader. You will then naturally be more open, compassionate and accepting once you understand this link.

Best Practices for Effective Communication

In 1936, Dale Carnegie wrote the then-seminal book for business relationships, *How to Win Friends and Influence People.* One section describes how to be a good leader.[72] The key, according to Carnegie, is to change people's behavior without giving offense or arousing resentment. Carnegie urges a team leader to consider *how* something is said to team members. While we may not know someone's back story or be able to fully anticipate how he or she will react to every communication, we can often avoid common emotional triggers by using communication "best practices."

Carnegie provides the following list of communication principles for leaders:[73]

1. Begin with praise and honest appreciation.
2. Call attention to people's mistakes indirectly rather than bluntly.

3. Talk about your own mistakes before criticizing the other person.

4. Ask questions that lead the group to your desired decision instead of giving direct orders.

5. Let the other person save face when you make a decision different from his or her point of view.

6. Praise every improvement.

7. Give the other person a fine reputation to live up to.

8. Use encouragement. Make the fault seem easy to correct so they take the initiative to correct it.

9. Make the other person happy about doing the thing you suggest.

You may notice three things about these communication principles. First, they are implemented with a positive goal of opportunity for improvement rather than criticism or punishment. They are unencumbered by negative experiences or outcomes that the speaker may have had in past interactions or relationships; instead, they seem to "start fresh" by assuming that the listener has the best possible intentions and will respond accordingly. Second, they reflect the fact that the speaker is mindful of the likely emotional reaction of the receiver. Finally, by embracing a positive tone, these practices are more likely to lead to the speaker achieving his or her desired outcome of improvement from the communication rather than a negative reaction or the receiver ignoring the content of the conversation going forward. These communication techniques create a win-win interaction between the two conversation participants.

It's Not What You Say, But How You Say It:

Communication at Work

How many times has your reaction to another person been significantly out of proportion to the actual event, either because of similar mistakes made by that person or even by others in your past? Some people yell; many others, however, would never allow themselves to yell at coworkers, but might speak in a frustrated, sarcastic, or disapproving tone of voice. Either way, coworkers hear the negative tone; this distracts them from hearing the substance of the message and leaves a lasting (negative) impression—much more lasting than the actual content of the discussion. It is generally more effective to resolve an issue with coworkers by discussing substance than by sounding accusatory, which causes them to become defensive and thus not be fully engaged in the resolution. The hard part is that you may not even realize you are doing this.

Exit interviews with departing employees sometimes amaze me because of what the employee remembers and highlights for "improvement." Outbound employees may describe a specific incident that left a negative impression on them that I, as the practice group leader, do not consider to be substantively important. It took me a long time to resist my urge to ignore such feedback, acknowledge to myself that I may frequently be unintentionally speaking with a negative tone of voice and instead seek to improve *how* I say and do things and to be more sensitive to others' points of view.

An effective leader should find an appropriate time to provide feedback and criticism; after due warning, sufficient opportunity, and reasonable assistance to improve, an ineffective worker should be let go. Those are decisions made by an effective leader. However, the percentage of time that feedback leads to successful change (rather than deteriorating into the need to terminate the relationship) can be improved by focusing on how you communicate your message and how carefully you listen to the person's response. It is important to provide substantive criticism not just at annual evaluation time, but close to the time of the occurrence of the growth opportunity, while the substance and context are still top of mind for everyone involved. Otherwise, the other person will blithely continue in the same manner without the opportunity to understand and improve upon his or her performance; in addition, this person will then be surprised (and, likely, resentful) if his or her performance is later questioned, particularly if that impacts his or her compensation. If the situation is emotionally charged, these conversations are generally more productive if held after "the heat of the moment" has passed but before too much time goes by; this is a fine line to walk, but the goal is to ensure that substance, rather than emotion, is the hallmark of the conversation.

Below are two potential communications delivered by an experienced lawyer to a young lawyer whose work requires revision. Can you feel the difference between the two? If you were the young lawyer, which communication would be more motivating and more likely to spur improvement in your job performance? If you were the experienced lawyer, which would be more likely to lead to the outcome you desire?

Communication #1: John, this agreement is unacceptable. You used inconsistent formatting, you spelled the name of the client wrong, and this definition of net profits makes no sense at all. I have marked up the agreement. Read my mark-up and ask me any questions you have. I want a revised draft on my desk when I get in tomorrow morning. Our clients expect a better work product from our lawyers. You are either going to improve or you are not going to make it here.

Communication #2: John, thank you for this draft agreement and for getting it to me within the time period I requested. I marked up the agreement and I'm returning it to you for revision. Overall, you did a good job describing the business and the purchase aspect of the transaction. I want to go over with you the net profits definition, which didn't quite work. I know understanding and integrating accounting principles into agreements with precision is difficult and takes years of experience. One idea may be to take an "Accounting for Lawyers" course, which many of our associates have found helpful. Also, my mark-up notes a number of typos and some inconsistent formatting, which is likely the result of cutting and pasting text from multiple documents. A consistently formatted document looks more professional. In addition, one of the lessons I had to learn (the hard way) is that clients seem to notice typos more than they notice substantive differences in legal documents, since they rely on us to handle the substantive content. I remember working really hard on a document when I was a first-year associate and was proud of the final work product; however, when it was sent to the client, he noticed only that his name was spelled wrong in two places. He then doubted my credibility and asked the partner to review all of my work before sending it to him. I was crushed and I don't want you to go through that experience, so please take notice of each person and entity name and double check it. When I create and edit my work directly on the computer, I always print the entire document and read it before sending it out. I find that I catch more mistakes that way than just reading the document on the computer screen; you will have to figure out what method works best for you, but consider at least trying that one. Let's go through my suggested changes page by page so I can explain my thinking with respect to each one. I would like to see a revised draft on my desk when I get in tomorrow morning so that we can meet the client's deadline. Overall, good job—but together let's make the next draft even better.

Of course, not all key work-related relationships are worker/supervisor. Effective leaders have the ability to develop and maintain effective relationships with peers, customers, vendors and others who provide value to an organization. Carnegie actually spends most of his book focusing on sales—a salesperson's relationships with current and prospective customers or constituents. In the past, these interactions most likely occurred in person. Today, a growing number of communications are by email or even text; what people write in a work email or text is often shocking. Sarcasm generally does not translate well in written communication. Rather, all communications with customers and other stakeholders should be professional and "forwardable" to others. Email and text are not good tools for emotionally-charged conversations.

The Carnegie method includes listening, paying attention, and providing support to the customer, both substantively and from a personal relationship point of view. It involves having back-and-forth communications and conversations in which you (i) really listen to what your customer has to say and (ii) are sensitive to respond in a manner that the other person is likely to hear and absorb, conveying in your reaction that you have heard and understood the message. We would now call this "empathetic listening" or "active listening."

For years, my wife, Stefanie, a former chief marketing officer at a major Philadelphia law firm and a natural empathetic listener, would frequently chastise me: "You're not listening." I would profess that I was, but it wasn't until years later that I understood the difference between hearing what the other person said and "active listening," a key component to mindful communication.

Quiet Your Mind ... and Listen

Mindful communication is facilitated by being genuinely interested in other people. Carnegie references former Harvard president and professor Charles W. Elliot: "There is no mystery about successful business intercourse... Exclusive attention to the person who is speaking to you is very important. Nothing else is so flattering as that."[74] Carnegie also references Henry James, one of America's great novelists, and his recollection of Elliot: "Dr. Elliot's listening was not mere silence, but a form of activity, He ....seemed to be hearing with his eyes as well as his ears." [75]

You can't hear if you don't listen. Stopping to listen, observe the other person's situation or nonverbal reaction, and being more present and aware allows us to spot the opportunities that are right in front of us, but we often don't recognize them until we are ready. Lisa Greenberg Gonzalez at Meditation4Leadership describes that her yoga training taught her that there are five levels of listening: (1) ignoring (don't hear the other person), (2) pretending (body looks like you are listening but mind is somewhere else); (3) selective (hear what you want to hear); (4) attentive (hear and are aware of the words) and (5) empathetic (hear with caring about what the person is saying). You can learn this mindful empathetic listening skill through the practice of meditation.

Mindful communication is a byproduct of meditative practices that quiet the mind and allow you to practice listening to what fills the void. During meditation, the "speaker" is your day-to-day thoughts. They come at you — thought, next thought, next thought. In a meditative consciousness, the thoughts coming in from the background come more slowly and seem different, generally more insightful. You have time to listen and observe and you care about doing so. You can then take the time to process those background thoughts and integrate them with your day-to-day thoughts. It is hard to describe, but universally experienced by those with a regular meditation practice. You can thus learn from meditation practice to be present and actually listen during listening time and think/respond during response time, both in connection with your meditation practice and in your life generally.

Notice what is going on in your mind during conversations with other people and incorporate into your response decision. Does your mind run wild, distracting you with its thoughts or planning the next thing you are going to say? If so, try instead to listen when the other person is speaking, pause, think, and then respond. Empathetic listening is not listening to advise, evaluate, probe or interpret; empathic listening is listening to connect.

Consider the similarity to our meditation practice focusing on connecting with your breath (except, in this case, the inhale is the focus on what the other person is saying, then the pause, then the focus on what you are saying, then the pause). Not only is this polite, but empathetic listening provides a better substantive result and allows you to develop deeper relationships with others, whether they are work colleagues, customers, friends, or family members. No one likes to hear or speak a half-hour monologue. Instead, engage the other person in conversation by mixing in relevant responses. Remember to pause. In my experience, the other person will view a conversation in which each person speaks roughly half the time as more satisfying than one in which one person (either person) speaks 90 percent of the time.

This ability to listen empathetically becomes easier when you are in an emotionally neutral or positive state. It is much easier to wait your turn to speak if the conversation is about something logistical or procedural. If the conversation topic or your feelings toward the other person are emotionally charged, then empathetic listening becomes significantly more difficult. Extending your empathetic listening ability to all situations requires practice.

Meditation To Clear Your Lens

The practice of listening from within during meditation also facilitates the ability to listen to others. What we notice in meditation is that sometimes the lens through which we see situations or listen to others is clouded by our own past. Our unprocessed emotions can cause us to hear differently than intended by the speaker and to speak differently than we intend. Listening to others with awareness of our own emotional reaction assists us in communicating to others in a manner that will ensure that they best receive the message and a connection is established or reinforced.

For many people, being sensitive to others' points of view is easy, but for others, it is one of the hardest leadership lessons to learn. By helping you become more mindful of emotions (both yours and other people's), meditation techniques can subsequently help you develop more mindful communication skills that are critical to effective leadership. More specifically, meditation techniques can help you learn to be present and recognize the emotions you are feeling or bringing to a situation; this recognition will make you much more able to communicate with someone in a way that is appropriate for the situation.

Meditation practices that involve rooting yourself in the present and being cognizant of your emotions will make it easier for you to recognize the likely emotion of the other person during potentially difficult interactions, enabling you to validate their viewpoint, either directly or subtly. You can also learn techniques to help you react more appropriately in frustrating situations, such as taking a deep breath before speaking. This will positively impact your content, tone of voice, and, therefore, others' reactions to you.

Most of us let our emotional states linger longer than necessary; as the Buddha said, "You will not be punished for your anger; you will be punished by your anger." Upon becoming angry, we tend to stay angry by replaying again and again the reasons we were made angry—the insult, the lack of desired compensation increase or bonus, or the rude behavior of a colleague or customer. We recall the insult and reconsider what we should have said in reply; in doing so, we resurrect the anger and keep it alive. However, we do have the power to change our emotional state; sometimes we do so voluntarily, and sometimes it just happens. For example, you may be angry over a client situation when a different client calls. You are able to "forget" your anger temporarily—you can set aside your angered state and focus on the content of the new telephone call. Does the anger come back? Maybe, maybe not. You have a better chance of ensuring that the anger does not return if you recognize the difference between "tanking" the emotion (burying it deep into your stored emotional warehouse) and feeling it and letting it go.

Each initial emotional reaction is actually quite brief, but we keep rerunning the loop every time we relive the situation in our mind. In other words, if something happens that makes us angry, the initial anger actually only lasts about 90 seconds.[76] Then, we repeat the event in our mind over again, continuing the anger for another 90 seconds. We may take a break to think about or do something else; we feel better until, for whatever reason, we decide to repeat the event in our mind and retrigger the anger. It's not clear why we do this . . . but most of us do. People you interact with do not know what is going on in your head (and don't know or can't fully appreciate your back story). What they see is your anger, impertinence or disapproval, or alternatively, your calm demeanor, and they react accordingly.

You can take control of whether the anger or another emotional state returns. Simply pay closer attention to the negative feelings themselves without judgment or resistance. How does the anger feel within you? How is it affecting your body? How is it affecting your normal pace of breath? What is it within you that is aware of or upset by this feeling? By investigating your emotional state in this way, with mindfulness, and bringing it into the forefront of your consciousness, you may discover that negative emotional states of mind vanish all by themselves. Once they vanish, you can rationally consider your desired relationship or response to the person who triggered the emotion in a manner designed to achieve your goal. With a calmer mind, you may decide what action to take with respect to the situation that made you angry, or you may decide to simply let it go and move on.

Once emotion dissipates from your end of the conversation, you will find it much, much easier to listen during listening time and speak during speaking time. This makes it easier to observe any emotional reaction in the other person and to address it or just dissipate it with your calm and possibly empathetic reaction.

Meditation does not make us "emotionless." It makes us more aware. We can choose to be happy, to experience joy and relax in a calm state of contentment. But we can't do so when anger, fear or shame are barriers.

Meditation teaches us the difference between reaction and response, and allows us to learn to accept "what is" without judgment (both self-judgment and judgment of the other person). The skills we practice during meditation are transferable to our daily lives. Learning to respond instead of react is how meditation can provide you with the power to influence your relationships with people and, from a leadership point of view, influence the effectiveness of your leadership.

During emotion mindfulness meditations, we attempt to focus on an emotion and bring that emotion into the front of our minds, from our subconscious into our focused consciousness. We acknowledge or express the emotion instead of further suppressing it.

Once you are mindful and have recognized the emotion, you can release the negative impact of the emotions and forgive yourself and ultimately others. Once you forgive, the past experience has less power over you—it goes from high-impact emotional baggage to a lower-impact part of your factual history. It no longer has the same influence on your future conversations and relationships.

Particular meditation practices help us become cognizant of our emotions. How do we learn to be more aware of our emotional state? Books by Dr. Deborah Tannen[77] and Dr. Brené Brown[78] have helped me become more aware of my emotional style by allowing me to identify or label what was happening. Even when we are aware, how can we learn to control the negative impact of certain emotions instead of allowing them to control us and our reactions?

I took an eight-week emotional mindfulness course and we discussed that emotions such as fear, shame, and self-doubt can inhibit us from realizing our purpose, both personally and professionally; these emotions are often described by popular psychology texts as "interconnected." Just as the primary colors on the color wheel combine to produce the secondary colors, the three core emotions of fear, shame and self-doubt combine to produce an onslaught of additional emotions. Anger can be defined as a defensive emotion triggered by a combination of vulnerability or self-doubt, mixed with a bit of fear and sometimes shame. The three emotional cousins of envy, jealousy and resentment intrigue me; they seem to be different manifestations of self-doubt mixed with shame and a dash of fear. Envy is the state of wanting what someone else has. When we envy, we are acting on a belief that this thing we want (promotion, money, corner office, etc.) will provide us greater happiness and that not having this thing diminishes us in some way. Jealousy carries with it more suspicion of another person—the thing we want is rightly ours and this other person is taking it away. Resentment is the festering of the envy (which can be accompanied by jealousy), which can cause anger or hate when directed at another person or group of people. Guilt is often a combination of fear and shame; when you feel guilty, you hold onto the past by regretting your actions. These emotions are often triggered by something from your past or uncertainty regarding your future. The emotions and your emotional reaction are real. Being mindful emotionally is noticing the emotion and being aware of the ramifications in the present moment as you experience the emotion and the emotional reaction. Too often, the reverse occurs, our emotional reaction clouds our view of a current situation creating delusion. A delusional view of a situation rarely creates the best result and more often creates unnecessary suffering.

You can free yourself from the overbearing grip of these emotions, and the resulting delusion and suffering, by bringing them to your present attention and engaging in self-forgiveness. You can then carry a lesser burden as you move on with your life. You can clear your clouded lens. Once your lens is more clear, you are able to be mindful both of what others are saying and the thoughts that come to you without one drowning out the other. It is this balance that facilitates effective communication.

Emotion-Focused Meditation Practices

Sometimes taking a few deep breaths or bringing your attention back to your breath can be sufficient to let go of the emotion of the moment, refocus on the present and clear your lens. At other times, a guided meditation to go deeper and reengage with your history and suppressed emotional baggage may be required.

Everyone has different emotional baggage based on his or her background. The emotion release meditation technique can work with any uncomfortable emotion: fear, shame, self-doubt, anger, guilt, jealousy and resentment.

The following meditation practices will assist you in becoming more aware of the impact of your emotions on your interactions with others, as well as being mindful of the feeling and expression of your emotions. In doing so, you can become more sensitive to the likely emotions of others in these situations. You can then practice meditation focused on releasing pent-up emotions below the surface of a current situation, and on forgiving yourself and others, so that you can approach new situations fresh and more emotionally aware. Although they can be uncomfortable at first, these meditations can help us dissipate the negative emotional charge instead of letting it fester and grow, which can impact not just our reactions to others but our physical health as well.

i. Feelings on a Cloud Meditation

This meditation helps us learn how to recognize and release emotions that are no longer serving our best interest.

Look inward and notice what is going on in your mind. What does your mind want to think about? View the thoughts without any emotional charge or judgment. Does your mind want to go along with your meditation practice, or distract you? No need to change anything, just be aware and notice.

Close your eyes, lower your gaze, or choose a focal point.

Focus on your breath.

The inhale, the pause, the exhale, the pause.

Create a rhythm with your breath. Try to even out the length of time for the inhale and the exhale. Notice the pause between the inhale and the exhale and even that out as well. Breathe comfortably.

Focus on what you are feeling. If nothing appears at first, be patient and conjure up the feeling that wants to bubble to the surface.

At some point, a feeling will appear. Observe it.

Really feel that feeling.

How does it feel in your heart?

Where do you feel it in your body?

How does it feel in your mind?

Then place that feeling on a cloud and watch it drift away.

At some point, another feeling may appear.

Focus on that new feeling.

Observe it.

Really feel that feeling.

How does it feel in your heart?

How does it feel in your body?

How does it feel in your mind?

Then place that feeling on a cloud and watch it drift away.

Repeat as desired.

When you are ready, focus again on your breath and return slowly.

Recognizing your emotions and then allowing them to drift away is a technique that can help us learn how to control our thoughts and emotions instead of allowing our thoughts and emotions to control us. Once you are able to do so, you will find that you have more open space for new personal growth and experiences.

ii. Emotion Warehouse Meditation

Some emotions can negate our happiness and instead cause us suffering, if we let them. These emotions often linger within us well beyond the event or other initial trigger event.

Let's recall certain common ones from earlier in this chapter.

- Shame
- Self-Doubt
- Fear
- Hate
- Anger
- Guilt
- Envy
- Jealousy
- Resentment

Choose one emotion for this exercise (and maybe a different one on a different day). (Note: A therapist friend once cautioned me not to choose fear as a beginning meditator, since this can lead to unexpected places you are not ready to go as well as to adverse reactions.)

Focus on your breath and center yourself. Take a few deep breaths.

As you go deeper into your awareness with each deep breath, visualize a row of warehouses and choose the one you will enter today—will it be the warehouse of your shame, self-doubt, fear, guilt, anger, sadness, jealousy or resentment? Stand in front of the one emblazoned with your chosen emotion on its side.

Open the door and enter slowly. All the cargo in this warehouse represents your personal life stories. Try to identify a specific example of a personal life story that triggers this emotion for you. You have been carrying it around for a long time. Replay that story in your mind.

Now picture yourself in front of a mirror reflecting your image. Concentrate on your heart and a healing green light that emanates from it. Say to yourself: "I hereby release this emotion from the warehouse. Watch it melt and fly away."

Now look deeper inside the emotion warehouse. What triggers the emotion? Find another story. What are the experiences that come to mind as you gaze around the warehouse? Consider whether the emotional reaction is a realistic emotional response that protects you, or one that holds you back.

Now picture yourself in front of a mirror reflecting your image. Concentrate on your heart and a healing green light that emanates from it. Say to yourself: "I hereby release this emotion from the warehouse. Watch it melt and fly away."

Repeat several more times until you feel you have completed this exercise.

When you are ready, exit the warehouse door. Notice that the row of warehouses is there whenever you want to return.

Ultimately, through this exercise we can learn to recognize and release, rather than suppress, the emotion deep inside each warehouse. By doing so, we allow it to dissipate instead of fester and grow inside of us.

iii. Shedding Skin Meditation

Part of the impact from eliminating barriers is the personal growth that can come from removing previous limits. You can witness what fills the space that was previously unavailable. One of my favorite metaphors for personal growth is the image of the snake.

You never see an old snake, because a snake is continually molting . . . shedding its skin and growing new fresh skin. The snake can teach us to shed the barriers, whether they be physical, emotional, mental or spiritual, so we don't carry them around like old skin.

People, like snakes, often go through several cycles in their lifetimes. In some South American tribal traditions, if you are feeling stagnant and the snake spirit animal appears, it is time to cast out the old and start anew. Don't waste any time being hard on yourself, or thinking that you are stuck in a rut. You don't have to be stuck; you're just in a phase. Snakes shed their skin for a few different reasons: to rid their bodies of impurities that they pick up from crawling on the ground, or because they have outgrown their previous skin. You can be like a snake and shed old habits, undesirable behaviors and physical, emotional, mental and spiritual barriers that hold you back.

This is not a particularly quick process, and a snake must often rub itself against rocks and other rough surfaces to escape the confines of its old and smaller self. You will need to leave a part of yourself behind if you really want to change. You may find some rocks or obstacles on your path to growth... consider them to be tools or resources that will help shed that extra weight you've been carrying on your shoulders.

Are you afraid of snakes? Have you ever considered life from the snake's point of view? Let's try that.

Close your eyes or lower your gaze. Focus on your breath. Picture yourself in your mind. Now picture yourself evolving into a snake . . . your two legs fused together below your torso, your arms down at your sides, melding into your body, so that you become one long being. Look into your snake eyes. What do you see in the reflection? If you could shed some objects, some barriers, from your life, what would they be? Maybe some debt, or a person or two, or a few pounds. What would you shed?

What stops you from doing so?

Now focus on your feelings. Look again into the eyes of your snake self. What do you see in those eyes? Do you see sadness, or pain, or fear, or resentment? What would it take to shed that feeling?

What stops you from doing so?

Now focus on your thoughts. When a snake is in its molting cycle, shedding its skin, it often stops moving and its eyes become translucent. What are the repetitive thoughts that hold you back, that keep you from taking the actions that you know your true self wants to take? Look again into the eyes of your snake self. Can you see the reflection of your true self in the snake, or do you just see a snake that you hardly recognize? Who is this snake you are picturing? Who are you?

Picture yourself shedding those barriers, pent-up feelings and repetitive limiting thoughts. Let them go forever.

Once you succeed, you will feel refreshed and invigorated. The cloudiness that obscured your vision will clear. You will be able to see yourself, and the world, through new eyes.

When you are ready, come back into consciousness and open your eyes. Remember this experience, and when you are feeling overwhelmed, consider what you can let go of to lighten your burden through your inner snake. Then come back to being you, after having released some of that burden.

iv. Happy Place Meditation

Everyone has a favorite safe and calming place, whether that is on the beach, near a lake surrounded by mountains, your childhood home, your favorite vacation spot or sitting in your favorite chair in your den. Identify your favorite of these choices as your "happy place" for this exercise.

Begin by sitting in silence, closing your eyes and focusing on your breath.

Picture your happy place.

Observe the sounds.

Observe the smells.

Observe how you feel situated in your happy place.

With practice, you can come back to this place when needed. Maybe you get stuck in traffic, or you take the brunt of a customer's dissatisfaction with a situation that wasn't your fault, or you are the victim of rude behavior or one of life's road bumps. Use these moments for a quick return to your happy place. See if it changes your mood or your reaction to whatever has happened and brings you back to a state of equanimity.

v. Integrating the Meditation Technique and Leadership Principle—Action/Reaction Meditation

One of the most complex business relationships is between you and the person who is your supervisor. Even the CEO has a board of directors to which he or she reports.

When we think about emotion focus and emotion release, we generally focus first on ourselves. As discussed, emotions can impact your thoughts and actions in the workplace and elsewhere. Your actions impact the reaction of the other person with whom you are interacting. In this exercise, you will focus not on yourself, but on the reaction to you by your supervisor, and then by someone you supervise or a colleague to whom you delegate tasks and then another colleague. The goal of this exercise is to bring these reactions into your awareness so you can engage in more mindful communication at work and improve your effectiveness.

Close your eyes and focus on your breath.

Focus on whomever you think of as your supervisor.

Consider an emotional interaction with your supervisor—whether it was you or him/her who was expressing the emotion.

Focus first on your emotion during that situation. Can you identify it?

Focus next on your supervisor's likely emotion during that situation. Is your first instinct to be unsure of your supervisor's emotion, or to think that your supervisor has no emotional reaction to you or your situation?

How do you think your supervisor feels about you? Do you think your supervisor generally likes you, or hates you, or is jealous of some of your traits, or is proud of your accomplishments? Do you think your supervisor doesn't care about you at all?

How do you feel while contemplating how your supervisor feels about you?

Consider whether that feeling impacts your relationship. Now that you are aware, is there anything you can think of to do or say differently to address this aspect of your relationship?

Next, focus on someone who considers you their supervisor or a staff person who provides internal support services for you (such as an information technology, human resources, or accounting staff member).

Consider an emotional interaction with your selected person—whether it was you or him/her who was expressing the emotion.

Focus first on your emotion during that situation. Can you identify it?

Focus next on this person's likely emotion during that situation. Is your first instinct to be unsure of your colleague's emotion, or to think that your colleague has no emotional reaction to you or your situation?

How do you think this person feels about you? Do you think that person generally likes you as a supervisor, or hates you, or is jealous of some of your traits, or is proud of your accomplishments? Do you think this person doesn't care about you at all?

This exercise can be repeated (or substituted) with a focus on a different colleague.

Upon completing the meditation, consider in your conscious mind how the newfound insight regarding the emotional aspects of your relationship with your supervisor and others may be impacting your work relationships. Then consider how, by being more aware of each of the emotional aspects of each relationship, you could modify your behavior or reaction to this person in a way that might improve the dynamic. You might want to review and consider some of Carnegie's suggested techniques to listen and express encouragement and appreciation.

VIII. ATTUNEMENT—
THE SURPRISING RESULT OF MEDITATION

If there is any one secret of success, it lies in the ability to get the other person's point of view and see things from his angle as well as your own.
Henry Ford, founder of Ford Motor Company

If you want to be happy, be grateful.
David Steint-Rast, monk and interfaith scholar

You are likely familiar with the Golden Rule: "Do unto others as you would like others to do unto you." Truly effective leaders follow what has become known as the Platinum Rule: "Treat others as they wish to be treated." Beyond empathetic listening, an understanding of others is a key component of making a lasting connection and motivating those that you lead. People are not created "one size fits all." I think of attunement as being aware of differences between another and myself rather than assuming that others are the same as I am—seeing situations exactly the same and having the same reactions. Being attuned means being in tune with another person which results from being both more aware and more connected at the same time. But, as a leader, do you know what motivates the people you lead (and whether it is the same or different from what motivates you)?

Your first reaction in business may be, "Of course: money motivates workers." "Show me the money" is the defining battle cry and motivational force for some. If a leader believes that people are motivated primarily by money, and by loss of money, that will certainly impact how an organization is led. No one can deny that money is a key motivator—we work to make money to feed our families, pay our bills and establish our standard of living. But there is also no denying that most people are motivated at work by factors beyond money.

Daniel Pink, in his book, *Drive: The Surprising Truth about What Motivates Us*, proposes that, rather than money, the freedom to grow and succeed is what motivates most white-collar workers.[79] According to Pink, too many organizations—not just for-profit businesses, but governments and not-for-profits as well—operate from assumptions about human potential and individual performance that are outdated, unexamined, and not rooted in science.[80]

Millennials are reportedly less likely to be primarily motivated by money than prior generations.[81] Aligning monetary compensation with success is certainly helpful, but Pink asks: "Which is the carrot and which is the stick?"

Money as a Motivator

Certainly, some people are motivated primarily by money—for these people, incentive monetary compensation is all that's needed. Sales people are the classic example where short-term financial incentive based on sales has been demonstrated to induce greater sales. In my experience, a perpetual focus on compensation just gets in the way of organizational success. Pink posits that a compensation system should be fair, but then should recede into the background.[82] If people do not believe they are paid what they are worth or are not adequately compensated for their successful efforts, they will find this to be demotivating and may leave the organization. This is consistent with Pink's acknowledgement that money (or compensation) is a denominator of value or success. However, many people with this motivation are more interested in how their compensation or raise compares with that of their coworkers (as a sign of their relative value to the organization) than the incremental buying power of the difference. In other words, they are dissatisfied not because of the actual dollar amount received, but because the result makes them feel devalued.

Pink offers a description of human motivation to differentiate those motivated by intrinsic rewards from those inspired by extrinsic ones.[83] Pink's theory is grounded in the science of human motivation and powered by our innate need to direct our own lives, to learn and create new things, and to do better by ourselves and our world.

Although Pink applies this theory to many different business situations, let's stay with the compensation system example. Pink's theory, which he calls the Zen of Compensation, is as follows.[84] Everybody wants to be paid well. The most important aspect of compensation is fairness, both internal (to reward relative value created) and external (compared to other organizations where the individual could work). Pink recommends being at the top end of "market" base compensation, as it takes the issue of external fairness off the table and eliminates the tendency to add small (ineffective) rewards. Compensation systems that are consistent with the Zen of Compensation do not involve paying everyone the same amount—that would be neither fair nor motivating. If one person has a relevant advanced degree or prior experience, it is fair to pay that person more than someone else in the same job category; if two people have similar backgrounds and one is working harder and/or makes a greater overall contribution to the organization, it is fair to pay that person more overall compensation.

The tricky part is the incentive portion. Pink notes that if you pay a product manager largely on a quarterly sales goal, he or she will naturally try mightily to hit that goal—but he or she probably won't be too concerned about the quarter after that, or the health of the company, or product innovation through research and development, or lowering costs, or expanding sales margins. Now imagine instead that you are a product manager and your bonus is determined by these factors: (i) sales of your product for each quarter and for the year, (ii) profit margin on those sales, (iii) overall company sales and profits over the past year, (iv) level of customer satisfaction with the product, (v) ideas for new products and new markets, and (vi) assistance given to co-workers. If you're smart, you will do the same beneficial things you were previously doing to maximize sales, but you won't cut corners that could hurt future performance and you will try hard to provide value to the organization in other ways. Equity (stock) incentive compensation can also add to the alignment of personal and organizational interests.

If you judge your job value only by compensation, you may "job hop" to get a bit more until you get to such a poor fit that other factors overwhelm the compensation improvement. Of course, there are legitimate reasons to switch jobs, and one of those reasons may be a material increase in compensation. The point is to look at compensation within the greater context of your work experience so that you make the best decision for you.

There are some excellent performers motivated primarily by money. We sometimes refer to those people as having "sharp elbows" in taking origination credit and boasting of their achievements to our compensation committee. Extra care has to be taken with those motivated primarily by compensation to make sure they know they are compensated fairly (or else they will leave). Relative compensation to the average (or the person next to them) is something they care a lot about.

One of my closest childhood friends, Jeff, would go to B'nai Mitzvah, look around the room at some of Philadelphia's most successful business owners and say to me: "I am going to be more successful than everyone in this room one day." And he is. He was driven in school and business school by his desire to learn in order to build a successful business. Jeff took six months after business school to figure out the best opportunity to start or buy a company to make his fortune. He identified a need in the early 1990s when computers became mainstream but software was sometimes hard to figure out and use. Microsoft and other software manufacturers provided insufficient customer support, and there was no Google or internet to provide answers to questions. Companies inefficiently hired their own internal "help desk" but needed multiple people not always fully utilized to cover knowledge of all applicable programs. Thus, Jeff formed PC Helps, an outsourced help desk staffed by people with deep knowledge of each major software program. Jeff appreciated money as a motivator in developing his successful business strategy. Instead of raising outside financing, he required his customers to pre-purchase support time, thus providing an incentive for customers to use pre-paid minutes and providing cash flow to run and grow the business. Also, he paid higher salaries compared with those of "in-house help desks" and thus recruited and retained quality people. It all worked.

Mission as a Motivator

If compensation is not an organization's primary retention tool, how does an organization create an incentive for its workers to stay? What is the incentive for an organization's workers to "give it all they have" in the best interest of the organization? Rather than focusing solely on monetary measures, I find that the most effective leaders articulate a compelling purpose for their organizations or group within an organization beyond a profit goal, and set annual or other periodic goals toward achieving that purpose. Beyond that, consistent with Collins' theories, hiring good people and allowing them the freedom to develop professionally, participate in developing goals and implementation plans, and then implement those plans together with colleagues is what creates great organizations.

Mission statements are a tool used to communicate the reason an organization exits. They provide unanimity of purpose and imbue employees (and often other stakeholders such as customers, suppliers and investors) with a sense of belonging and identity. They can become a creed or mantra. They have to be clear and memorable to be useful.

An organization's mission statement may spell out the context in which the organization operates and provides employees with a tone to follow within the organizational climate. The mission statement can serve as a focal point that allows individuals to identify themselves with the organization and get high-level direction to keep them centered on the communal purpose. This creates organizational culture and differentiates one organization from others that may appear to be providing or selling the same service or product.

For example, Whole Foods, as a healthier grocery store, incorporates social responsibility and support of organic farming as core values. Whole Foods intentionally seeks employees (called Team Members) who are passionate about healthy food and active in community service in the local store areas. The Whole Foods website notes, "Without our Team Members we are just four walls and food." Whole Foods expresses that it cares about how it treats its employees and our planet, and that it wants its employees to bring their passion into the workplace. Whole Foods employees are then part of the differentiating edge with customers. The healthy food branding, enjoyable shopping experience, and faith in the integrity of the products sold at Whole Foods not only engender customer loyalty but a willingness to pay premium prices for some special but mostly commodity products. Whole Foods is also known for treating its suppliers well, including supporting start-up healthy food and beverage products, giving many companies the head start they need to succeed. This is all part of Whole Foods' differentiable mission. It will be interesting to see what happens to its mission and culture following its acquisition by Amazon, a company with a drastically different organizational culture and organizational mission.

Attachment to an organizational mission can be a powerful motivator. Many people choose to work or volunteer at non-profit organizations. In almost all instances, the position does not maximize that person's financial remuneration, but being part of a communal group seeking to accomplish a common mission is more compelling.

Validation as a Motivator

Oprah Winfrey notes that beyond money and mission, validation as a primary motivator for high achievers. "I've talked to nearly 30,000 people on this show, and all 30,000 had one thing in common: They all wanted validation. If I could reach through this television and sit on your sofa or sit on a stool in your kitchen right now, I would tell you that every single person you will ever meet shares that common desire. They want to know: 'Do you see me? Do you hear me? Does what I say mean anything to you?'… Understanding that one principle, that everybody wants to be heard, has allowed me to hold the microphone for you all these years with the least amount of judgment. Now I can't say I wasn't judging some days. Some days, I had to judge just a little bit. But it's helped me to stand and to try to do that with an open mind and to do it with an open heart. It has worked for this platform, and I guarantee you it will work for yours. Try it with your children, your husband, your wife, your boss, your friends. Validate them. 'I see you. I hear you. And what you say matters to me.'"[85]

Validation is such a strong motivator, applicable to all of us. Does what we do matter? Are we doing our job well? It takes such little incremental time, but so many of us and so many organizational leaders are so poor at making the effort, to express gratitude and appreciation to our co-workers for the effort and value they create.

When my wife took a break from working outside the home, she would often comment that what she missed most was the validation from doing a good job and being appreciated for doing a good job. It is probably not uncommon in today's world for children not to express appreciation to their parents (even if they thought about it). This probably also holds true for spouses. Consider the impact expressing more appreciation could have.

Attunement as a Motivator

I struggle with my desire to better understand what motivates me and others in the workplace. I know compensation is a part of it. I know enjoying the day-to-day challenges of the job is a part of it. I do care about our mission and I know that many of my friends who work at non-profits and as positive impact entrepreneurs are highly motivated by their organizational mission. I appreciate that being validated by success at work is motivating. I came to realize that not only are different people motivated differently, but I myself have been motivated differently at different points in my life and often wish to fulfill a complex set of work needs and goals (which are sometimes even contradictory). There is so much give and take between each of us, the organizations in which we work and the leaders within those organizations. What does it take to effectively lead others?

In his 2012 book, *To Sell is Human: The Surprising Truth about Moving Others*, Pink posits that in the Information Age, we are all salespeople selling our ideas. We spend a significant amount of time and effort trying to coax others to a different point of view or to part with monetary or other resources. "We're persuading, convincing, and influencing others to give up something they've got in exchange for what we've got," Pink writes.[86]

Pink's theories seem to suggest a fine line between a positively-perceived motivation and negatively-perceived manipulation. To me, the critical difference is your intention, integrity and goal. If your intention is pure, then your use of these tools to motivate others consistent with that intention is positive—but you do have to remain aware of the difference. Many of the world's great motivating leaders did not have pure intentions, which in some cases resulted in devastating consequences.

Pink cites a study based on the *What Do You Do at Work?* survey.[87] Two main findings emerged. "People are now spending an average of 40 percent of their time at work engaged in non-sales selling—persuading, influencing, and convincing others in ways that don't involve anyone making a purchase. Across a range of professions, we are devoting 24 minutes of every hour to moving others' mindsets in this way."[88] Motivating others to do what you want has become crucial to effectiveness.

Pink cites examples that we might not think of ordinarily as "sales." A teacher giving a science lecture is selling students the accuracy of the information conveyed as well as the idea that the lecture has sufficient value to warrant paying attention. A physical therapist is selling patients the value of performing the prescribed exercises daily despite the cost (time, attention and effort) of complying. In both of these examples, the recipients will benefit from compliance, just as product purchasers will purportedly benefit from owning and using the product. A compliant student or patient will achieve a better result, which in turn reflects positively on the performance of the teacher, doctor or other professional.

All of us in leadership capacities spend a portion of our work time persuading a group to follow our lead and, together, to accomplish our organizational goals. One interesting observation from Pink's work is that as one climbs the corporate ladder (which Pink describes as "injections of power"), one often becomes less likely (and perhaps less able) to incorporate someone else's point of view in setting up team action plans.

However, by being aware, we can change that natural phenomenon to achieve optimal results.

Pink focuses on the importance of being in tune with the constituents hearing the message (similar to the Platinum Rule).[89] How one achieves attunement most effectively depends in part upon one's personality. While one normally thinks about extroverts as the best sales people, Pink notes that extroverts are geared to "respond" while introverts are geared to "analyze." Selling of any sort—whether traditional sales or motivating others to incorporate ideas—requires a delicate balance of listening, analyzing and responding. "Ambiverts", people who are neither overly extraverted nor wildly introverted, find that balance; they know instinctively when to speak and when to listen. Most of us are somewhere on the spectrum of introvert to extraverts and can become more aware, and with practice, become more balanced as ambiverts.

Pink has specific suggestions to help you as a leader become more attuned to your employees. The first is to increase your power by reducing it. [90] Pink notes that as power increases, those with power become less likely (but not necessarily less able) to attune themselves to people with less power. The key then is to be aware of the power difference and connect, notwithstanding that difference. The second tip from Pink is to express empathy, balancing your response from your head and your heart.[91] Taking the perspective of the other person into account makes it significantly more likely to achieve a mutually satisfactory goal. Pink's third tip is to mimic strategically.[92] If you observe how the other person speaks and acts, and you mimic that style you (and your message) are more likely to be positively received.

Most of us have taken personality quality tests, some of which were discussed in the self-awareness portion of Chapter IV, to better understand ourselves. Human Capital consultants have adapted their leadership development training methods to focus on these principles of applying what was previously thought of as self-awareness attributes to others in order to be more attuned with them and more able to motivate them to accomplish your organization's goals.

Pink tells a story of how Jeff Bezos, the founder of Amazon, would leave an empty chair at all meetings. The theory was that the empty chair represents the customer and the customer needs a seat at the table. As a result, the Amazon decision making group was attuned to the customer throughout their decision making process.

One example of customer attunement is the Container Store. The Container Store doesn't sell stuff you want; it sells the boxes and storage cabinets that hold the stuff you want. Kip Tindell in his book, *Uncontainable: How Passion, Commitment and Conscious Capitalism Build a Business Where Everyone Thrives*,[93] explains how great sales people are the key to the store chain's success and how he recruits and motivates them. Tindell notes that one great sales person equals three good ones in terms of productivity.[94] Thus, the Container Store decided to pay one and a half to two times prevailing retail wages to recruit great sales people. They then keep these great people focused on principles of attunement to the customer, communication, creating solutions for customers and what they call an "employee first" culture investing an average of 300 hours of training each employee. The Container Store has an employee turnover rate of 10% per year compared with a retail industry average of about 100%.[95] It is an inspiring success story of effective leadership in a company without a sexy mission. Remember, this company basically sells empty space—containers—but they are sold using motivated, effective sales people providing a solution to a customer problem, thereby creating an innovative concept and successful brand. The Container Store hires people who are attuned to the mission and attuned to the customer (and they specifically train for that attunement).

What Motivates Millennials and Future Generations

After law school graduation, when many in my graduating class started practicing law at big law firms, most of us set a goal to become partners at those firms. We knew that most of us wouldn't succeed in that career goal, and less than 10% of our class stayed at the position long enough to be made partner at their initial law firm. However, it was a goal that motivated our performance, which included long hours, seemingly unreasonable demands (and sometimes rude behavior) from clients, adversaries and even partners. We would "suck it up" and keep in mind the potential career goal.

According to the Deloitte Millennial Survey,[96] two-thirds of millennials express an intention to leave their organizations within three years. Businesses must adjust how they motivate shorter-term workers, consider how to nurture greater loyalty, and use better knowledge management resources to institutionally adjust to a more transient work force.

In the Deloitte study, millennials cite a perceived lack of leadership development, feelings of being overlooked, and desire for greater flexibility and work life balance, along with a desire to align personal and organizational values.[97] Interestingly, over the years the millennial survey has been conducted, millennials don't seem to shift away from these early values as their careers progress. These issues are solvable with organizational recognition of employee desires and relatively moderate changes to adapt to their different motivations. Instituting leadership development programs (possibly incorporating a bit of meditation technique training), greater expressions of gratitude and appreciation for their efforts, and greater flexibility in scheduling (while ensuring effective work completion) will go a long way.

Millennials also express their desire to be proud of their organization and its ethics. Millennials in the survey overwhelmingly perceive their organization to be all about profit instead of equally about mission and people.[98] Millennials want their organization to make a positive impact upon wider society. Perhaps they are right. Perhaps, without sacrificing profit, most business organizations need to change to take greater account of its decisions' impact on its mission, people and greater society. The wisdom that comes to me through meditation tells me that creating greater employee motivation and customer loyalty will in fact be worth the effort, both in terms of overall organizational impact and, ironically, maximizing profits for the organization over the long-term.

Generation Z (those born 1995 and later) are now entering the work force. Gen Zers are very tech savvy but also impacted by the ancillary impact of technology with a full 40% self-identified digital device addicts.[99] Early input from Gen Z is that they value feedback, not just annually or semi-annually, but on a real-time basis. They are generally less focused, with shorter attention spans, but are also better multitaskers. Gen Z has witnessed the disruptive change that can come from implementation of new technology and are both more entrepreneurial and have higher aspirations than millennials of what they can accomplish. Gen Zers are also more global in their thinking, interactions and relatability.[100]

Being attuned to generational norms is important. Being attuned to individual preferences is even more important.

Every Body (Everybody) is Different

I have heard several yoga teachers espouse the lesson that everyone's body is different and you have to adopt the base yoga postures to your unique body as part of the yoga practice. Everybody is different and what motivates each of us will reflect that difference. I am never a fan of personality tests that ask 100 questions, then group everyone into four or so groups based on common characteristics. If there are 100 characteristics, we are each on a scale of 1 to 10 in each of the 100 (with some ability to change over time), thus making us each unique. While we may have some success over time understanding ourselves well, we can't fully know what makes someone else tick. Thus, the best we can do is listen empathetically to a colleague, get to know them, be as attuned as we can to the other person based on our observations and, once attuned, respond as best we can to a particular person, group or situation.

Put simply, different people prefer to be communicated with differently and prefer to manage equivalent projects differently (with each style potentially being equally effective). If you aren't aware of the differences, you will likely only work effectively with some people and not others. For example, two managing directors at a private equity company that I work with, Managing Director A and Managing Director B, are extremely smart and substantively agree with each other almost all of the time; however, they prefer to be communicated with differently. I have observed that many people, both within their own organization and ours, work better with one versus the other. I am one of the few who really enjoys working with both of them, possibly based upon awareness of a key communication style difference. Managing Director A wants to have the issues identified, be presented with all of the alternatives and participate in the resolution. If you simply present a resolution, he will almost always challenge it to engage in dialogue, after which he has participated in the resolution. Managing Director B also wants the issues identified for him, but prefers to hear about them after you have a proposed resolution so that he can understand and approve it (which he often will without further discourse) or provide additional ideas for consideration. If you simply present all of the alternatives without a recommended resolution, he considers you unprepared. Both achieve excellent results.

I was recently influenced by Sheryl Sandberg's book, *Option B: Facing Adversity, Building Resilience and Finding Joy*,[38] that told her story and lessons learned following the death of her husband. One line that influenced me was the subtle difference between someone greeting, "How are you?" (of course she was horrible—her husband had recently died) and "How are you *today*?" (which acknowledges that she is doing horribly but expresses hope that today is a bit better). Sandberg observed that the subtle difference in greeting drew out a dramatically different reaction from her. As President and Chief Operating Officer of Facebook, many of her relationships changed based on how they reacted to (or avoided) the death of her husband. We engage in these types of interactions every day and those who do so well, succeed. Thus, mindful communication is not just about listening to what the other person is saying but being sensitive when communicating to that other person of how that other person will hear you.

I don't recall the source, but I remember reading an article on leadership that described the difference between good and mediocre bosses and the difference between playing chess and checkers. In checkers, all pieces are the same and move in the same way. In chess (and life), each piece has a unique movement, unique value and unique limitations, but all pieces play a role on the team and are thus important. In other words, you don't treat your knight, your queen and your pawn the same way if you want the best results.

Gratitude as a Motivator

The one motivational technique that I find works on almost all types of people is appreciation. All the time, almost as a habit, effective leaders say "thank you" and find ways to express appreciation to their employees and to others who provide value—particularly as it relates to accomplishing the organizational mission. Sometimes, this appreciation is in the form of a personal thank you, while at other times the appreciation is publicly expressed, such as during a meeting or in a group email. Expressing gratitude is a simple concept and requires little time and effort, yet too often is forgotten in the chaos of the day; thus, it is important to remain attentive to situations that warrant gratitude, and to become comfortable expressing it. The key is to express gratitude often, but only when it is sincere. Expressing gratitude as part of organizational culture builds community and organizational loyalty and motivates more of the positive behavior that gave rise to the expression of gratitude.

The bottom line is this: we all respond to praise and appreciation; when we receive it, we are highly motivated to continue the actions that resulted in praise. The simplicity of gratitude belies its power. As for me, while I like to think I try my hardest for all my clients, I have noticed that—whether consciously or subconsciously—I "go the extra mile" for people who express appreciation for my efforts. Note that this has nothing to do with money.

Attunement and Gratitude Meditation Practices

My favorite meditation technique for practicing attunement and emotional mindfulness is the "Replay the Story—Put Yourself in Others' Shoes" meditation. The practice includes not just contemplating what the other person might say, but what the other person is feeling when he or she says it. If during an interaction with another person you can pause for a moment to contemplate what the other person may be feeling and what his or her reaction might be before you say something, logic follows that you are more likely to say the right thing. By practicing attunement, you will develop an instinct for how to interact with other people in ways that will lead to positive outcomes. Also, remember that you don't really fully know what other people are thinking or feeling or their own personal life battles, but you will be more effective by being more aware of their reaction to your actions. By practicing meditation, awareness and empathy are enhanced and so is the trait of attunement.

For me, there is no meditation practice that produces better results than a gratitude practice. Instead of focusing on what I don't have, I focus on what I do have. Instead of focusing on what needs to be corrected, I focus on what is going right. Instead of focusing on myself, I focus on what I appreciate in others. Gratitude meditation puts the mind in a position to be more empathetic and more attuned to the person to whom you are expressing gratitude.

However, unlike lovingkindness and forgiveness meditation practices (where it is enough to send out your lovingkindness and forgiveness to the universe), in a gratitude practice you recognize the areas of gratitude during meditation, but then you need to express your goodwill to the other person. Gratitude practices can also help us transform from "grasping" or "always wanting more" (which causes unhappiness and suffering) to gratitude (which causes joy). Below are several meditation techniques that can enhance your sense of attunement and gratitude.

i. Emotional Mindfulness—Replaying the Story

The replaying the story meditation facilitates learning from our experiences so we don't make the same mistakes over and over again.

Focus on your breath. You don't have to change your breath.

Close your eyes. Relax and center yourself.

Replay 1. Think of one event that happened during the past week or so that is fresh in your mind and created a strong emotional reaction in you. Identify and put a label on that emotion.

Once you have identified the event and emotion, relive it in your mind, with all its details and vivid emotional charge.

133

Replay 2. Now, replay the same event in your mind but try to detach yourself from the emotion of the event. Imagine that you are omniscient—that you can create the event again impartially and without the emotion.

What happened differently? Look at the event in an analytical way. See all the conditions and factors that came together to make this event possible. See all the consequences for yourself. What emotional baggage did you bring to the original event? What happened in your past that influenced your role in this event or, if you were not the primary actor, your reaction to the event?

Replay 3. Replay the event one more time from this new place of perspective. This time, again replay the event from your perspective (rather than the omniscient viewpoint); however, this time, you are aware and in control of your emotions and your reaction, with the ability to make changes in how you would like the interaction to occur. How does the situation play out differently? How are you different?

Over the course of the next week, you may encounter a negative interaction with a co-worker, family member or close friend. That evening, try this exercise again and see if it makes a difference the next time you see that person or face the same situation.]

ii. Count Your Blessings Meditation

Counting your blessings is part of many religious traditions and recovery programs. In Judaism, the Talmud teaches us to recite 100 blessings a day in which we thank God for all that God has blessed us with. If that works for you, then continue it (or commence it).

Becoming aware of your gratitude, bringing it to the surface, is more important than whom you are thanking or what you are thankful for. You can be grateful for big things like the love of your spouse and family or life itself, as well as little things like finding an open checkout line in the grocery store. A friend of mine decided to consciously count 100 blessings every day as part of his recovery program and found it highly effective.

Try this gratitude meditation at night before you go to sleep:

Close your eyes, lower your gaze, or choose your focal point.

Focus on your breath. The inhale, the pause, the exhale, the pause.

No need to change the pace of your breath, just notice it.

You are perfect just the way you are. Be aware of your perfection.

Ask yourself: What am I grateful for?

Pause 10 seconds, and listen.

What am I grateful for?

Keep going for several minutes. If nothing comes to mind, ask the question again. The answers can be tangible or intangible, big or small, mundane or insightful.

Drift off to sleep with gratitude forming the last thoughts in your mind and see if you feel any different the next morning.

iii. Make Every Day Thanks Giving

Gratitude can include both being thankful for what others are doing for you as well as for the ability to give of yourself, for which someone else should and will be thankful (whether or not they express it). Just like the Thanksgiving holiday, gratitude can create balance.

When you are ready:

Close your eyes, lower your gaze, or choose your focal point.

Focus on your breath. The inhale, the pause, the exhale, the pause.

No need to change the pace of your breath, just notice it.

Consider something that went well today (or yesterday, if you are medi-tating in the morning). Try to relive that experience.

Smile.

Who inspired you or did something positive for you today?

Say "thank you" out loud.

Who did you inspire or do something positive today?

Say "good job" out loud.

When you are ready, return your focus to your breath and then to the room.

This practice works best if repeated for a number of days over a week or a month (and then periodically). Eventually, you will find yourself saying thank you more often to people during the day and being more aware of the positive aspects of your life.

iv. Integrating the Meditation Technique and Leadership Principle: Gratitude at Work Meditation

Close your eyes or lower your gaze to avoid distractions.

Focus on your breath. No need to change your breath, just notice it.

What are you grateful for in your workplace?

Consider individual people who support you and your work, whether internal employees or external suppliers or advisors to your organization.

Consider customers (whether internal or external) for whom you are working.

Consider any benefit to the world from what you and your organization produce.

Consider that you are paid money for what you do in the workplace and appreciate for a moment that you are making more money than many others in the world.

Consider some of the things you most cherish that are purchased with that money.

Consider the personal relationships you have developed with people you have met in the workplace. Think about what they have added to your life and support system.

Note a few of the people for whom you feel most grateful during this exercise.

Return to your breath and to the room. Write down the names of the people for whom you felt most grateful.

Within the next few days, express your gratitude, whether in person or by text, email, or phone. No one ever resents someone coming to them, seemingly out of the blue, and saying, "Thank you. I appreciate what you have done for me and/or our organization."

Try this practice whenever you are feeling negative about your workplace (or family or any other setting).

With practice, gratitude can become more instinctive and the "thank yous" more spontaneous and in the moment. You may notice a better reaction from those to whom you express gratitude. The expressions of gratitude may motivate them, consciously or subconsciously, to do more of the action you expressed appreciation for.

IX. DEVELOPING RELATIONSHIPS—USING MEDITATION AS YOUR SECRET OF SUCCESS

Everything in the universe only exists because it is in relationship to everything else. Nothing exists in isolation. We have to stop pretending we are individuals who can go it alone.

Margaret Wheatley, author and management consultant

I work with many entrepreneurs who have "hit a wall" in their growth. They have a great idea, they are focused on moving the business forward, their idea is innovative, and they are able to communicate effectively and be attuned with others. The problem is that there is only so much one person—even the most talented, driven, hard-working person—can do.

Effective leaders require the ability to develop and maintain successful relationships—with subordinates, with peers, with superiors, with customers/clients, with vendors who provide valuable products and services to the organization, and with other external stakeholders. To some degree, all of these people have an impact on the professional success of the leader as well as on the ability of the organization to achieve its mission. Thus, it stands to reason that a leader can only be successful if he or she has the personal will and skill to build these relationships. But, can this skill be learned?

In his book, *Never Eat Alone: And Other Secrets to Success, One Relationship at a Time*, Keith Ferrazzi (co-author with Tahl Raz) focuses on the importance of developing a network of business relationships. Although Ferrazzi stresses the business aspect of relationships, his lessons are applicable to relationships in all aspects of life.

Ferrazzi stresses that every event is an opportunity to network and every relationship has the potential to be important. He considers relationship development to be more of a lifestyle than an activity. Like Dale

Carnegie, Ferrazzi stresses the importance of showing genuine interest in other people and maintaining an active presence during a conversation. Personally, I like to think of business relationships being relationships first and business second: a certain percentage of relationships will *lead* to business, either directly or through referral, and the others are just nice to have. We have no way of knowing in advance which ones will be which.

As an illustration, consider the following example from my own experience. I worked on a legal project for which I devoted only a small amount of my time (1/10th of 1% of my billable time for that year. The client was pleased with the result, the service and the cost, which came in at the budgeted amount (his prior law firm had greatly exceeded the budget on his last project, which is why he switched). A few months later, that client was asked for a legal referral by a friend who was pursuing his first acquisition for his new private equity firm, but the law firm he usually used was engaged by the other side. I got the referral from this small but satisfied client, completed that larger deal successfully—and that second client ultimately became the largest client of my career (in some years, 25-50% of my time and revenue generated). Thus, I reaped significant benefits from paying attention to what seemed by all accounts to be a "minor" relationship.

Building Relationships through Networking

As Ferrazzi emphasizes, relationship development is a way of life for effective leaders of all types. In business and in life, developing relationships often occurs through networking. He points out that your network is your destiny. Studies in social networking and social contagion theory find that your reality is greatly influenced by your relationship network.[101] In business, we often are only as valuable to an organization as the people with whom we interact. Ferrazzi even developed his own formula: [102]

Success in life = The people you meet + What you create together

Ferrazzi stresses that follow-up with potential network members should become a habit following each new meeting. Follow-up may involve a substantive connection via a follow-up meeting or lunch or simply a LinkedIn message or email to keep you connected. Relationships are based much more heavily on the quality rather than the quantity of time spent together. You may have only one or two conversations as part of a business relationship; some interactions will be forgettable, but if it is a quality interaction, then the person will likely remember you and will be amenable to creating a deeper relationship at a later time. Follow-up is critical to turning 100 meaningless handshakes at an event into a meaningful few that will be remembered.

One networking tip from Ferrazzi is to network in a way that feels most comfortable to you. Different people have different styles and levels of intensity in their follow-up; intensity and success don't necessarily go hand-in-hand. I am not very aggressive, so I find that a short, simple follow-up email noting something from our conversation (with no "ask" included) is enough to develop a relationship until the next time our paths cross or the person needs services that I can provide. I find that networkers who are overly aggressive can undermine their own best interests, since people tend to avoid those who pursue relationships too forcefully—particularly those who don't back it up with substantive value. In general, people network most successfully by ensuring that their networking efforts are consistent with their personality and comfort zone. Initially networking within a "safe" network, such as a college alumni group, social club, or community group or trade association established for networking, can often be most comfortable and most successful.

When I was a senior associate seeking a promotion to partner, I developed a "relationship action plan" as suggested by Ferrazzi.[103] I started with a core group of people who I believed could refer business to me in the future. These were not primarily clients, although a few were employed by clients, but were thought leaders in their industry. The others were investors, accountants, and financial printers (who print public company annual reports and proxy statements) who wanted to get to know—as I did—leaders of emerging companies that might one day go public or grow and sell their company. The list also included friends who were not yet in a position of responsibility but who I expected would be one day. I tried to find an excuse to reach out to each person quarterly with something (for example, a news article) I thought would be of interest. I would also send a "Wishing You Well for the New Year" message to everyone in January (to avoid getting lost among the Christmas season well-wishers). When I met new people, I incorporated them into the relationship action plan.

I was also blessed to have a mentor, Steve Goodman, who was a legend in Philadelphia for "knowing everyone." Before Facebook and LinkedIn, he maintained a personal relationship network of thousands of people and would try to help every one of them. They, in turn, would try to help him by referring him business, making Steve one of the most successful lawyers in Philadelphia history. These interactions were pure of heart; Steve Goodman was such a genuinely nice guy that you felt great after each interaction with him, and he was an outstanding substantive lawyer so referral sources were confident they were "referring to the best." In return, his own relationship-building efforts were sincere. He genuinely cared about each relationship. I could never duplicate the style and success of my legendary mentor. However, the goal isn't to repeat what someone else does, but to be aware and incorporate as best you can what you learn from others into your own style and behavior.

Ferrazzi stresses a second tip that Steve Goodman practiced regularly: give to others without expecting something in return. This tip can be extended to the organizations you lead. Successful leaders act wholly and consistently in the best interest of their organization; those who jockey for promotion or view their co-workers as competitors are less likely to be trusted, and therefore are less likely to get the position they covet. Over the long term, relationships developed for the simple purpose of having them are often stronger and provide more value.

We often have an intuition about a person when we meet him or her that this is someone with whom we seek a relationship. I have learned to go with that intuition and stay in touch with people who "feel right" without knowing an end goal. Some of these "connection" relationships have resurfaced years later. These are the people you never forget and are glad when your paths cross again. There are hundreds or thousands of others you meet and just don't feel the same intuitive connection. I have learned to let those interactions go, while remaining open when another person follows up with me, as I may have missed the potential connection.

Steve Goodman introduced me years ago to Wayne Kimmel, a natural networker—one might even say professional networker—who turned his network into proprietary deal flow for the venture capital funds he founded, now known as Seventy Six Capital. In his book, *Six Degrees of Wayne Kimmel*[104] Wayne notes the pattern of successful start-up entrepreneurs who are able to collaborate, make contacts and develop relationships. He shares his personal story, his networking philosophy and how he created the "Wayne Kimmel" brand. Wayne also articulates a lesson I have observed and Ferrazzi notes in different words, which is that "relationship development is a marathon and not a sprint."[105]

I mentor associates by explaining that you don't just make partner and generate a legal practice. It generally takes three to five years of advanced relationship development to begin to develop a practice, followed by a lifetime of continued relationship development to maintain and grow that practice. Start connecting early. Relationship development simply becomes a part of how you live your life. Over time, your relationship network can become one of your biggest assets, can complement your skills and substantive experience, and can be the most satisfying part of your work life.

The Karma of Relationships

Ultimately, what Ferrazzi means when he talks about networking is the ability to build meaningful connections with other people. Connecting is giving and receiving. It is a constant process of asking for and offering help. By putting people in contact with one another, and by sharing your time and expertise freely, the pie gets bigger for everyone.

One Thanksgiving, during my morning meditation, I was contemplating the word "thanksgiving." I had always thought of the meaning of that word as a time for giving thanks. However, as the words split in my mind ("thanks" and "giving"), I saw them balanced, each with six letters, sitting on an old-fashioned scale—THANKS on one side and GIVING on the other. On one hand, I felt thankful for that which I had received, and on the other, I felt equally grateful for that which I have to give. The Thanksgiving holiday became for me a karmic balance between giving and receiving.

We don't think of karma as a leadership principle, but it does seem that "what goes around, comes around" in terms of relationship development. The business person who helps others succeed may be more likely to have others help him or her be successful. While the power of generosity may not always be fully appreciated in the short-term, the long-term benefits are undeniable to those who have used networking and relationship development to become leaders.

The karmic balance of giving and receiving only works on a macro-level scale: you will give to someone and you will receive from someone. It doesn't work on a micro-level scale where you "keep score" of what you give me and what I give you. Giving and receiving on a micro-level generally becomes petty and, inevitably, the proverbial scale tips one way or the other, with one party becoming resentful. The relationship is ultimately undermined.

The macro view of giving and receiving is particularly important in today's work world, which is characterized by job transience. The evolution of the workplace has replaced what William Whyte called "The Organization Man" in his 1950s bestselling book of the same name. That worker started and ended his career in one workplace. Today, employers offer little loyalty and millennial employees seem to give less. Although we still value loyalty and generosity, we associate them more strongly with our web of personal relationships rather than with long-term corporate allegiance. This can involve a personal kind of loyalty or devotion to one million Twitter followers. Either way, as Ferrazzi notes, we have each become our own brand. In this light, an organization becomes an ever-changing collection of personal brands that combine for a moment in time in order to achieve the organization's purpose.

Lovingkindness and Relationship Building

What prevents us from developing more effective relationships? Is it just time? I don't think so. Often it is our own fears and limitations, sometimes directed at a specific person and sometimes at "strangers" in general. Sometimes, as discussed in the prior chapter, it is our emotional baggage from past situations, maybe past rejections.

Lovingkindness meditation practice teaches us the value of all relationships and subtly and indirectly reinforces the humanity of all people by wishing all people well (a macro-level concept). Lovingkindness meditation generally consists of a four-stanza saying or mantra focused in the following order:

- You
- Dearly beloved—someone who is a close family member, friend, teacher or with whom you have a positive feeling
- Neutral person—someone you know but have no special feelings towards (e.g., a person who serves you in a shop)
- Hostile person—someone with whom you are currently having difficulty
- Everyone

The practice always begins with developing a loving acceptance of yourself. If you experience resistance, you may harbor feelings of unworthiness. No matter; the practice itself is designed to overcome feelings of self-doubt or negativity. Direct benevolent feelings toward yourself. Once you can do this, then you are ready to systematically develop acceptance, compassion, goodwill, and lovingkindness towards others. In fact, while on the surface lovingkindness appears focused on others, in reality it is a focus on ourselves and our attitude toward others. The focus is on you and your reaction to other people—although a change in your action may alter the other person's reaction. By sending out into the universe your best wishes without any expectation of receipt or response, you actually feel more loving and more kindness (in essence, more goodwill) toward others.

Practice of this meditation can develop the quality of acceptance. When lovingkindness practice matures, it naturally overflows into compassion, as one empathizes with other people's difficulties. Lovingkindness meditation can be a tool to permit the release of long-harbored negative emotions such as guilt, resentment, anger, and jealousy. Lovingkindness meditation has helped me break through some of my barriers and come to the realization that everyone is good, or can be good. It is really not for me to judge others, but rather to be open to the intersection of our interests.

The benefits of lovingkindness meditation are powerful; the Pali Canon, an ancient Buddhist text, says that lovingkindness meditation (Metta Bhavana) helps us to sleep well, to wake well, to avoid nightmares, to be closer to other people, to feel a sense of emotional protection, to feel closer to others, and to develop concentration. Richard Davidson, a neuroscientist and Director of the University of Wisconsin's Waisman Center, conducted research involving functional MRI scans of monks who had been meditating for many years. The research revealed that lovingkindness has a profound impact on specific areas of the brain: it significantly heightened the monks' compassion for others as well as their own levels of joy, happiness and contentment.[106]

Self-Forgiveness Opens Space for Others

Forgiveness is the gift you give yourself more than the person you are forgiving. When hurt or injured by another, we keep reliving that hurt, and it is the reliving that has the continued negative impact — the barrier. Forgiveness releases that replay cycle, thus releasing the barrier to developing or enhancing that relationship and similar ones with others. Multiple times in my career, lawyers I trained and groomed to be successful partners departed to join competitors. I was hurt and angry and disappointed and sad, even though I knew intellectually people depart for many reasons and it wasn't about me or any lack of appreciation for whatever value I had added to someone's career. However, until I was able to forgive, I wasn't fully able to train and nurture their successor relationship. I offered no value to myself or my organization by holding onto resentment. The value came from using meditation practices to let go of that resentment.

Meditation techniques for embracing forgiveness and compassion are core tenants of Christianity and other faiths as well. We seek the strength to forgive others and pray for God to forgive us.

During forgiveness meditations, we attempt to first identify and then release the emotions that we have retained about ourselves or another person. Once we release, we forgive, and past experiences have less power over us. Through self-forgiveness, we can escape the clutches of guilt and self-condemnation; instead of dwelling on the "what ifs," we can concentrate on the "what nows." Regardless of age, our ability to learn from our past experiences and to apply these lessons to our present is vital to help us grow as both people and as leaders.

The past can be a teacher for the present. When you hold on to emotions that weigh you down, you hold on to the past rather than learn from it.

Lovingkindness and self-forgiveness meditations are not intended to change others. The result of these meditation practices is to clear our own lens (distorted by our trapped emotions), at least for a moment in time. With a clearer lens, we can better see and choose which battles to pick with others and, ultimately, maybe see that there don't have to be battles at all.

Once we have forgiven and released, there is an opening created for improved relationships, deeper relationships and new relationships.

Relationship Meditation Practices

In order to glean the benefits discussed above, practice the lovingkindness techniques below when you need your lens cleared (and, like eyeglasses and car windshields, everyone does, periodically).

i. Lovingkindness Meditation

There are many lovingkindness sayings, blessings, prayers, and mantras. The following is based on a lovingkindness meditation taught to me by well-known author and meditation teacher Sylvia Boorstein. Sylvia has a calm style that evokes both wisdom and compassion; she is one of the most compelling people I have met during my lifetime. Sylvia's version of the lovingkindness meditation is as follows:

> May you be protected and safe
>
> May you be contented and pleased
>
> May your body support you with strength
>
> May your life unfold smoothly with ease

Sylvia encouraged us to create our own version of a lovingkindness meditation. I have adapted the meditation as follows:

> May you be protected and safe
>
> May you feel joyous and pleased
>
> May your mind be receptive to wisdom
>
> May your life unfold smoothly with ease

To me, feeling contented and pleased sounded like the same thing and not enough. I want joy. I also found the first and third stanza focused on physical presence and I was seeking more emotional and mental openness and balance, so to me (and for me), my adaptation fulfills me physically, emotionally, mentally and spiritually. The point is, it doesn't matter which lovingkindness variation you choose (and there are many). I encourage you to use the version you prefer, or to develop your own.

Start by using the pronoun "I" and repeating the blessings four times using that pronoun, preferably out loud. Remember, it is important to extend lovingkindness to ourselves before we are ready to fully extend it to others. As the Buddha reportedly said, "You, yourself, as much as anyone else, deserve your love and compassion."

> May I be protected and safe
> May I feel joyous and pleased
> May my mind be receptive to wisdom
> May my life unfold smoothly with ease

Then focus on a loved one such as a family member, mentor, or very close friend. (Traditional Buddhist teaching would have you start with your teacher or mentor.) Recite the blessings using that person's name. Then wait as the idea for the next loved one pops into your mind, substituting the general pronoun with the name that you call this person.

> May Michael be protected and safe
> May he feel joyous and pleased
> May his mind be receptive to wisdom
> May his life unfold smoothly with ease

> May _____ be protected and safe
> May he/she feel joyous and pleased
> May his/her mind be receptive to wisdom
> May his/her life unfold smoothly with ease

Now move on to showing appreciation for those in your life with whom you have significant contact but about whom you feel neutral. You wouldn't mind feeling more warmly towards these people, but you don't yet fully "click" with them, although they mean you no harm.

> May _____ be protected and safe
> May he/she feel joyous and pleased

May his/her mind be receptive to wisdom

May his/her life unfold smoothly with ease

Next, focus on a person towards whom you feel unease or hostility. Try to state the lovingkindness refrain with the same vehemence and focus that you used for the people you named earlier. You may wish to repeat the verse for that person more than once until you begin to feel more compassion toward him/her.

May _____ be protected and safe

May he/she feel joyous and pleased

May his/her mind be receptive to wisdom

My his/her life unfold smoothly with ease

We always end our lovingkindness practice with a verse addressed to everyone

May everyone be protected and safe

May all feel joyous and pleased

May all be receptive to wisdom

May everyone's life unfold smoothly with ease

Although this exercise appears benign, you will be amazed at the warmth, openness, compassion, and, yes, even lovingkindness you feel afterwards. You may be surprised by which names surface into your consciousness in which categories. Over time, this exercise may even dissipate the built-up hostility you have toward the difficult people in your life (after many practice sessions). You may be amazed that you perceive others differently, once your lens is clearer, and you may notice how many of their attitudes and actions really have nothing to do with you personally. It's an exercise you must experience to appreciate its impact.

ii. Forgiveness Meditation

Forgiveness meditation works best if, in advance of the exercise, you choose an event or relationship that sets off an emotional reaction as your intended focus for the meditation exercise. Keep in mind that the forgiveness is for your benefit—it actually has nothing to do with the other person. Just focus on one event or person in each meditation session; you may choose to focus on this event or person in multiple meditation sessions until you perceive an impact.

Once you choose a focus event or person, begin to relax your body; you may find that you tensed up just by choosing your focus event or person.

Focus on your breath and center yourself.

Focus your breath around your heart. Breathe deeply into and out of your heart center.

Now bring your attention to your focus event or person. Remember that you are in complete control of this experience. You can replay a story or conversation in your mind or just focus on the essence of that person or event (maybe a visualization, smell, or background scene that puts your focus in that place).

Consider a message of apology and/or forgiveness and let it go with the following affirmation:

> I am (on the inhale)
>
> Sorry (on the exhale)
>
> I am (on the inhale)
>
> Forgiving (on the exhale)
>
> I am (on the inhale)

Letting go (on the exhale)

There is no need to direct your affirmation; it will know where to go.

Now, replay the same story or conversation in your mind or just focus on that person or event. Focus your breath on your midsection around your heart. Breathe deeply into and out of your heart center. This time, picture green healing and forgiving light emanating from your heart. Say the following affirmation:

I am (on the inhale)

Sorry (on the exhale)

I am (on the inhale)

Forgiving (on the exhale)

I am (on the inhale)

Letting go (on the exhale)

Feel free to say this affirmation multiple times or stop if that is sufficient for you.

Bring your focus back to your breath, and open your eyes when you are ready. Notice if you feel different.

iii. Relationship Perspective Exercise

In today's Information Age, the difficulty is not finding more information, but rather sifting through the information we have in order to prioritize our actions. Similarly, rather than treating all of our relationships the same, we can benefit by identifying our priority relationships and ensuring that we regularly focus on further developing and nurturing these relationships.

In doing so, remember that relationships are a two-way street. The best relationships are ones where each person gives and each person gets and you share meaningful experiences together, whether professional or personal. This is often hard for "givers" who only want to focus on giving and are uncomfortable focusing on getting, but the truth remains that a relationship will be more fulfilling if you both give and get from that relationship.

Close your eyes or lower your gaze to avoid distractions.

Focus on your breath.

Ask yourself, "Who can be my most important relationships?"

Wait 10 seconds and observe what fills your mind. Then ask:

"What can I do for them?"

"What can they do for me?"

Wait 10 seconds and observe what fills your mind.

Then repeat again:

"Who can be my most important relationships?"

"What can I do for them?"

"What can they do for me?"

Repeat 5-10 times.

If something interesting or insightful comes to mind, make a note to remember it. After the exercise is complete, feel free to write your insights down to remember later, and follow up with those people.

iv. Integrating the Meditation Technique and Leadership Principle: Lovingkindness at Work Meditation

We can apply our lovingkindness meditation to our workplace. However, just as you should require nothing in return for reaching out to others with whom you are in a relationship, so you should want nothing from your colleagues. The goal is to send out lovingkindness and to release any inhibition or built up resentment you may have. While you may get a benefit, it is not a benefit created by wanting something specific in return from another person.

> May _____ be protected and safe
> May he/she feel joyous and pleased
> May his/her mind be receptive to wisdom
> May his/her life unfold smoothly with ease

Start with yourself, then move on to your favorite work colleagues—showing appreciation for those who "have your back"—the people who assist you every day, whom you feel warmly towards—and then extend your thoughts to a key customer or vendor. Then move on to those to whom you are neutral (other colleagues, customers or vendors). Consider moving around the office or focusing on those within your smaller work division. Then, with special focus, send lovingkindness to those at work with whom you have difficulty. Then, work your way up (regardless of your personal sentiment) to your boss and his/her boss until you reach the top of the organization. If you are the CEO, apply this to your board of directors and send them lovingkindness. Finally, focus on everyone in the organization, sending everyone your lovingkindness.

When you are finished, take a few moments to observe whether you feel any differently about your organization and working there than you did before. This is not a one-time exercise. Repeat as frequently as needed.

X. TEAM ORIENTATION — THE ZEN OF SUCCESS

As we look ahead into the next century, leaders will be those who empower others.

Bill Gates, Founder and CEO of Microsoft

There is a fine line between telling others what to do and creating an atmosphere as a leader where everyone knows what to do and supports each other's success. As we discussed in prior chapters, there is only so much one person can do, even a superstar. Success requires a team. Ideally, that team comprises not just your employees, but thought leaders in the industry, customers who want to buy the product/service, and suppliers and vendors who enable the organization to produce its innovative product or service most efficiently or integrate it with their own product or service offering. Many times, CEOs have told me that despite the fact that they are the company founder or person in charge—and possibly the hardest worker in the building—many employees seem not to always listen or be engaged. Just because you are in charge or have a title doesn't mean that others will follow . . . and, without followers, there is only so much impact you can have as a leader.

Effective leadership is about creating an atmosphere where each person knows what to do, knows how to do it and supports each other's and the organization' successes. Sometimes, to maximize your effectiveness as a leader, you have to be the coach rather than the star player.

I love watching Oprah's "Super Soul Sunday." I recall an episode interview with Phil Jackson. The Hall of Famer and most decorated coach in the NBA sat calmly in a sports jacket and a pair of Nike sneakers. Jackson is well-known for his Zen-like approach to basketball. Oprah was intrigued by the connection Jackson had drawn between basketball and spirituality. Jackson has led some of the biggest stars (and egos) in the NBA to victory, including Michael Jordan, Dennis Rodman, Kobe Bryant, and Shaquille O'Neal.

"What's the difference between spirituality and religion?" Oprah asked him. "Doctrine," he replied.[107]

Jackson recalled his strict religious upbringing and the "rude spiritual awakening" he encountered when he went to the University of North Dakota. During college, the young man who had grown up in a traditional religious Christian household and who had memorized 175 scriptures learned about Darwinism. Suddenly, he had a different perspective on the creation of our world. With this new perspective, he sought to learn more about people with varying beliefs. He became fascinated by Native American tribes (particularly the Lakota) and the tribal spiritual practices that led to unity. He was also introduced to Buddhism.

Buddhism is a religion that is based on the teachings of Siddhartha Gautama (commonly known as the Buddha), who taught people how to achieve enlightenment through their own direct experiences, rather than through formal dogma or faith in an external God. By practicing to achieve enlightenment, Buddhism practitioners seek to live their lives with wisdom, compassion, and peace.

In fact, Jackson traces a key part of his basketball philosophy to the principles of Zen Buddhism, a branch of Buddhism. Practitioners of Zen Buddhism focus on observing the breath and practicing mindfulness. A Zen Buddhist can achieve enlightenment and self-knowledge by accessing his or her mind and nature directly through intuition rather than through the intellectual analysis of feelings and thoughts. By focusing on one's own true nature, Zen Buddhists are able to free themselves from labels and logic and just accept "what is."

Over the years, Jackson embraced this new Zen Buddhist perspective of the world while not abandoning his Christianity. Ultimately, he developed a philosophy of leadership that was imbued with spirituality and acceptance of "what is." Jackson's philosophy is that there is only so much that can be taught, only so much a parent or teacher or coach can do; after that, the coach must let the team play and have confidence in its ability to succeed. Maybe he was just lucky enough to coach Michael Jordan and Kobe Bryant, two of the greatest basketball players of all time; certainly, teams need talent to win an NBA basketball game. But it was the string of consistent wins and consecutive championships in a sport where every team has talent that made Jackson's championship runs so impressive. When he accomplished this with two different teams — the Chicago Bulls and Los Angeles Lakers—it seemed like there was a component to Jackson's team successes other than just having talented players.

One aspect of Jackson's core leadership philosophy that I find fascinating is that he draws upon the most salient messages from his Christian upbringing, study of tribal cultures, and Buddhist teachings to create his own approach and style of leadership that he uses to open space for others to grow to achieve their individual and group potential. Jackson correctly observed in his Oprah interview that there is nothing about meditation antithetical to any religion. Meditation can deepen your religious beliefs in any religion (although admittedly, everyone's experience differs and there were aspects of his religious upbringing that Jackson did seem to reject; whether that was due to meditation or otherwise is unclear).

Lessons from Tribal Leadership

Jackson penned the New York Times best seller, *Eleven Rings*,[108] in which he shares his thoughts on the relationship among sports, spirituality, and leadership.

In the book, Jackson summarizes the five stages of "tribal leadership" formulated by Logan, King, and Fischer-Wright in their book, *Tribal Leadership*, which explains the mentality and culture of tribe members, and describes how these stages were relevant to the teams he coached throughout the years.

- Stage One is shared by groups, such as street gangs, who have a "life stinks" mentality.
- Stage Two is characterized by apathetic people with a "victim" mentality (such as the characters from the popular workplace mockumentary *The Office*).
- Stage Three is driven by individual achievement and includes individuals with the "I'm great; you're not" mentality.
- Stage Four reflects a sense of unity and group pride among individuals who have a "We're great; they're not" mentality.
- Stage Five is characterized by a strong belief that "life is great" or can be great. Jackson cites the Michael Jordon-led '95-'98 Chicago Bulls as a rare example of a Stage Five team. A Stage Five business team can do well while also doing good for the broader world.

In a perfect world, all groups would thrive under a Stage Five tribal leadership paradigm. However, our egos and personal biases make that nearly impossible, and most organizations remain stubbornly rooted in Stage Three or, in rare circumstances, rise successfully to Stage Four. A pessimistic outlook on life can keep us from advancing. While we wallow in our own misery, we can fall deeper into the depths of the Stage Two or

Stage One mentality, dragging down an entire organization. In this way, we fail to grow, both individually and collectively.

Like Steve Jobs, Jackson applied his passion for spirituality to an organization that seemed anything but spiritual. The NBA, like any of the four core American sports leagues, is full of famous faces that double as brands. For example, you can find a Jordon Bulls, Shaq Lakers, or LeBron James Cavaliers jersey anywhere around the world. These athletes are marketing machines in a fast-paced, multi-billion dollar industry.

Jackson didn't care if he was coaching the new face of Gatorade or the revered spokesperson of Nike; he wanted those egos checked at the door. He refused to be swept up in the chaos and held true to his spiritual routines and practices.

Before the '95-'98 Chicago Bulls could achieve Stage Five tribal leadership status, they had to first go through a difficult transition and begin to practice techniques that would facilitate their growth as a group. The year was 1987; Jackson had just become assistant coach of the Chicago Bulls and Michael Jordan was showing the shooting and playmaking skills that would lead him to achieve superstardom. Jackson's interactions with the superstar were limited, and he instead bonded with newcomer forward Scottie Pippen. Unlike Jordan, Pippen worked closely with his teammates and easily adapted to Jackson's triangle system. (The triangle system does not have many set plays, like many offensive systems; rather, players are positioned properly to read the defense and react appropriately.) After Doug Collins was fired as the Chicago Bulls head coach and Jackson took over, he knew he faced a long road ahead to transition the team from a group of individual players to a championship team. Over the next six years, the Bulls coaching staff repeatedly tried to build a team around Jordan. ". . . [W]e had the talent in place to win a championship," remarks Jackson, "but there was an important piece missing."[109]

Jackson wanted to grow the Chicago Bulls to become a Stage Five tribe. Jackson had to first transform his team of Stage Three "lone warriors" into a Stage Four "we" team. Much of the team embraced this unified, tribal mentality. Jackson realized he would have to do a little extra work to get three-time scoring title recipient Jordan to score less and allow other team members to contribute to the offense in order to keep the other team's defense from converging on Jordan. Jackson describes Jordan's response as "surprisingly pragmatic," although Jordan expressed his lack of confidence in his teammates' relative abilities. Jackson retorted, "You can't defeat a good defensive team with one man."

Jackson began to assimilate Lakota tribal practices into team practices, subtly at first. Team members would gather in a circle at the beginning and end of each practice in order to bond them together in a circle without a beginning or an end. Jackson notes, "Lakota warriors always gathered in circular formations because the circle was a symbol of fundamental harmony of the universe."[110]

Jackson also incorporated other Lakota customs. He beat a drum when he wanted the players to come together in the "tribal room" (more commonly known as the "video room"). If the team lost a game, Jackson would light a sage smudge stick to "purify" the air in the locker room. Jackson also compiled clips from the television program "Mystic Warrior" (the story of Crazy Horse, the Native American war leader who led his tribe to victory against the U.S. Government in the Battle of Little Bighorn in 1876) and showed them to the team in an attempt to exhibit the power of unity and how it can lead to success. In addition to embracing Lakota customs, Jackson had his team attend yoga, tai chi, and other similar activities in order to hone their spirituality and develop their "oneness," which would lead to their ability to experience oneness as a team.

These practices likely seemed silly to some of the players (and maybe even to some of you reading this book), but Jackson was instilling into the minds of these athletes that these customs exist for a reason. They nurture the unity that comes with being a tribe.

Jackson's main goal was to have the team "lead from within." He was assertive during practice, and hands-off during the game. The players took responsibility on the court for the team as a whole (not just for themselves), and the process ingrained in them the interests of the tribal team. The Chicago Bulls began to gel as a result and became three-time NBA champions.

Hall of Famers Kobe Bryant and Shaquille O'Neal joined the L.A. Lakers in 1996. When Jackson became coach of the L. A. Lakers in 1999, they were feuding and it didn't appear that they could play together with only one ball. Jackson implemented his tribal methods to deal with the egos of these basketball titans. In the first season of the Jackson era, L.A. finished with a 67-15 record (the best in the NBA and the second-best all-time Laker record). That does not mean that there wasn't adversity. In Game 7 of the Western Conference finals (winner moves on, loser goes home), L.A. was down 15 points with 10 minutes left to play. Jackson expressed his continued support and encouragement to focus on each possession (score on offense, stop the other team on defense). The Lakers won that game and went on to win three championships in Jackson's first three years coaching the team. After a rough 2003/2004 season, Jackson left the team for a year. Bryant and O'Neal again appeared unable to play on the same team, and O'Neal was traded to Miami. Jackson returned to the team after a year off to start the rebuild and the Lakers again won two more championship titles in 2009 and 2010.

Principles for Leading With A Team Orientation

Jackson applied the tribal lessons and basic principles of mindful leadership over time to transform disorganized teams into champions. He lists eleven principles that leaders can use in all types of organizations to support team achievement:

1. **<u>Lead from the Inside Out</u>.** Most people do what others are doing—they lead from the outside in. That strategy may work in the short term, but inevitably has limits. Effective leaders seem to take the best of others and combine those traits and practices with their own personality and inner wisdom.

2. **<u>Bench the Ego</u>.** The "my way or the highway" leader also has limits. That strategy may work in the short term, but ultimately the best people hit the highway after their creativity is stifled. Effective leaders listen and take the best ideas from everyone inside and outside the organization regardless of attribution.

3. **<u>Let Each Player Discover His [or Her] Own Destiny</u>.** You can't effectively force your will on other people. As a leader, you can provide guidance and share "best practices," but ultimately you have to delegate and trust good people to do their job well. Great leaders inspire greatness in others and then give them enough room to carve out a meaningful role and achieve success. An insightful leader recognizes and utilizes what is unique about each member of the team and uses that insight to maximize performance from each individual and from the team as a whole.

4. **<u>The Road to Freedom is a Beautiful System</u>.** Jackson describes his application of the values of selflessness and mindful awareness to basketball. Mindful court awareness is the core of his triangle system of basketball strategy. Great leaders don't just dictate but continuously react to the needs and desires of others—whether they are employees, suppliers or customers—to take advantage of available opportunities.

5. **<u>Turn the Mundane into the Sacred</u>.** This is the essence of transforming a group of disparate people into an organization where they connect

to something bigger than themselves. The essence of being an effective leader is to get those in your organization to wholeheartedly agree to being led, and then offer them a sense of their destiny as a collective organization.

6. One Breath – One Mind. Jackson introduced his teams to mindfulness meditation. One exercise that he often had them perform on the basketball floor in a dark stadium was to synchronize their breathing while holding hands. The practice of quieting the restless mind and focusing on the present moment is extremely valuable during times of chaos, helping people to keep perspective and weave effectively through the chaos. Keeping your team on the same page in mission fulfillment is key to a successful effort.

7. <u>Compassion</u>. Jackson repeats a new adaption of the Chinese sacred text of Tao Te Ching by Stephen Mitchell:

> "I have just three things to teach.
> simplicity, patience and compassion
> These three are the greatest treasures.
> Simple in actions and thoughts,
> you return to the source of being.
> Patient with both friends and enemies
> you accord with the way things are.
> Compassionate toward yourself.
> You reconcile all beings in the world."[111]

"Compassion" is a word not often bandied about either in the locker room or in the board room. However, Jackson notes that a few kind, thoughtful words can have a strong transformative effect on relationships, even those with the toughest people. Great leaders take the time, as Dale Carnegie recommends, to express appreciation and compassion to those within the organization trying their best to overcome obstacles and succeed.

8. **Keep Your Eye on the Spirit, Not the Scoreboard.** Jackson repeats a story from Stephen Covey, who tells a Japanese tale about a samurai warrior and his three sons. The samurai wanted to teach his sons about the power of teamwork, so he gave each son an arrow and asked them to break it. They each did so easily. Then the samurai gave them a bundle of three arrows and asked them to break them, which they couldn't. The lesson is that if you stick together, you will not be defeated.

Jackson notes that this story reflects just how strong a team can be when each of its members surrenders their self-interest for the greater good of the team. If an organizational leader can institute that level of teamwork, the organization is much more likely to be successful than one that motivates individuals to make individual efforts.

9. **Sometimes You Have to Pull Out the Big Stick.** As far back as the Old Testament, leaders have had the power to use the carrot or the stick—to lead through incentive or to lead by force. While Jackson generally promotes leading by incentive, he notes that sometimes an effective leader must keep everyone in line toward the goal. He notes that coaching, like any leadership position, requires toughness. No matter how nice a leader may be, sometimes that leader will have to be tough on people (including replacing members of the team) in order to achieve the greater good. Someone who needs to always be liked will find it impossible to lead effectively.

10. **When in Doubt, Do Nothing.** Jackson notes that on some occasions, the best thing to do as a leader is absolutely nothing. A corollary lesson is to pause before taking action: respond instead of react. Relaxing the mind during a time of chaos is a way to take that pause and contemplate the best reaction before doing so. Jackson notes that the unconscious

mind is a terrific solver of complex problems when the conscious mind is busy elsewhere, overtaxed, or just plain stuck. Effective leaders know when to act and when to wait; often, issues will resolve themselves (or others empowered to resolve them will do so) in a manner more effective than top-down action.

11. **<u>Forget the Ring.</u>** While it is important to be competitive, the focus should be on the journey rather than the goal. This is consistent with basic yoga philosophy: effort without attachment to result. While an effective leader can at times motivate an organization with a focus on future goals, the day-to-day tasks generally need to remain the focus if the organization is to be successful in achieving the goal.[112] Letting go of the day-to-day focus on the goal can actually help achieve that goal.

All 11 of Jackson's leadership principles are consistent with his philosophy of supporting achievement with a team first orientation by guiding individual players as best he can and then just letting them each do what they do best within a mutually understood game plan. He puts the players in a position to win as a team — and sure enough, they often do.

In his interview with Oprah, Jackson indicated that he still believes in God and in Christianity. He doesn't find the practice of Zen meditation and Christianity to be inconsistent. Jackson was able to combine his religious upbringing, his Zen style of learning, and his personality with his meditation practices and his general awareness that arose from that meditation practice. With this greater awareness, Jackson was able to teach and lead others as the most effective NBA coach of all time.

As the Dalai Lama has said: "Don't try to use what you have learned through Buddhism to be a better Buddhist, use it to be a better whatever-you-are."

Lessons from Buddhism

The four noble truths are the truths or realities that one fully under-
stands, and thus lives, once one has become enlightened. The four
truths, described below, express the basic orientation of Buddhism.[113]

Dukkha (the truth of suffering). We crave and cling to impermanent
states and things that we are incapable of satisfying. This causes us suffering. For example, if we want to be thinner, have a bigger house, or
make more money, we will never achieve everything we want. (If we
achieve something, we want more).

Samsara (the truth of understanding the cause and condition of suffering). The continued arising of Dukkha keeps us in an endless cycle
of repeated rebirth, Dukkha and dying again until we learn to release
the clinging and craving. This craving and clinging produce karma,
which keeps us trapped in the reincarnation cycle of rebirth and
renewed dissatisfaction.

Niroda (the truth of the possibility of the cessation of suffering). There
is a way to reach happiness, which is by stopping the craving and the
clinging. This is when Nirvana is attained, no more karma is produced,
and the cycle of rebirth and dissatisfaction ends.

Magga (the truth that the Buddhist path can lead to the end of suffering).
There is a path to cessation of or liberation from the craving and clinging
called the Noble Eightfold Path. By restraining oneself, cultivating discipline, and practicing mindfulness and meditation, the craving and clinging can stop and rebirth and dissatisfaction end.

The Buddha purportedly spoke directly of the four noble truths, and they
represent the awakening and liberation of the Buddha and a roadmap for
all people to achieve their own spiritual awakening and liberation. My

favorite summary description of the Buddha's roadmap is that suffering is necessary until you realize that it is not necessary.

More on Buddhism—Schools of Buddhist Thought

Buddhism does not describe a singular worldview; like many other religions, Buddhism split into various schools of thought over time. There are three main schools of Buddhist thought, which all share a common core of fundamental ideals and principles.

Buddhism originated in northern India, where Theravada Buddhism originated through the teachings of Siddhartha Gautama, the primordial Buddha. This school of thought, often referred to as the most orthodox within the realm of Buddhism, is characterized by inquiry into the understanding of human nature, and presents a meditative approach to obtaining this understanding[114]. This school spread throughout southern Asia, before evolving beyond the Buddha's fundamental teachings into other disciplines.

The earliest segmentation in Buddhist practice became known as the Mahayana Buddhism , and is popular in Tibet and Nepal.[115] Another major branch of Buddhism, Vajrayana, is also rooted in Tibet. This practice centers around a religious figure known as a "lama" and contains four lineages of Tibetan Buddhist practice. The Dali Lama is from the Gelug-pa tradition of the Vajrayana school, and is the recognized leader of all four Tibetan traditions.[116]

Buddhism spread to Japan, where it further segmented into multiple schools of practice, the most popular of which is Zen Buddhism. In its earliest forms, Zen Buddhist practice avoided the intellectualism and scriptures of earlier forms. Instead, this practice is often based in extensive silent meditation, and aims to transcend linear thinking.[117]

There is no single Buddhist view of the world. Buddhism split into different sects over time. As a result, just like there are Catholic and Protestant Christians, Reform, Conservative and Orthodox Jews and Sunni and Shia disciplines of Islam, there are distinct branches of Buddhism that differ in particular points of doctrine and style of teaching, but share a common core of fundamental ideas.

Within Buddhism, there are at least five different sects (some of which have sub sects). *Theravada Buddhism* is prominent in Southeast Asia and includes very specific rituals practiced precisely. *Mahayana Buddhism* reformed the "right" rituals required by Mahayana Buddhism. *Tantric Buddhism* (sometimes called Tibetan Buddhism) arose in Tibet and Nepal. *Zen Buddhism* arose in China and became popular in Japan and, in the 20th century, in the U.S. *Pure Land Buddhism* is a sect whose basic premise is that heaven on earth leads us to a place with no pain.[118]

One common Buddhist tradition, originally practiced only by Buddhist monks and then spread to the masses, is daily meditation, often in the morning. Buddhists attempt to carry out the mindset gained through morning meditation throughout the day.

The Leap From Buddhism to Teamwork

My brief study of Buddhism guided me to two basic lessons. The first is that my suffering stemmed from wanting to control the uncontrollable and "feel in control" of my life. Trying to be in control all of the time is a lot of pressure (and creates stress). Realizing that there is an impermanence in everything (internal and external) helped me to stop believing I had to be in control (or subordinate to someone I had confidence in who was in control). Replacing control is "acceptance and choice." I can choose to act, react or not act. I can choose to take control in a situation or not. If I am aware of more choices and in the present moment when making them, I make better choices. As will be discussed in Chapter XIII, once you accept that you are making choices, you are willing to accept responsibility for those choices knowing that some will work out well and some will not.

My second basic lesson from Buddhism is that what I can achieve alone is so much less than what I can achieve in relationship with my connections. It comes back to the Ferrazzi success formula (success = the people you meet + what you do together). When we are connected to our personal and organizational mission and others as a team, we both achieve more and enjoy the experience. The Buddhist philosophy of "lack of self" focuses on each of us as simply a small part of a connected universe. We can better address the causes of our suffering together, connected.

Jackson used his personal Zen meditation practices to develop and successfully implement his leadership principles and, as a result, to make the teams he coached more successful. He also shared some of these practices with his players who bonded to a certain extent just by participating and, to varying degrees, benefited from the meditation exercises being practiced.

Religious and Tribal Meditation Practices

Phil Jackson practices Zen meditation. Zen meditation is the practice of calming your body and mind and opening yourself up to discovering insight into the nature of your being. As you sit in prescribed positions, you close your mind to thoughts and images; after a period of time, your heart rate will slow, your breathing will become shallow, and you will pass into a reflective meditative state. With the use of Zen meditation, deliberate thought, contemplation, and reflection, you can create a synergy that connects all aspects of your being—the body, the mind and the soul. In your practice of Zen meditation, your mind is only in the moment. You are not thinking about the past or the future. You are not thinking about how to get your work done or what you should have said to that guy who cut you off in the grocery line. You are thinking thoughts that appear to randomly float through your mind like, "my nose is itching," "my leg hurts in this position," or "the sun is beautiful."

You are in the moment, only reacting to what is happening now. You are not ruminating about things you should have done or will do tomorrow. You are not reflecting on or planning your life.

You are making the choice to stay, to not scratch the itch and not let your mind take you away from your present moment. You are choosing each moment to control your mind and not vice versa. You are practicing key lessons that translate to effective leadership.

i. Zazen Meditation

Zazen is the generic term for seated meditation in the Buddhist tradition, but in the modern Zen tradition it is often referred to as "just sitting." It is a minimalist kind of meditation, done for long periods of time, with little instruction beyond the basics of your physical posture (sit with your back straight) and generally to keep your eyes half open with your gaze down. There is no particular attention to the breath, nor an attempt to change the breath. Zazen is the "anti-method" approach to meditation, but it is often done in conjunction with a concentration on a certain aspect of Buddhist scripture, or a paradoxical sentence, story, or question (called a koan). Zazen is very difficult to learn, and it is very difficult to make progress with this method alone because it frequently requires guidance on how to do the practice. Also, it was developed for a monastic setting, making it difficult to adapt to an active life in the world. However, there are many who think that this is what meditation is or is meant to be, and the lack of a requirement to do anything but sit works for them with practice. If you don't like the distraction of the instruction or other concentration techniques, try to "just sit."

ii. Meditation within Judeo-Christian Religious Traditions

Mother Theresa wrote: "We need to find God, and He cannot be found in the noise and restlessness. God is the friend of silence. See how nature— trees, flowers, grass—grows in silence . . . the more we receive in silent prayer, the more we can give in our active life. We need silence to be able to touch souls. The essential thing is not what we say, but what God says to us and through us. All our words will be useless unless they come from within—words which do not give the light of Christ increase the darkness."[119]

Contemplation is a foundation of both Christian and Jewish mysticism. Prayer and moments of silence after prayer focus one's attention to achieve unity with God. Many rituals, such as counting rosary beads, require intense focus to prevent distraction.

While silent prayer is the most obvious form of meditation within a service, all prayer can be meditative. Saying the words of prayer is only part of a prayer practice during a religious service. The harder part is paying attention while doing so—in other words, being aware and in the present moment with complete focus on the prayer. Mindful prayer is, in my experience, when prayer becomes meaningful. These are the lessons we practice and learn through meditation and can then apply to all aspects of our life, including our religious practice.

Christians, Jews and other religious practitioners often speak of meditation practice as a component in maturing, reinforcing and deepening their faith as their wisdom within confirms they are on the right path. Meditation can be a method for breaking through human defense barriers and opening the heart to intimacy with God. Meditation can also be a way to quiet the day-to-day chatter of the mind, which is focused on worldly issues, to leave room for spiritual contemplation and gratitude for what God has given us.

Meditation is a particularly overt part of services in certain sects of Christianity such as Benedictine and Trappist monasticism, the Eastern Orthodox church and Quakerism, and certain sects of Judaism such as Chassidism. The Jews under Moses walked through the desert for 40 years, and Jesus himself is said to have walked through the desert while fasting for 40 days. These are meditative moments for the participants in religious history, and practices that are a lot more difficult than the ones described in this book. The practice of Salah five times a day is an obligatory religious duty of every Muslim. This meditative prayer ritual is practiced at particular times, raising the collective energy and connection of those practicing together.

However, there are those within many religious authority structures who do not favor meditation because they do not believe or desire to encourage a direct relationship between practitioners and God. There are others who believe that an empty mind is fodder to be filled by Satan.

Ultimately, following your own instinct and your own religious beliefs is your best guide. To me, meditation is neither a religious practice nor a nonreligious practice. It simply is. It is an act that takes on whatever intention you've given to it. Being more in the present moment and more aware is fairly consistent with all religions, as are loving kindness, gratitude, empathy and support for others.

Recite a favorite prayer, either once or a few times. Then sit for 10 minutes and see where it leads.

iii. Create a Meditative Ritual

Meditation is common in tribal practices around the world. I had the opportunity to take a trip to Peru to visit the Incan sites, including Machu Picchu, with an Incan Shaman guide, Malku. Malku took our group on a journey to perform traditional Incan rituals at the sites in which they were performed historically. He taught us about the Andean culture and its theory of spiritual development through the ages.

The Incans, like most tribal cultures, focused on what they knew and extrapolated their belief system and customs from there. The four elements of Earth, Water, Fire and Air that are essential for human existence are part of the core practice. Rituals surrounding each of those four elements developed (slightly differently in different regions and tribes around the world but with the same intent) to encourage practitioners to be more aware and focused on each element with expressions of wonder and gratitude. Spirit animals or power animals are often symbols of desirable human characteristics by tribal cultures, and stories are created to learn and teach lessons relating to these characteristics.

Most tribes developed some version of a shaman or special leader who can speak with the spirits, interpret their messages, and provide guidance to the people. These special leaders engage in meditative practices, often leading their tribe in these practices. There is faith in the wisdom that comes during these sacred rituals.

Ultimately, whether the wisdom came from the ancestors or the spirit animals or just the inner voice within the leader, it was sufficiently wise that the tribe followed, and the tribes that utilized these practices survived and thrived for many centuries.

Create your own ritual using Earth, Water, Fire and Air (or something that represents them such as a brown, blue, yellow and white stone) and honor the elements with your ritual. Maybe do it as part of a group for bonding or team building from shared experiences. Have fun. It is the journey that matters, not the destination.

iv. Integrating the Meditation Technique and Leadership Principle—Group Meditation

One of the techniques Phil Jackson used with his team to promote connection and support for teammates is to simply hold hands with another person (or hold hands as a group in a circle) in silence. While you may not be ready to try this practice in the board room, this is a great practice to try with your spouse and/or entire family.

Put away the cell phone and other electronics.

Dim the lights.

Stand, sit, or lie in bed together.

Hold hands.

You may begin with an affirmation such as "I support you," or not.

Maintain silence for 5-10 minutes.

Focus your attention on the other.

Feel the other's hand and the physical and energetic connection.

Smile.

Appreciate.

Enjoy.

Meditation does not have to be a solitary practice. Like many things, there is joy in sharing and support in community.

Building the Pillar of Connection

In business, connection is everything. It is how customers and employees are satisfied, how sales are made and how brands are built.

Effective leaders are able to communicate well with others and listen at least as much as they talk. Too often, a barrier to effective communication is the baggage we bring to an interaction from our past experiences. Meditation can clear your clouded lens to facilitate more and closer connections.

Once the lens is clear, it is easier to observe others with greater attunement. What we observe is that different people are motivated differently and have different communication styles. Being aware of those differences can assist you in more successfully motivating others.

There is only so much we can accomplish alone. Effective leaders develop successful relationships. An organization's overall success is based on the relationships created within the organization and with important stakeholders outside the organization. It takes a team and a team orientation to succeed.

Meditation can help you practice listening, learning to respond instead of react, developing relationship intuition as to who should be a focus for relationship development and team building. As a result, meditation facilitates your ability to develop more meaningful relationships.

BUILDING THE PILLAR OF PERSPECTIVE

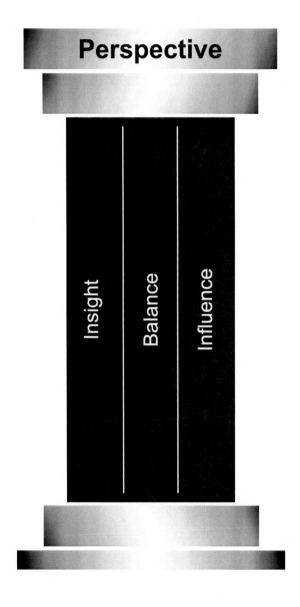

XI. SEVEN HABITS OF HIGHLY EFFECTIVE MEDITATORS—THE ROAD TO INSIGHT

Transformational leaders serve a transcendent purpose,
pointing the way to a new reality.

Dali Lama, spiritual leader

We have focused on our self, using meditation to create greater awareness, focus, and creativity. We have used meditation to improve our connection with others by communicating more effectively, developing more and better relationships, being more attuned with our key relationships, and supporting the success of organizational teams. The transformation from your meditation practice comes from seeing things and people closer to how they really are, and observing the wisdom within when the day-to-day chatter of your mind is quieted. That is when a changed perspective creates your new reality.

Perspective is the capacity to view life experiences in their true relationship or relative importance. Maintaining perspective requires a focus on the larger goals while carrying out day-to-day activities. Effective leaders maintain perspective within the chaos of every-day life.

Leaders can spread perspective to others throughout an organization. This is why organizations create mission statements and often have slogans that seek to externally communicate and internally reinforce the organization's most important goals. A well-crafted mission statement helps employees and other stakeholders develop a shared passion for the organization's purpose, and leaders can encourage employees to keep that shared mission in mind in order to maintain perspective.

Perspective is derived from a combination of insight (an accurate and deep understanding) and wisdom (a combination of knowledge and experience). We will further explore these terms and how the practice of meditation can lead to greater insight and wisdom as you build up the foundational pillar of perspective. Perspective is bigger than just work or performance goals. We will also consider stress reduction and work life balance as part of your overall perspective and greater overall perspective leading to greater influence, both at work and in the other communities in which you live.

7 Habits of Highly Effective People

I first read the book *The 7 Habits of Highly Effective People: Powerful Lessons in Personal Change* by Stephen Covey[120] in my 20s. I even had the opportunity to hear Stephen Covey teach the course, and I used his planner notebook for about five years (this was before the time of smart phones as organizational tools).

Covey focuses on habits that permit each of us to organize our lives for success. Covey defines a habit as "the intersection of knowledge, skill and desire."[121] These life habits are as important today for developing positive leadership as they were 30 years ago. They embody the essence of personal character and are influential in creating a team based on mutual respect and acting with integrity to fulfill the organizational mission.

In some respects, perspective requires the development and integration of the other leadership traits discussed previously in this book. Covey's habits include tools for increasing awareness, staying focused, enhancing creativity, and developing relationships. Meditation practices can reinforce Covey's habits and help you integrate them into your life.

Covey's first three habits of highly successful people involve taking control of your mind and actions. They involve being proactive in setting intention and keeping your goals in perspective while seeking to fulfill them. These habits emphasize that, instead of just going about your daily tasks mindlessly (doing, doing, doing), you should strive to bring important items from your subconscious (background) to your conscious (foreground). Once an idea is in the front of your mind, you are more likely to act on it. Covey's first three habits of effective people are:

Habit 1: Be Proactive[122]

When given responsibility—a task or position—proactive people take responsibility for crafting and organizing a detailed implementation plan, getting supervisors to approve the plan, making implementation choices, and accepting the consequences that follow. Being proactive does not mean "doing whatever you want." There will be times when you must implement what your supervisor (or the board if you are a CEO) assigned you to do. It means a mindset of doing what you can do in the best interest of the organization. Part of being proactive is to get tasks done. Another part of being proactive is to actively choose not to be a victim, not to be reactive, not to blame others or the organization itself for what you can't do, and not to give up on yourself or the organization following setbacks

Proactively plan to meditate daily. This is my key habit. It makes a big difference if you commit to meditate daily, even if only for 10 minutes a day. Daily discipline shows your mind that your meditation practice is a priority. Once the practice of meditation becomes a daily habit, the lessons learned become habits incorporated into your daily life.

One of my teachers said that everyone should meditate daily, and those who have no time to meditate daily should meditate twice a day. If, like virtually all of us, you have what seems to be an impossibly busy schedule, it is often hard to believe that you have the time for meditation. Keep reminding yourself that you will feel less pressured and become more efficient if you put aside a short time each day for your meditation.

It helps to meditate at the same time of day, in the same location, and in the same position, as this trains your mind and body to be prepared. When choosing a time of day, place, and position that is right for you, consider when you are most aware. You can use the time, place and position that you intuitively sense is best for you, or you can use a trial-and-error method to find what you like best. Don't worry if you change. Observe and do what is best for you at this time without worrying about "rules"— as long as you are meditating daily. Once you are in a meditative state of consciousness during meditation, you are no longer proactive, but instead simply observing.

Habit 2: Begin with the End in Mind[123]

Create a mission statement at a macro-level (a mission statement for your life) and at a micro-level (a mission statement for important projects). For the macro-level mission statement, envision the ideal characteristics for each of your various roles and relationships in life. For the micro—level mission statement, envision for each project the results you desire, and then create a step-by-step implementation plan to achieve project success. This doesn't mean that you won't pivot along the way. However, if you keep the end in mind, you develop the perspective to better see when you are deviating from your path to success. It is then much easier to consider the changes necessary to get you back on that path.

Before each meditation practice, set an intention. You might be seeking something; it might be stress relief, relaxation of the body, release of an emotion or an emotional reaction to a relationship, or a problem you wish to contemplate. The intention may be to have no intention—just to see what happens. Be aware of that need in setting your daily intention. Start with your habit for quieting your mind — the place and position you take each day — an initial focus on your breath, and then move forward with intention. Setting an intention and choosing the right technique consistent with that intention is different from attaching to a result. It is important to allow the meditation to unfold naturally. I find that I am more likely to achieve value if I set an intention before starting, but then remain flexible as to what actually happens.

Habit 3: Put First Things First[124]

Prioritize, plan, and execute your week's tasks based on importance rather than urgency. As Collins also noted (and as will be further emphasized in Chapter XIV), focus on your biggest opportunities, not just your biggest problems. Evaluate whether your efforts exemplify your desired character values, propel you toward goals, and enrich the roles and relationships you identified in your macro-level mission statement from Habit 2. This is the "connecting the dots" step to get you from here to there. Live and be driven by what matters most, not just by the forces around you that require the short-term actions that usurp most of your time.

Learning to be in the present moment is one of the consistent themes of meditation you utilize. It is putting first things (the present moment) first. Meditation keeps you in the present moment, whether it is a focus on a mantra, counting, or simply your breath. One mantra recitation at a time. One number at a time. One breath at a time. You are not getting caught up in the past or the future, but practicing focusing on the present and over time simply being more often in the present moment. This may lead to helping you actually listen when someone else is speaking or helping you stay focused on a task without distraction. Your everyday thoughts seem to fade away. What replaces them is more insightful. You have to experience it to fully understand the benefit.

Covey's next three habits deal with interdependence (i.e., working with others). These habits help us keep the importance of our employees, customers, clients, patients, key vendor contributors, friends, family and other relationships within our broader perspective.

Habit 4: Think Win-Win[125]

If a business leader can create win-win situations for employees, customers and the organization as a whole, he or she can exceed expectations and make a substantial positive impact. Genuinely strive for mutually beneficial solutions and agreements in all of your relationships. Value and respect people by understanding that a "win" for all is ultimately a better long-term resolution than if only one person gets his or her way. Focus on opportunity rather than competition. Recall that every relationship can be an important one—you just don't know which one will turn out that way while you are developing them. Ask "How can I help you?" rather than "How can you help me?"

For some people—the runner who gets in that meditative run every morning or the disciplined Zazen meditator with a repeated meditation ritual or trigger—using the same technique every day works best. However, for many other people (like me), life gets in the way. Sometimes combining meditation with something else you are already doing can teach you to regularly create win-win scenarios for yourself. For example, try a flossing meditation. Look at the floss, focus on your breath, focus on the floss. Instead of just doing a 10-second floss, take your time. Start on the upper left side and feel the floss between your teeth. Shift the floss to the left and to the right. Feel the difference between moving fast and slow. Notice when something is dislodged by the floss. Keep focusing on each tooth as you work around your mouth; if you lose focus, come back to the floss, come back to your breath. Reach a meditative state, observe and have clean teeth—win-win. Remember that meditation is not the end in itself. The technique is a means to facilitate a meditative state, so do whatever is working for you, whenever you can do so.

Habit 5: Seek First to Understand, Then to Be Understood.[126]

Covey accurately observes, "Most people do not listen with the intent to understand; they listen with the intent to reply."[127] Use empathic listening to be genuinely influenced by people and what they are saying, which provides an incentive for them to reciprocate the listening and remain open to being influenced by you. This creates an atmosphere of caring and positive problem-solving. Once you understand the other person's point of view, it is easier for you to make your point of view understood because you know how best to phrase your thoughts based on your heightened understanding of the listener. Effectiveness lies in blending the listening and a well-framed response together.

Insightful moments during meditation allow you to practice listening without immediately and instinctively responding. When an "ah ha" moment during meditation occurs, your instinct may be to think too quickly; once you open up the door for the brain to analyze it, your mind shifts back to every day consciousness and you may lose that place that generated the insight, for that session at least. When you notice something insightful, try to say to yourself, "That is insightful; I will remember that" or just write it down without analyzing it and continue. Learning to separate your witness "self" (that part of your subconscious that observes what is going on) from your thoughts, actions and feelings is a key result from a regular meditation practice.

Habit 6: Synergize[128]

Leaders who create synergy put others in a position to succeed and thus succeed themselves, ultimately helping their organization succeed. Synergy is a key concept in merger and acquisition (M&A) discussions. How can the buyer obtain more value from the business than the seller?

Both parties benefit—the buyer reaps the benefits from the synergistic value to be created and is thus willing to pay the seller an extra amount for that value. The seller benefits from the higher sale price. Effective leaders combine the strengths of people through teamwork so that together they can achieve goals no one person could have achieved alone. Effective coordination among team members starts with the leader's realization that he or she is not perfect or always right and can't do everything himself or herself. A synergistic working group allows the strengths of some to compensate for the weaknesses of others (and everyone has strengths and weaknesses) to optimize the performance of the team.

Wisdom emerges when we synergize the insights gained through meditation into the practicality of our lives. As we become more aware of the difference between our thinking mind and the space behind these thoughts during meditation, the answers come to us. After each meditation session is over, come back to those insights for a few moments and remember and analyze what sticks in your mind; then try to integrate these insights into your conscious mind and life action plan. This works at a micro level with respect to a particular issue, and at a macro level as you transform your world view from one of isolation and chaos created by your conscious mind to one of connection, clarity and compassion (at least for moments in time), whether during meditation or during daily activities, and then integrate these observations. When you utilize the lessons learned during meditation into your daily life, you are more often aware in the present moment, with a clearer lens and you observe and act with greater perspective. This is how meditation makes you a more effective leader and better person.

The final habit is vital for all of us: to view your role in the organization in the context of your whole life, while at the same time cultivating perspective and finding time for creativity.

Habit 7: Sharpen the Saw[129]

Effective people constantly renew themselves by "sharpening the saw" in four basic spheres of life: physical, emotional/social, mental and spiritual. I think of these spheres not as independent but more like overlapping concentric circles. Renewal increases your capacity to live all of the other habits more effectively.

Hitting the "refresh" button renews your resources, energy, and health to create a sustainable, long-term, effective lifestyle. This applies both to you personally as a leader and to your organizations. It is why the annual corporate retreat or company picnic is worth the time and expense. It is why vacations actually make us more effective in the workplace. Balance will be further emphasized in Chapter XII. Without balance, we have difficulty upholding the other habits over time.

Meditation is a practice that facilitates insight and invites growth. Even though I meditate regularly, have taken many meditation courses, and teach meditation seminars, I sometimes get into a rut. How do I get out? I attend a weekend retreat. My preferred places include the Omega Institute for Holistic Studies in Rhinebeck, New York (http://www. eomega.org/) and the Kripalu Center for Yoga and Health in Stockbridge, Massachusetts (http://kripalu.org/). All of my life's problems seem to dissipate when I enter these retreat centers, which gives me the perfect backdrop in which to learn, renew, and refresh. Many people sharpen their saw by attending a weekly religious service. Others prefer to read a book or attend a weekly yoga class; whether or not these are directly meditative, the escape renews them. In order to sharpen your saw, you may periodically return to the meditation techniques from this book that worked for you. I have also started to access online guided meditations and related practices for use when I am in a rut without even leaving my home.

Finding Perspective ... and Then Finding Your Voice

The seven habits together emphasize obtaining and retaining perspective, and Covey in his workbooks provides the organizational tools to achieve it—not just in the workplace, but in your life. Covey is observing that as leaders and as people, we need to keep things in perspective. We should make it a habit to view work as one element of our life, which includes other elements such as family, fun, commitment to community, physical health, spirituality, and all the other things that we do and want to do. This is perspective.

What made Covey one of the most brilliant teachers of leadership is how he applied the knowledge he gathered as he became older and more experienced and gained greater perspective. After promoting his seven habits for many years, Covey observed that many people feel frustrated, discouraged, unappreciated and undervalued, with little or no sense of voice or unique contribution. Covey's eighth habit is his answer to our yearning for greatness, the organization's imperative for significance and superior results, and humanity's search for its "voice."[130]

The search for voice integrates not just the first seven habits, but all of the previously discussed leadership traits (and a few to come). This eighth habit is key for leaders who have already integrated the first seven habits into their daily lives.

The essence of this habit is that you will find your voice when you can say you are 100% involved in your life, so that your body, heart, mind and spirit are all engaged in whatever is important to you. To find your voice, you need to examine your natural talent, what you absolutely love to do from your core, what your inner voice tells you is the right thing for you to be doing. Covey states that we were born with three gifts that allow us to find our voice: (i) the freedom to choose[131], (ii) the natural laws or principles that dictate the consequences of behavior (i.e., positive consequences come from fairness, kindness, respect, honesty, integrity, service and contribution)[132], and (iii) the four intelligences — physical (great achievers develop physical energy into discipline), emotional (great achievers develop emotional energy for passion), mental (great achievers develop mental energy into vision) and spiritual (great achievers develop spiritual energy into conscience or meaning within the universe).[133]

When you find your voice, your gut, heart and mind merge to permit you to act with insight. When you have found your voice, you can inspire others to do the same. This is really what leadership is all about. Effective leaders inspire people. They surround themselves with the best people available and let go of the fear that they may be outshined and instead excel together. The achievements of others reflect positively on the leader and do not diminish her or him. That is how a leader facilitates an organization fulfilling its potential. A group of inspired employees can do a lot more than one person, even the most talented and hard-working person. Organizations that have truly found their collective voice go on to succeed.

Insights From Meditation

How do we hear our voice? We quiet the chatter of the mind and take the time to listen. Listening to the voice that remains—our inner voice—during these moments of calm and quiet is often our time of greatest insight.

Listening to that inner voice tells you when you or a colleague may be in need of praise and positive reinforcement, when to call a client or customer because you sense something is wrong, when you need a break, when to call Mom, when to spend time with your child, or when to take a vacation. Giving your mind a break from daily thought routine can help you become more effective, because stepping back provides incremental perspective.

Through meditation, we also realize who it is that is doing the listening. You may recognize that it is your true authentic self that becomes the witness during meditation. You may then begin to contemplate who that "self" really is and why are you here. You may observe that your true self is not isolated or independent from others. These observations can create a broader perspective and may help you fit better within the larger context of your life. You may find more meaning in your life or be better able to point yourself in that direction.

Covey emphasizes that it is important to take the time each day to practice the habits so that they actually do become habitual. Once they become more intuitive, we have successfully incorporated these good habits into our daily life.

The same can be said for meditation. Practicing meditation regularly can teach us to change our perspective from an ego (self) perspective to a more insightful broader perspective by being more aware of what actually is. The practice of being in the present moment during meditation can become a habit of being in the present moment while living all aspects of your life. It can help us find our most authentic voice. This is how a meditation habit can dramatically improve our effectiveness and the impact we can make in an organization.

Insight Meditation

Insight meditation is another name for the meditation technique known as Vipasana, which roughly translates to "to see clearly" derived from Thereruada Buddhism. Insight meditation is often taught in week-long (or longer) retreats based on a talk by the Buddha called the Satipatthana

Sutra, which roughly translates to "discourse about mindfulness" and is designed to awaken the practitioner to the true nature of reality. These "silent" retreats generally involve alternating sitting meditation, walking meditation and sessions with a teacher providing periodic "Dharma talks" that are both informative and spark questions further contemplated during meditation. The basic framework of these talks relate to insight from the "three marks of existence": impermanence, suffering or unsatisfactoriness, and the realization of non-self.[134] The basic framework and the questions come from the teacher, but the "insight" comes from within. This is not a "10 minute a day" practice but an intensive focused contemplation that is said to often lead to a revealing of aspects of truth about existence, in turn leading to a sudden awareness or insight of the true nature of reality. After experiencing this insight, the change in life perspective can be transformative.

Meditation Practices For Insight

Life is a journey and meditation is a practice. We all veer off course. It is human to lose focus. We need to find a way back to center to bring us back on course to be the best "self" we can be.

One of my closest friends growing up was my neighbor, David Newman. We played ball daily in the cul-de-sac, rode bicycles around the neighborhood and, as he learned to play the guitar, sang songs and listened to music (Bruce Springsteen and Jim Morrison were favorites). His father was the area's most successful plastic surgeon, and his mother went to law school while we were in elementary school and became the first female Pennsylvania Supreme Court justice. As he matured, David wanted to follow his passion and connect to people through his music. He is a talented musician, a sage lyricist, and an authentic connector— that is who he is at his core. He turned that passion, talent and growing skill into becoming one of the top 10 Kirtan chant musicians. He also founded a yoga studio and wrote a book about his personal journey through enlightenment called *The Timebound Traveler,*[135] in which he observed: "There is something powerful happening—people are waking up and the only requirement is to want it—unless of course, you already have it, which, of course, you do. Waking up is not a spiritual path, but a simple recognition of who you are."[136]

To gain this insight, we can focus on the big "W" questions. Who am I? Why am I here? If you keep the answers to these questions in the front of your mind, you will be much more likely to live your life with perspective.

i. Who Am I Meditation

The Who Am I meditation is an attempt to draw aspects of our identity from our subconscious mind into our consciousness. Instead of sitting for 10 minutes, find a quiet place for an hour, maybe outside in nature.

Eckhart Tolle notes: "Your innermost sense of self, of who you are, is inseparable from stillness. This is the *I am* that is deeper than name and form."[137] You may find that your deeper self has nothing to do with the past or the future or the factual events of your life. Your deeper self witnesses those events.

Since you will be sitting longer, make sure to find a comfortable position. The traditional seated meditation posting of cross-legged with back upright and straight and support under your tail bone to lean a bit forward works best for most people, but any supportive position is fine.

Take a few slow, deep breaths with a pause between breaths.

For five minutes, at the top of the inhale, ask yourself "Who Am I" and pause.

If there is no answer after a couple of full breaths, ask again.

Usually people start with descriptive answers like . . .

"Mother"

"Daughter"

"Lawyer"

"Catholic"

"Irish American"

. . . but then you start to surprise yourself with some of the words that come out, perhaps involving emotions you are feeling or concepts of human existence.

When new answers dry up, contemplate intuitively (rather than intellectually) and in silence the difference between who you are physically, who you are mentally and who you are spiritually. If your mind wanders off topic, just come back gently to "Who Am I?"

If you prefer, after a while just come back to your breath with no further intention and look within to witness what passively passes through your mind as your essence within the larger context. It is okay if you don't have words for what you are observing.

Note which of your insights surprised you most.

Sometimes these types of contemplative meditations help us break out of our daily roles and consider the potential that was always there, who we are down deep, not limited by the constraints put on us by ourselves and others.

As we become more in touch with who we are (our "true self"), we notice that our conscious mind (our ego) seems to be doing our daily thinking, dominating our brain and thus our actions. We also notice there is an area behind the conscious mind that is able to witness our consciousness. It is that behind-the-scenes witness that I identify as my true self (in response to a "Who Am I"). I don't have the experience to lead you down the path of a Buddhist Insight Meditation journey. However, if you are drawn to this line of meditation, follow your instinct and seek out an Insight Meditation retreat. You may even progress to experience the Buddha's concept of "non-self." Accept your own experience as your best guide as to who you are.

ii. Why Am I Here Meditation

Sometimes understanding a situation (particularly one you are close to) requires looking at it from an entirely different perspective in order to gain insight.

Two books that helped me gain perspective, each of which contains a philosophy of the world, are *The Life You Were Born To Live, A Guide to Finding Your Purpose,* by Dan Millman[138] and *The Instruction* by Ainslie MacLeod[139]. Each provides a framework to determine where in the universe you may fit. I also had the benefit of learning in a retreat session with each of them, both of which was transformative. However, the greatest insights have come not from the framework of others but simply by looking within periodically during meditation practice and understanding how different parts of my past may fit in with my future. It amazes me how the pieces of the puzzle often seem to fit together when viewed in retrospect and converge with my then-present moment.

This next meditation requires you to suspend your belief or disbelief of religion and your world view for the duration of the meditation. (Whether the perspective is "true" or not is irrelevant; it is simply an exercise that prompts you to look at yourself from a different perspective.)

Imagine having the free will before we are born to choose the life into which we will be born. Once we are born, we no longer have recollection of having participated in that decision; we simply live our childhood. We then have the opportunity as adults to contemplate our lives and make decisions about how to move forward. This exercise can help you gain insight as to why you are here and take responsibility for your life and future actions. Whether or not there is any reality in this perspective or point of view, let it be your reality for the next 10 minutes.

Close your eyes or lower your gaze in a manner that best permits you to focus.

Start by focusing on your breath.

Focus on the feeling of your breath leaving and entering your mouth or leaving and entering your nose. If you get distracted, just go back to your focus point.

Pause.

Now, imagine your soul looking down on earth just before you are about to be born. Look down at your birth parents from the proverbial 30,000 feet level.

Why did you choose to be born to these parents?

Why did you choose to be born in your birth country, town or city?

Pause.

What about your childhood most impacted who you are today? It may be positive or it may be an adversity that you had to overcome.

What personal growth came from that childhood experience?

What damage was created that requires growth to forgive, to release, to move on?

Now consider a person or event in your adult life—maybe meeting your spouse or an unexpected trauma.

What personal growth came from that experience?

Was any damage created that requires growth to forgive, to release, to move on?

Hold on to those thoughts about growth lessons, either those that have occurred or those you have yet to learn.

Did your soul know you needed to learn those lessons? Could your soul have chosen to put you in that situation?

Would that fact change or help you overcome your anger, your resentment, or your guilt?

Focus again on your breath.

Now consider: when others chose their lives from 30,000 feet before they were born and they chose their life path to interact with yours, why did they do so?

Consider a child, a childhood friend, your spouse, a work relationship, or just someone who keeps popping up in your life, almost as if it were fated for your lives to continue to intersect.

Take a moment to choose someone (note that we are going to do this several times), then focus on your breath and contemplate why that person chose you. What does he or she receive from their relationship with you?

Pause for a minute.

Now, choose someone else. Focus on your breath and contemplate why that person chose you. What does he or she receive from their relationship with you?

Pause for a minute.

Before coming back to our reality, reflect on "Why am I here?"

Open your eyes and begin to come back to consciousness.

Consider the adage "everything happens for a reason." Sometimes we know the reason, sometimes we don't. Maybe we each have multiple potential paths, but I have observed that certain paths seem to naturally converge. When you are sufficiently aware, you can instinctively feel the difference when you are moving down the right path versus the wrong one.

iii. Candle/Fire Foreground/Background Meditation

We have so much information stored and floating around in our minds. How do we retrieve it? How do we shift information from the background to our foreground consciousness at just the right time?

Meditation can help us practice this shift.

For the next exercise, choose a focal point and concentrate on it. It is a lot easier if the object interests you.

Consider focusing on a fire. The way the flames go higher and lower and change in shapes is interesting and mesmerizing.

Find a candle and matches and take them into a darkened room (no need for it to be pitch black).

Light the match and move it towards the wick of the candle.

Notice how the wick catches the flame from the match.

Place the matches out of the way in a safe place.

Either sit or stand in a comfortable position with your legs apart the same distance as your hips. Settle into a place where your body can be comfortable for ten minutes.

Focus for a moment on your breath to help center you. There is no need to change your breath. Just feel the air coming in through your nose, filling your lungs, coming back through your throat and out of your body.

Now look at the flame in front of you. Try to focus your attention on the flame. Keep a soft gaze; it is not a staring contest with the flame.

Notice what you observe. The colors, the shape, the heat.

Try to keep your attention on the flame. If your mind wanders, bring your thoughts and focus back to the flame.

If it helps, you can focus on your breath and the flame, or alternate your attention to your breath, then the flame, then your breath, then the flame.

Do not make a judgment on your thoughts. Maybe note if a thought is interesting and then let it go as you bring your focus back to the flame and/or your breath. Maybe note a feeling or sensation in your body.

Don't analyze it now; just remember it and maybe come back to it after the exercise and wonder about it.

Note the movement of the flame and the changes in shape—never the same from one moment to the next.

Note the colors of the flame. Maybe you see some yellow and some orange and some blue. Wonder what causes those subtle changes in color.

Simply keep your attention on the flame and your breath as you view the flame.

When you notice yourself losing attention, bring your attention back to your breath and slowly end the exercise.

Notice the rest of the room behind the candle. Notice how the rest of the room became background and you didn't even notice it while you were focusing on the candle.

Notice how when you are viewing the rest of the room, the candle, which demanded your attention for the past few minutes, is now background.

Notice how you may have forgotten that you are continuing to breathe.

This shifting focus from foreground to background is one of the key lessons that allows me to be aware of differences in physical perspective and thereby achieve better overall perspective. Other people also come into the foreground of our lives and drift into our background (and we in theirs). In prior exercises, we witnessed how specific emotions that are usually in the background can be brought back into the foreground either to be addressed and released or to drift back again into the background. This is not an exercise of change but one of observation so you can be more aware and thus gain greater perspective in the moment for use in future moments. It is also about taking control of what is in the foreground and what is in the background in our lives and daily thoughts and actions. As my friend David Newman further notes: "We are the dreamer rather than the dreamed, the seer rather than the seen, the vast sky rather than the weather."[140] We each simply need to have the perspective to realize it.

iv. Integrating the Meditation Practice and Leadership Principle—Step Back Meditation

The seven habits are not an intellectual exercise. You have to live them—not just read about them—in order for them to become habitual. A contemplative meditation gives us a vehicle to practice and to learn experientially rather than simply theoretically.

Focus on your breath. Listen to the sound of your breath. There is no need to change your breath. Simply focus on it; be aware of it.

Bring into your awareness the organization in which you work or an organization in which you volunteer or even your family organization. This one organization is your focus for this exercise. Bring into your awareness the leadership team, maybe the physical office space or the location where you most often do this work. Be aware of your feelings as you enter this place in your meditation.

Bring your awareness to the physical space in which the organization resides. See yourself within this physical space. Notice any observations. See others with whom you work in this physical space. Notice any observations. See the leaders of this organization in the physical space with you. Notice any observations. Extend to see the customers or patients or members or extended family this organization serves. Notice any observations. Extend to see the suppliers, the vendors and others who provide products and services to this organization. Notice any observations. Notice how many people are impacted directly or indirectly by this organization. Consider the impact you have on these people—on the organization. Is your value appreciated? Can you have a bigger impact? Can you see more clearly by stepping back to see more of the whole? Observe carefully. When you are done observing, open your eyes and consider what insights you may have learned.

XII. MEDITATION AS A PATH TO THE BALANCE NECESSARY TO THRIVE

Life is about balance. The good and the bad. The highs and the lows. The pina and the colada.

Ellen DeGeneres, Seriously... I'm Kidding

Perspective comes from a heightened level of awareness—the clarity that comes from stepping back. Once we take a step back, and then approach an issue again, we can sometimes see it differently. We can see more. We can see the issue within the context of a bigger picture. So, as we consider leadership, the leadership lessons that can be learned from meditation and the third pillar of perspective, let's take a step back.

Why do we work? Money is certainly a part of it, but we already established that money is not most people's sole, or maybe even primary, motivation. Many of us do not work at the job that maximizes our potential compensation or seek the position that maximizes our compensation if we are compensated adequately and satisfied by the experience. Many of us do meaningful unpaid or underpaid work for non-profit organizations or devote our time, effort and energy to our family organization. We work to make a contribution and, at least in part, to bring meaning to our lives. How do we define success?

A decade ago, as the newsprint industry began to decline from being our primary source of news and information to one of many, online news sources began to thrive. In 2005, Arianna Huffington had the vision to identify this trend before the rest of us. She launched The Huffington Post, which has become one of the most popular online news sources in the world.

In her 2013 commencement speech to the new graduates at the all-women Smith College, Huffington stressed the importance of re-evaluating how we define success. Huffington told the women, "Commencement speakers are traditionally expected to tell the graduating class how to go out there and climb the ladder of success. But I want to ask you instead to redefine success. Because the world you are headed into desperately needs it. And because you are up to the challenge." Huffington then reassures them, "You can work in any field, and you can make it to the top of any field. But what I urge you to do is not just take your place at the top of the world, but to change the world." [141]

Huffington was promoting the following idea: spend time creating your own vision for what your success will be, and then go out and implement it with a view toward positively impacting the world. Thus, perspective (or awareness within the realm of the bigger picture) is important, but using that perspective to form an action plan is what will ultimately enable you to lead with greater effectiveness. An important factor in achieving success is defining what success means. Is your success measured just in money or the power of your job position, or something more?

In her book, *Thrive: The Third Metric to Redefining Success and Creating a Life of Well-Being, Wisdom, and Wonder*, Huffington equates money and power to a "two-legged stool." She claims, "[Y]ou can balance on them for a while, but eventually you're going to topple over." [142] Huffington articulates a third leg to this stool, a metric required for success that she calls "thrive." Seeking to thrive while still profitably running the Huffington Post organization became her personal vision.

Huffington notes four components of success that form the Thrive metric:

1. Well-Being
2. Wisdom
3. Wonder
4. Giving

In Huffington's vision of success in the information age, human capital (her own and others) is as important as financial capital. Thus, as leaders we need to do everything we can to nurture our human capital to achieve success. How do we nurture human capital? Huffington's three-legged stool analogy brings equanimity into the mix.

Equanimity is one of my all-time favorite words. Equanimity is the state of having an even mind and heart, a state of mental and psychological stability and composure that is undisturbed by experience or exposure to emotions, pain, or other phenomena that may cause one to lose the balance of the mind. Equanimity is like balancing your body on one leg. You can do it for a short period of time, but that is the best you can do. With practice, we can stay in equanimity longer and get back into that state when we become aware we are out of balance. To relate Huffington's thesis to the stool analogy, equanimity is when all three legs of the stool are the exact same length and firmly on the ground. When we are in a state of equanimity, we are in balance—we have perspective—we Thrive.

Well-Being

Try not to become a man of success, but rather a man of value.
Albert Einstein

In addition to articulating her positive Thrive vision, Huffington also notes what holds us back—in particular, our high levels of stress. Some of this stress is imposed by our workplace; some is a residual from our childhood; some results from the difficult situations we find ourselves in; but much of it is self-imposed. The negative impact of stress can range from physical manifestations (such as my decade of back pain), to shutting down emotionally, to a life of addiction.

Huffington opens *Thrive* with a story of how she collapsed and hit the corner of her desk on the way to the floor, ending up with a large cut near her eye and a broken cheekbone. She was working 18 hours a day, trying to build a business and bring in investors. The two-legged stool had finally toppled over for Huffington; money and power were no longer enough to keep her standing. Collapsing was her "wake-up call."[143]

Ultimately, Huffington discovered that meditation was a great way to keep her well-being in check. Meditation gave her the tools to pause and, in doing so, to gain greater perspective, to step back and gain more equanimity in her life. As a result, she developed her Thrive vision.

Huffington tells an inspiring story acknowledging the stigma that is sometimes associated with meditation in a section of her book entitled, "Meditation: It's Not Just for Enlightenment."[144] Huffington originally found the concepts of meditation and mindfulness to be perplexing, equating her mind to a "household junk drawer" into which she crammed things but hoped that it would still function properly. It wasn't until she read the writings of renowned mindfulness teacher, Jon Kabat-Zinn, that she discovered why mindfulness is so important. Kabat-Zinn writes, "In Asian languages the word for 'mind' and the word for 'heart' are the same word. So when we hear the word 'mindfulness,' we have to inwardly hear 'heartfulness' in order to grasp it even as a concept, and especially as a way of being."[145]

Although Kabat-Zinn's explanation resonates, I am partial to Huffington's own interpretation: "When we are all mind, things can get rigid. When we are all heart, things can get chaotic. Both lead to stress."[146] Huffington goes on to describe how she found the balance between mind and heart in mindfulness meditation. Mindfulness is about keeping our heart and mind in balance and developing an appreciation for the present. Life is too short to not appreciate and cherish our present moments, no matter how trivial they may seem on the surface. This is because even the most trivial moments with someone can become special moments we reminisce about later in life. The moments I reminisce about include playing "car games" to pass the time during long car rides on family vacations, unplanned moments where the ordinary became memorable, or the "obligatory" weekly Sunday morning brunch I had with my grandparents that at the time seemed a chore but now are a nostalgic part of my childhood. The present truly is a "present" and should be treated as such. Before we regret not cherishing these moments, we should learn from our lack of appreciation and improve upon it. Breathe in the ocean air on that summer day at the beach, feel the leaves crunch under your feet on a cool fall afternoon, watch the beautiful snow blanket the earth on a winter morning, and envelop yourself in the aroma of the blooming flowers on a walk around the neighborhood in the spring. Avoid electronic stimuli such as your phone or television and just take a moment to fully appreciate all of the beauty in the world. The worst thing people can do is put themselves on auto-pilot to just "get by." Mindfulness is our portal to a more beautiful life. Meditation is a way to practice mindfulness, and a focus on mindfulness can be a meditation technique in and of itself.

Huffington recalls that her mother taught her to meditate when she was around age 13. "…[f]inding time for my meditation was always a challenge" starts Huffington, "because I was under the impression that I had to 'do' meditation."[147] This is a common misconception; meditation could not be more distant from "doing." As noted earlier, meditation is about coming into a state of "being" rather than "doing." Meditation is much more than sitting lotus style on a mat or staring at a candle. Huffington notes that a friend's comment that "we don't do meditation" but rather "meditation does us" helped open the door to the practice for her.[148] Huffington finds that we can meditate in even the shortest periods of time or while on the move. Instead of thinking of breathing as simply "breathing," she instead sees it as "being breathed." She notes, "At any time we choose, we can take a moment to bring attention to the rising and falling of our breath without our conscious interference."[149]

ABC news anchor Dan Harris' book *10% Happier—How I Tamed the Voice in My Head, Reduced Stress Without Losing My Edge, and Found Self-Help*

That Actually Works—A True Story, is one of the best books about the impact of meditation that I have read. Dan also had his "wake-up call" when he froze on air due to greater and greater self-imposed stress during his quest to go from reporter to anchor.[150] The book discusses his journey to pursue regular meditation practice, resulting in a thriving career.

What I particularly like is Harris's conclusion that meditation doesn't magically solve all of your problems; it doesn't cause a complete dissipation of suffering or result in instant and total happiness. Rather, meditation facilitates your becoming "10% happier."[151]

While some stress is positive in that it motivates you and your employees, too much stress leads to lack of focus, inefficiency, and ultimately burn-out, which can cause the loss of good people from an organization. It can also lead to mistakes and bad decisions.

I have met many young lawyers, accountants at large firms, and investment bankers with a lot of stamina and drive who are not only able but eager to put in a 15-16 hour day. That works for a while (for some). Inevitably, in the short term, when they read the work product the next morning with clarity, they find mistakes. Inevitably, over the long term, most drop out and choose a different career path. There are very few "over 40" investment bankers and those who survive find a way to work differently as a senior banker (although they still seem to put the junior bankers through the same rigorous process). There is a key difference between providing your clients with the perception that you are always available for them when needed, versus actually always working.

For example, paradoxically, Huffington—the founder of an online 24-hour news provider—believes in keeping her bedroom a "device-free zone" as a stress reduction technique. This may be less feasible in a professional services business, but even for service providers, some boundaries are appropriate and essential for long-term well-being.

Using meditation techniques such as refocusing on the breath or repeating a mantra in your head a few times are useful to take a break and bring you back into a place of balance, equanimity and perspective. That is what a runner does during his or her morning run, and how people reap the benefits of taking a yoga class in the middle of the week or attending church every Sunday. That break, whether for a moment or an hour or a day, is rejuvenating.

Taking a break to rejuvenate is not a new idea. Taking time out of our busy lives to rest dates back at least to the Ten Commandments, when God commanded the Israelites to "Remember the Sabbath and keep it holy"—six days of labor and one of rest. For Jews, that period of rest is from sundown Friday to sundown Saturday. For Christians, it is generally on Sunday, and for Muslims, Friday. Each of these major religious traditions recognized that a weekly break is vital to our well-being. Each of these traditions also includes a daily prayer ritual. Daily prayer can serve as your meditation technique. If it is not your preferred route, this book provides many different choices.

Finding some way to take a short daily break from your routine when you need it and taking one day a week to rejuvenate in some manner are key to well-being. This will help you regain overall balance and equanimity, which leads to reducing stress. I find that remembering to pause, along with adequate sleep and sufficient exercise, leads to well-being.

Without having found a way to de-stress and refocus on my well-being, not only would I not be as effective, I might not even still be in this world. You can't make a positive difference when you can't even show up.

Wisdom

The intuitive mind is a sacred gift and the rational mind is a faithful servant. We have created a society that honors the servant and has forgotten the gift.

Albert Einstein

Huffington indicates that she now embraces two fundamental truths about human beings. First, we all have within us a centered place of wisdom, harmony and strength. Second, we veer away from this place again and again and need to develop tools to return to it.[152]

Huffington points out that life is a classroom. We continually engage in learning facts and lessons that can lead to greater wisdom. However, Huffington also notes that sometimes, like rats in the famous B.F. Skinner groundbreaking behavioral theory experiment about reward-based learning, we press the same levers again and again even though there is no longer a real reward.

Wisdom allows us to instinctively know the difference and break free of the maze when it no long suits us. Many of life's lessons that shape our wisdom are not pleasant and may involve defeat, failure, divorce, career setbacks or death of loved ones. As the country song says, it sometimes takes an illness to "live like you are dying"[153]—in other words, to live life to its fullest and to appreciate what we have. Meditation is a tool to return to that place of wisdom and perspective in the face of adversity.

You can't force wisdom. Wisdom can be learned, but it can't be taught.

Wisdom is more than knowledge. Knowledge can be taught. Wisdom is knowledge with the perspective of experience. Since we all have somewhat different perspectives based on who we are, wisdom is expressed differently in each of us.

Wisdom can be a practical application of knowledge, or it can be considered our own "truth" within our personal awareness and perspective. Proverbs 4:10-19 states: "Wisdom provides guidance in the way of righteousness." This implies an overarching value judgment that wisdom is correct and, thus, acting consistently with wisdom will be effective. However, unlike knowledge, wisdom is not obtained by simply reading a book. It requires experience.

Many people identify a difference between their thoughts about information (knowledge) and their intuition, which seems to be pulling from somewhere beyond those thoughts. I believe that intuition pulls from your wisdom.

Successful innovators often create from a place of intuition. Steve Jobs stated that intuition is more powerful than intellect. Many artists, authors and musicians report that when they are in the creative flow their art seems to just come out and appear to them. Both Huffington and Jobs developed such faith in their intuition that each noted that they would plow forward even when others asserted that something was impossible or that there was no current market for a new idea.

Huffington notes that Steve Jobs asked that *Autobiography of a Yogi* by guru Paramahansa Yogananda be distributed at his memorial service. Yogananda focused on the role of intuition in our lives. Huffington quotes Yogananda from his 1946 autobiography: "Nearly everyone has had the experience of an inexplicably correct hunch or has transferred his thoughts effectively to another person. The human mind, free of restlessness, can perform through its antenna of intuition, all of the functions of complicated radio mechanisms sending and receiving thoughts, and tuning out undesirable ones."[154]

Huffington also points out: "Intuition is about connections—but connections that can't be reasoned into existence."[155] Intuition connects us to our inner self and to something beyond our self that we can't fully explain, but seems to be the source of wisdom beyond our individual life experience. That wisdom can be accessed; we can hear it when we silence our minds in meditation or even, as previously noted, during a run, in the shower, or at other moments when the conscious mind is distracted and thus quieted.

Learning to follow their intuition or "inner wisdom" had a big impact on Jobs' and Huffington's success. We are most in tune with our intuition when we are in a state of balance and equanimity. In the quiet of meditation, balance and equanimity become the norm. At that level of inner consciousness, there is perspective and recognition of what matters. There is access to different information. You then can bring that different information into your conscious mind, analyze it in context, and achieve greater wisdom.

When I think about my entrepreneurial clients who have built successful businesses worth tens or even hundreds of millions of dollars, many did not complete college or were not challenged by college if they completed it. Formal education did not motivate them. However, they are all "street smart" with keen awareness, focus, drive and wisdom. Entrepreneurs know themselves, are driven by their entrepreneurial vision, and motivate others to participate, often at lower than market short-term compensation. Entrepreneurs more than people in many other professions seem able to achieve using wisdom and gut instinct.

Meditation is our tool to increase the scope and scale of human achievement. Through meditation, we can access our own inner wisdom and perhaps even a collective wisdom, as believed by many tribal cultures and modern philosophers. Once we are able to tap into that wisdom on a regular basis, it is expressed to us through our instinct—that feeling in the gut or the heart or thought that pops into your head, seemingly from nowhere but instantly right. As you learn to be aware of and follow your instinct, you notice that your instinct tends to have a much higher likelihood of being right than your more detailed thought processes. Also, there is nothing wrong with observing your instinct, taking a few moments to think it through, and then have your conscious thinking mind validate the conclusion before acting. That is often the process of a wise and highly effective person.

Many times I hear a wise person say something and instantly know it to be true, but I just hadn't thought about it in that way; once aware, I will always notice it in the future. That is how wisdom accumulates in society.

Wonder

Imagination is everything. It is the preview of life's coming attractions.
Albert Einstein

Wonder is not just a product of what we feel when we see something magnificent; it is our state of mind when we are looking at it. Two people can see the same thing—for example, a lake surrounded by mountains. One person just views the physical landscape, and the other sees it from a state of inspiration-inducing wonder, perhaps noticing the ice-capped mountain top creating a stream running down to fill the lake while hearing birds chirping in the background. Children seem to have an innate ability to see things through the lens of a state of wonder. Many of us lose that over time.

The state of wonder in business execution leads to vision . . . the kind of vision that Jobs demonstrated in creating the personal computer and the iPhone, that Huffington had in creating *The Huffington Post,* and that Phil Jackson had in putting together his championship teams and his triangle offense.

Huffington's vision was not just the wisdom to create electronic delivery of news content, but the wonder to think completely outside the box to create a virtual organization. *The Huffington Post* site started as an alternative to both traditional printed press and to online news aggregators, publishing original content online. Some of the content was isolated in geographically-focused editions, and some carried across all editions. *The Huffington Post* eventually added vertically-focused editions such as Gay Voices, which is dedicated to LGBT-relevant articles. Some of the contributors work full-time and some are part-timers. Huffington was able to articulate clearly her new organizational vision to a wide variety of stakeholders in a way that facilitated *The Huffington Post's* success and, ultimately, its multi-billion dollar sale to AOL.

Visionary entrepreneurs seem to have that sense of wonder. They wonder, if we do "x" differently, will it be better. I am blessed as a business lawyer to be exposed to thousands of entrepreneurs who have imagined that which is beyond my imagination; many of these entrepreneurs also had the other leadership traits that enabled them to successfully implement their ideas, but many others did not. I have never lost my sense of wonder and excitement in learning about their new discoveries.

Wonder is all around us. We don't experience it when our day-to-day thoughts so distract us that we are not able to be fully aware. Meditation can both open up the path to wonder when it is blocked and assist in applying the wisdom in the context of this wonder, in order to make sense of the sometimes vague path from idea to implementation.

Meditation can be focusing mindfully on the colors of the trees in the autumn on your way to work—the same trees you might otherwise drive past without noticing on another day. Meditation can be awareness of a sunset (that happens every day) while considering the wonder of where the sun goes, or how you manage to stand on a planet that is continually spinning without losing balance. Meditation is quieting your thinking mind for a few moments and letting your imagination take over to fill the void. All of these practices fill us with a state of wonder that can lead to creativity in approaching situations and new solutions.

Giving

Only a life lived for others is a life worth living.
—Albert Einstein

Huffington notes that well-being, wisdom and wonder are all critical to redefining success and thriving, but they are incomplete without the fourth element of Thrive. We thrive when we use our wisdom in our state of wonder from a place of well-being to provide service to others.

Huffington tells stories of the contributions made to others during personal or natural disasters,[156] but giving can be part of everyday life. As we previously discussed, Ferrazzi karma of relationships teaches us that giving for the sake of giving has its own long-term rewards.

Giving can involve money, it can involve time, and it can involve simple support to another human being through listening. This applies to both work and non-work environments. A giving mentality focuses on using your resources to create value for others. By-products are satisfaction, joy and, often, being able to receive when you are in need. The relative amount of "giving" compared to that given by someone else does not matter. You thrive by giving what you are able to give at the time.

I am rarely envious of people (particularly entrepreneurs) who make a lot of money. I am envious of those who give whatever they have available to really make a difference and I want to be in that crowd. I also marvel at the creativity of giving. One of my favorite giving stories involves a client, Scott Zucker, who wanted to set up a scholarship at his college alma mater to assist people "like him." So he set up a scholarship to pay for a portion of the last two years of college for students who demonstrated significant academic improvement during their sophomore year compared with their freshman year. I bet that motivated quite a few students who had struggled (and maybe lost their initial scholarship grants) adjusting to college and inspired them to do better, not only because of potential scholarship money, but because they know someone who was in their position had turned it around after starting their college career with a 2.03 freshman year GPA and become hugely successful. Scott is giving hope, not just money.

Giving is a core part of a Buddhist practice and part of all religious traditions. Giving material things, whatever they may be, creating karma, is the first level. Giving the gift of teaching (dharma), secularly translated as "conveying wisdom to others," is the second level. Giving the gift of peace (nirvana), secularly translated as "just listening and being with someone in need," is the third level. Judaism promotes Tikkun Olam, translated as "repairing the world," creating an ethical duty and purpose of our lives to improve the lives of others. There is also the biblical practice of tithing by returning 10% of your blessings to God. In all these religious traditions, giving is a key part of a balanced life.

Some people seem to be wired so that giving just comes naturally. My wife is like that. But the more natural perspective for many of us is focusing on our own self-interest—what might be called "taking." Ironically, balancing giving with taking can lead to more success than either just giving or just taking. I have found that with better balance I actually receive more (and as a result have the ability to give more), staying in balance with greater regularity.

When contemplating the wisdom that comes from meditation, you may think that you would always apply that wisdom toward yourself. What will pop into your mind when your mind is quiet is the answer to each of your problems that your thinking mind simply couldn't solve. I have observed that when ideas pop into my mind during meditation, the origin of the idea often has no basis that I can understand logically or through my personal experience. It is never "buy Google at the IPO price—this stock could go somewhere." In most cases, the beneficiary is someone else and I feel like the conduit. Maybe that is why I am a professional counselor. Over time, I have developed the experience to recognize these moments, the faith to believe, and the courage to follow through. There is nothing more satisfying than helping someone else and knowing that you have made a positive difference in the life of another. That is ultimately "success."

Meditation Can Help You Regain Balance

Meditation is a key tool to facilitate the ability to regain balance and to thrive. We all fall in and out of balance, in and out of equanimity. Creating and sticking to a daily meditation practice can be difficult. It requires a change to your daily habits. While meditation is a habit that supports your health, well-being and effectiveness, even good change can be messy, difficult, and at times, you may want to quit. One of my teachers described change as hard at first, messy in the middle and beautiful at the end. We are in the messy middle and need reminders to bring us back, to keep the value of daily meditation in our perspective so it becomes a healthy habit. We need triggers to bring us back.

If, by definition, balance and equanimity are fleeting, experienced for only a moment in time, how do we return to that state of mental balance when we need it? It would be nice if we could stop our life for a full seated meditation session any time we wanted to return to balance, but that is not practical. However, a practicing meditator can develop triggers that once aware you are out of balance, you notice the trigger and can with intention seek to return to balance.

i. Mantra Meditation Practice

Mantra meditation can be effective in only a few seconds and can, with practice, be used as your reminder to bring your mental and emotional state back to its place of equanimity when you need it. Mantra meditation is the focus on a word, phrase or saying that returns one to a state of balance and equanimity. Sometimes a mantra is simply a series of sounds or vibrations. Sometimes the mantra itself has deep meaning, such as Thrive. Sometimes the mantra may not sound profound, but the mantra that brings back our perspective and thus becomes meaningful.

Your thoughts are generally not rhythmic. Accordingly, a mantra serves three primary purposes: (i) rhythm, (ii) meaning, and (iii) focus. By reciting the same word or phrases over and over again, rhythmically with your breathing, you can use the mantra to quiet the chatter of your mind. This is similar to the impact that classical music can have in taming the mind (or wild beast) and inducing a relaxed state. Repeating a mantra draws meaning from that mantra back into your awareness. Repeating a phrase with positive meaning reinforces the importance of that meaning in your mind. By focusing your mind on the repetitive activity, like with the other focus meditations discussed earlier, you can quiet your day-to-day thoughts by reciting the mantra. Mantra meditation can help us not only focus, but also re-focus after being distracted—which is an increasingly common peril of our technology-besieged lives. Eventually, we continue to recite the mantra but the mantra shifts to the background and the wisdom is able to enter into the foreground.

To start, you will need to choose a mantra. You don't need to use the same mantra every time you practice, but because you are creating a reminder to return to balance and perspective, it helps to choose one and stick with it for a few weeks, months or years until you find a new one, and then stick to the new one for a few weeks, months or years.

Below are a few categories of mantras. Pick the category that feels right to you, and then choose a mantra from within that category. You may also create your own variation of the mantras listed, or create one from scratch, or use a segment from a song, poem or prayer. The key is to alter your attention from its current focus to your mantra word or phrase. This will change the way your mind is functioning to facilitate different thought patterns and access to inner wisdom from those thought patterns. Over time, the mantra becomes the reminder to bring us back into balance and equanimity.

Affirmation Mantras

Affirmation mantras tend to have both vibrational significance and positive meaning. Reciting these mantras creates a vibration of the vocal cords and channels your positive thinking, creating physical energy.

- Om (or Aaaaaaaaaaaaoooooooooooooommmmmmm): This is one of the most ancient Hindu and Buddhist mantras. The sound is held for as long as possible in a single breath. Om is simple, calming and is thought to symbolize the sound of creation. It is often recited at the beginning or end of a hatha yoga class.
- I Am: This is a simple affirmation of your self. You can also add a third word (for example, I Am Strong) that works for you at a particular time on a particular day. You can either use the same word daily or rotate words to create the affirmation that is right for you.
- Align With the Divine: This is a mantra that works for me. When I say it repetitively, it can bring me into a state of greater perspective. When I am in a mildly frustrating situation (such as a slow supermarket check-out line), it can calm me, balance me, and bring the situation into perspective that this is merely

an inconvenience that is really insignificant and not worthy of stress. No one around me knows what I am repeating in my head.

- Thrive (thriiiiiiiiiiiiiiiivvvvvve)
- Equanimity (eq uan im ity). Say it four times with different emphasis, one on each syllable to create balance physically, emotionally, mentally and spiritually.

Religious-Based Mantras

Religious-based mantras include, but are not limited to, the following:

Maranatha (Come Lord): This phrase is from the New Testament and is a frequently-used Christian mantra.

The Father, Son and Holy Spirit: This mantra reflects the Christian doctrine of the Holy Trinity.

Sh'ma Yisrael Adonai Elohanu Adonai Echod (Hear O Israel the Lord our God, the Lord is One): This is a traditional Hebrew chant and prayer.

Sabbe Satta Sukhi Santa (May All Beings Be Happy): This is a Tibetan lovingkindness mantra.

Ayatul Kursi Full and *Durood Shareef*: These are two Muslim mantras.

Namu Amida Butsu (Homage to Infinite Light): This is a mantra chanted in Japanese Buddhism.

Examples from Poems or Songs

Mantras can come from poems or songs.

Prayer of Protection (attributed to James Dillet Freeman)

The light of God surrounds me
The love of God enfolds me
The power of God protects me
The presence of God watches over me
Wherever I am, God is.

I changed a few words to make this mantra more meaningful for me; the following became my daily mantra for a while:

The light of God surrounds me
The love of God engulfs me
The power of God protects me
The presence of God is within me
Wherever I am, God is,
For I am one with God

Lead Me From Ignorance to Truth (a traditional Hindu Prayer)

From ignorance, lead me to truth
From darkness, lead me to light
From death, lead me to immortality
Om, peace, peace, peace

As you can see, there are infinite possibilities in creating your mantra. Look around, and maybe the right one for you will appear.

A mantra does not engage the mind more than necessary. It is a focal point for the mind. This focus brings the day-to-day mind to stillness. We then listen and observe what arises during the periods of stillness.

Song choruses can make excellent mantras with a built in rhythm and melody. I love Kirtan chants, which are rhythmic Sanskrit words not too long to remember, generally with meaning (although I don't always understand the meaning) and often sung in groups in call and response style. A group Kirtan chant clears my mind and opens me up to new insight virtually every time.

To create your mantra "habit" simply repeat your mantra during your 10 minutes of meditation until it does become habit and fades into the background. Then whenever you need it during the day, bring it back to the foreground. Even 30-60 seconds can be enough to restore you to the balance and equanimity you feel following your longer meditation practice.

ii. Transcendental Meditation

In the 1950s, Mahesh Prasad Varma, who later became known as "The Maharishi" or "Giggling Guru," entered a cave in the Himalayan Mountains for a period of spiritual study. There he developed the meditation practice that would become known as Transcendental Meditation (TM). TM is a practice that emerges from the mantra meditative tradition. TM became a mantra meditation organization launched by the David Lynch Foundation originally in the U.S. and is now spreading throughout the world. In fact, many celebrities from Paul McCartney to Jerry Seinfeld are on *YouTube* promoting the experience, which involves going to a free seminar, paying for three private lessons, and then participating in TM group activities to continue building a personal daily TM practice. The David Lynch Foundation has also sponsored many studies demonstrating the benefits of this technique and meditation in general.

In TM, you sit with your back straight (ideally in the lotus or half-lotus posture), and use a mantra. This is practiced twice per day. Your focus is on rising above all that is impermanent and "self-transcending" to a level of the mind that is always calm, settled yet aware and awake, and filled with creativity and wisdom. At the more advanced levels, TM focuses on the breath (either in addition to or in lieu of the mantra) and changes the breath to change one's state of being. TM is a practice that is complimentary to mindfulness and part of the broad group of techniques referred in this book under the broader heading of meditation.

Consider the organized TM group approach or creating your own mantra meditation practice.

iii. Big O Mantra

One of my favorite children's books I read to my daughters is Shel Silverstein's *The Missing Piece Meets the Big O*. In that story, a character shaped like a slice of pie keeps looking for other pieces to fit together to recreate a pie. However, it keeps finding that the pieces don't fit or they fit for a moment in time and grow to no longer fit. Finally, the missing piece meets an 'O'-shaped character that encourages the missing piece to roll down the hill and round out its edges and become self-sufficient. It is only after doing so and becoming 'O'-shaped and independently complete that the missing piece character is happy and rolls away, hand-in-hand, with the Big O character.

The lesson from that story is that we have to round out our own edges (and not rely on others to do so for us) and ultimately become comfortable that we are what we are and we are good enough on our own. It is after that realization that we can develop more healthy relationships with others.

Rather than rolling down a hill, try the following affirmation mantra in sync with your breath, with "I am" on the inhale and the next verse on the exhale.

I am (on inhale)

Enough (on exhale)

I am (on inhale)

Whole and complete (on exhale)

I am (on inhale)

Who I am (on exhale)

Repeat the affirmation 5-10 times before moving on.

iv. Feel Some Awe

Nothing brings a sense of awe or wonder like nature. Sometimes, it's the big things. How do you feel when you look down from a mountain? Have you ever gone scuba diving and explored the richness of the sea? It fills me with awe to realize that there is an entire ecosystem under the sea that we don't see every day and, for the most part, don't think about; furthermore, the creatures who live under the sea are not aware of our land existence. What else is happening that we are not aware of?

Other times, we can be in awe of the little things in nature: the bird walking in front of you looking for a worm, looking up to see you and then flying away (maybe even scared of you), or the way in which flowers bloom in the spring, survive the heat of summer, lie dormant through the winter, and bloom again the following spring.

The first step is to become more aware of the awe-inspiring aspects of nature. This next step is to be grateful for them after you are aware.

This is a meditation better done with your eyes open than closed.

Go out into nature, or simply look out the window on your drive to work or while bringing your kids to soccer practice, and notice something. You may enjoy a beautiful sunrise or sunset, spot the first star in the sky, look at the raindrops and wonder where that water came from, notice the colors on the leaves as they turn in the Fall, get lucky and catch glimpse of a rainbow following a storm . . . or notice any number of amazing, awe-inspiring things that occur in nature every moment of every day.

Don't just notice them for their physical beauty, but be grateful for nature's ecosystem and that you are part of it. You are an integral part of nature, just like the leaf and the sun and the stars. Dwell on your role in nature. Appreciate the wonder to be a part of it. Devote yourself to making a positive contribution and being grateful for the positive contribution of other creatures to nature and to life.

v. Integrating the Meditation Technique and Leadership Principle—Thrive Mantra Meditation

Consider the four pillars of *Thrive*: well-being, wonder, wisdom and giving. Which pillar requires focus today? It may be different from moment to moment, from day to day, and at different times in your life.

When you want to return to equanimity during the day, repeat the pillar of your current focus such as "Giving" a few times (roughly ten times per minute) as your mantra, or choose "Thrive" if your pillars are in balance.

Remember to breathe as you repeat your mantra. Use your breath to keep your rhythm. Repeat multiple times until you begin to feel equanimity.

If you are not sure where you should focus, try meditating on that question.

How can I thrive in well-being?

How can I thrive in wonder?

How can I thrive in wisdom?

How can I thrive in giving?

Try not to "think" the answer, but allow a five or so breath pause and witness what fills the void; it can often be quite insightful. Repeat every five breaths for a few minutes.

In the future, return to what you found insightful. You may choose to return to this experience not by posing a question, but by remembering your insight as a reminder to recapture your equanimity.

XIII. USING MEDITATION TO DEVELOP INFLUENCE

You do not lead by hitting people over the head —
that's assault, not leadership.

Dwight D. Eisenhower,
General and President of the United States

Meditation can facilitate improving your relationships, help you to develop greater insight and equanimity, and therefore increase your perspective. Instead of drifting through your day, you become more aware of the choices you make—your actions, reactions and non-actions. Through the greater awareness and wisdom from your meditation practice, you can have greater positive influence on everything you do and care about. The goal is not to simply bolster any one or combination of leadership traits in isolation, but to have a positive impact from the lessons and wisdom from meditation practice in all aspects of your life as you continue to integrate meditation into it. Once you are comfortable you are making more choices with greater awareness, you become more comfortable taking responsibility for your choices and the resulting impact.

Covey provides an intellectual organizational habits framework to acquire and maintain greater insight. But this framework alone is limited to our intellectual analytical thought process. Huffington's Thrive opens us up to perspective physically, emotionally and spiritually in addition to mentally, allowing us to create personal equanimity. How do we bring the lessons from both these frameworks back to the office to be more effective leaders to develop greater influence to create better organizations?

Over the past 30 years, John C. Maxwell has written more than 40 books about leadership, relationships, and attitudes that provide a context for being more effective. Similar to Collins, Maxwell begins with the premise that everyone can be a leader and that most leadership in an organization occurs not from the top but from the middle of an organization.

Since most organizations have only one top leader, what do you do to add leadership value when, like me, you are not that person?

In Maxwell's well-known leadership guide, *The 360 Degree Leader,*[157] Maxwell claims that anyone can seize the opportunity to be an influential leader, regardless of where he or she works within an organization.

Maxwell notes that leadership is more than management.[158] Leadership is:

- People more than projects;
- movement more than maintenance;
- art more than science;
- intuition more than formula;
- vision more than procedure;
- risk more than caution;
- action more than reaction;
- relationship more than rules; and
- who you are more than what you do.

A 360-degree leader is not associated with a specific title or a position in the organizational hierarchy. A title does not automatically make someone a good leader. Maxwell posits that the true measure of leadership is *influence*, and that influence extends up, down and all around.

Effective Leaders Lead Up, Down and All Around

"If you take the approach of wanting to add value to those around you," says Maxwell, "you have the best chance of influencing them."[159]

When you lift people up, whether it is your supervisor, your peers, your subordinates, or your customers, they can't help but notice it. Even if others in the organization aren't aware, the person being lifted is. Lifting others shows that you are a team player. It demonstrates that you are grateful for being a member of the team and you recognize that you are part of something bigger than yourself. If you practice this regularly, good things happen (similar to Ferrazzi's karma of relationships principle discussed in Chapter IX.) You don't really know which action will be recognized or by whom. However, when you are a person who lifts up those around you, you will eventually be noticed and compensated. The lift you give others is often returned when another lifts you.

Maxwell suggests that "leading up," is the most challenging component for a 360-degree leader. How do you effectively lift the load without being seen as a "suck up" to the boss or being disparaged for extending yourself beyond your position level? Maxwell suggests that you should first focus on doing your own job well. Be good at what you do every day, and do it with a great attitude. When you find a problem, provide a solution. Don't just find fault, find an answer. But in doing so, communicate your proposed solution in a modest way without showmanship. In this same vein, tell supervisors what they need to hear (that is how they receive constructive feedback); don't just say "yes" to their instructions. Again, how you say it is at least as important as what you say. Go the extra mile when something needs to be done; don't limit your role to the specified instructions if doing more can add value to a project. If you don't know what you can do, ask the other person how you can lift his or her load. Most of the time, people respond positively to this request. All it takes is for you to ask.

There are also significant challenges to "leading down." How many times have you had a good idea or tried to implement a new "best practice" or policy that's simply not followed? There is a certain immediate resistance to change, even if the change is objectively for the better. This is particularly true when there is a short-term inconvenience or effort required to achieve the long-term benefit of the proposed change. Unless required or convinced, most people will continue to pursue their past activity pattern. Getting people to change is difficult, even those who report to you and are "supposed" to follow. I certainly observe this as a manager. A 360-degree leader will use influence rather than authoritative power to achieve the desired change. The difference is in the method of communicating and implementing the instructions that will lead to the desired outcome.

Leading peers (such as law firm partners) as a manager can also be very difficult. You have no positional authority over them. A frequent reaction to a peer's request to support a new idea may be polite conversation with no meaningful change in behavior or progress for the organization. (I have been on both sides of that conversation). Attempting to lead peers can invoke emotions of jealousy or resentment, although sometimes the resistance is simply inertia and lack of willingness by successful people to change long-time practices. Maxwell also includes others such as your boss' peers and your subordinate's peers in his matrix. Maxwell's best practices for a 360-degree leader can help all of us model the change we'd like to see in others.

For years, starting as a relatively young partner and middle manager leading the growth of one of our office practice groups, I had an annual lunch with our firm Chair. He was a prominent employment litigator with a strong presence; he ascended to the leadership of our law firm and remained there for about 15 years until his retirement. I am not sure how these lunches started or what I originally thought the purpose might be, but I learned a lot over the years. My most vivid memory of these meetings was during one lunch when he explained how difficult it was to implement change. I had always assumed that he was in charge, so if he wanted something to happen, it happened. I perceived him to have almost unlimited influence because he was our firm Chair. From his point of view, it was almost the opposite—change happened in the organization only when the managers, partners, and other lawyers and staff were on board (or at least not opposed to the change). He recognized that his influence arose not from his title but from the process of decision-making and implementation.

Becoming a 360-degree leader is within the reach of all of us who are willing to work at it. What separates effective 360-degree leaders from those who are not? Maxwell offers myths, challenges and principles to guide us to becoming a 360-degree leader. To me, it boils down to the following:

- Self-Manage
- Handle Setbacks
- Accept Responsibility
- Develop Influence

Effective Leaders Take the Initiative to Self-Manage

Lead yourself. That's where it all starts. Besides, if you won't follow yourself, why should anyone else?

John C. Maxwell

Source: John Maxwell - The 360 Leader - Developing Your Influence from Anywhere in the Organization

"If you take the approach of wanting to add value to those around you," says Maxwell, "you have the best chance of influencing them."[160]

Maxwell notes that you must learn to effectively lead yourself before you can influence your superiors, subordinates or peers.[161] Good leaders begin by managing themselves well and exercise leadership in how they manage the decision making process and decision implementation.

Becoming a good leader is a lifelong process. In all likelihood, no one at work is going to sit you down and teach you how to be a good leader. You may read books such as this one or any of the others profiled here, but to be an effective leader you have to integrate the leadership principles into your daily life. Many more people read leadership books than are effective leaders. A daily meditation practice was key for me to be able to step back and see things from a bigger picture perspective more closely to how they are rather than from an egocentric perspective. I used to perceive things were as I wanted them to be and was repeatedly frustrated when that was not accurate. Meditation practice can facilitate being able to self-manage and take action that will have the intended impact.

Maxwell claims self-management to be the most crucial component of leading oneself and then others successfully. He notes, "People put too much emphasis on decision making and too little on decision managing. As a result, they lack focus, discipline, intentionality, and purpose in making key decisions."[162] Frequently, it is not the substance of the decision that requires change, but how it is made and how it is communicated that will determine whether the change is implemented successfully or ignored by others. In other words, it is imperative that enough people who are affected by the change are engaged in the decision-making process. How one gets to the decision impacts how the decision affects the behavior of others as well as the perceived influence of the decision-maker.

What stops us as leaders from better managing decision making? Time? This is usually my initial response, but it may take less time overall to get input up front than extend the implementation timing and communication process. It often comes down to lack of awareness that we are rushing things. Short-term focus on other priorities and misplaced confidence that only the substantive result matters, can be detrimental to successful decision implementation. As decision maker, you can also add value to a decision making process not just by your own ideas but by providing positive reinforcement to others for their ideas and giving them responsibility to implement them.

If you are making the final decision or making a recommendation to the person making the final decision, consider with greater awareness from where the input from that decision is coming. Is support broad based or did you more expediently just pull together your own ideas that you believe are right and are trying to push them through? In doing so, consider whether you are being a good decision manager in addition to decision maker. Consider whether you are adding all the value you have to give to a decision making process led by others.

Maxwell notes that we each can self-manage becoming better leaders wherever we are in the organization by more fully participating in decisions that impact the organization even when you are not the decision maker.[163] In doing so, you can have influence and change people's lives, whether in the middle or at the top of an organization.

Meditation is not just about quieting your mind to allow the "big ideas" to come to the surface. Most of our wisdom presents as small, incremental steps. By quieting the chatter, the next incremental step rises to the surface. You become aware of what was blocked out by the noise. Different solutions come from a different level of consciousness. Once you lead yourself from within, you are in a better position to lead others. You are also in a position to release the frustration of being in the middle of managing others and being managed. You are more able to be comfortable with some of your ideas not being implemented and implementing others' ideas. You are less focused on external validation (although some appreciation from others is always nice) and more satisfied with internal validation that you are contributing value from your wisdom within. This is how meditation facilitates your ability to self-manage and, in doing so, puts you in a better position to be more influential in your organization.

Effective Leaders Handle Setbacks

I've never known a person focused on yesterday to have a better tomorrow.

John C. Maxwell

Life is not just a series of kumbaya moments of awareness, wonder and connection built through meditation. Life is chaotic and full of adversity. All of us will deal with career setbacks during our lifetime (such as being passed over for a promotion, or the loss of a job), organizational setbacks that may impact us (such as loss of a key customer or client or the rise of a new competitor) and personal setbacks (such as the sickness or loss of a loved one or a failed relationship). When you are losing, everything hurts. If you are going to fail, and everyone does, it really is best to recognize it as a learning experience. Why did that client go to another provider? Could I have said or done something to prevent the loss of this relationship if I were more aware it was at risk? Why did one my best workers choose to take a different job? Why did we not meet our revenue growth or profit expectations? Why isn't my family more grateful for my efforts?

Every good leader in every organization runs into the proverbial "brick wall" from time to time. You are doing everything right (or trying to do so), wanting to accomplish what is in the best interest of the organization. You perceive you are adding value, but no one seems to recognize it or, worse, your "good" ideas are rejected and/or your efforts are criticized. Senior managers may or may not have all the relevant facts and may or may not have a larger, more important contextual goal from their perspective, but they may set guidelines that prevent you from implementing what you believe is in the best interest of the organization. This is, to say the least, very frustrating, but it happens to all of us.

The way we handle these misfortunes, setbacks and brick walls can either cripple us or help us grow. Unfortunately, many people at some point get frustrated and "give up." They blame the organization and its leaders (and maybe even their parents) and, instead of leading, they retreat narrowly into performing their responsibilities, getting paid, going home and being unsatisfied with the work and career that once interested them. They may even job hop frequently looking for a "fresh start."

An effective leader also comes to understand that being effective at leadership is not the same as winning every battle. Sometimes, there are boundaries of decision-making authority that cannot be overstepped. Particularly when leading from the middle, you have to know when to give up a point and come back a different day with a different idea for change.

Pushing too far can be a significant source of loss of influence. No one wants someone to "go over their head." If you choose to do so, expect a loss of trust and perhaps even retribution. Be aware of the potential consequences, and whether you might win that battle but lose the war.

The hardest lesson for me was to acknowledge my mistakes. Everyone makes mistakes. It took me years to recognize that loss of reputation and influence results when people try to hide instead of admitting their mistakes, or put their egos and their own ideas ahead of institutional group decision-making processes. No idea is foolproof and no one is perfect.

As Maxwell notes: "Successful leaders make the right move at the right moment with the right motive."[164] I would supplement that the right move is only judged in retrospect and that makes it even more important to retain the right motive in seeking to make the right moves. Keep trying to make the right moves even when some of what you consider your best ideas are rejected. Hang in there after getting passed over for a promotion or not receiving the bonus you would have liked — there will be future opportunities.

This is where the importance of already having a habitual daily meditation practice is imperative. It is virtually impossible, if not impossible, to start your daily meditation in the face of setback, although it is more possible to return to a prior established practice when setback arises. Your meditation time can be a time of reflection to gain insight from your inner wisdom as to what you should do in such a situation. You may also choose a mantra meditation to change your focus or even a lovingkindness or forgiveness meditation to seek to clear any barriers created by the setback, recollection of similar setbacks and fear of future setbacks so you can move on more quickly.

As discussed in prior chapters, handling setbacks does not mean pretending they didn't happen; it means maintaining your awareness of what is actually happening and experiencing the emotions of the situation, overcoming them, and letting them go, rather than stuffing them deep into your mind and body. It means taking a step back to gain perspective and learning from the setback. It also means using your relationships to support you. For many of us, it is easier to give than to receive. A 360-degree leader learns how to receive support from others during times of setback rather than just give it. Even lifters sometimes need someone to lift them. What helps us overcome setbacks is community. Left to ourselves, we often want to flee, to give up. Our community of family, friends and work colleagues can help support us to overcome inevitable setbacks. It is up to us to be open enough and share enough to let them. This can seem awkward or scary. I can't recall a time when I was rejected after I opened up, or rejected someone at work who opened up about his or her issues, frustrations or even mistakes. We can't help but temporarily lose perspective in these moments of setback. It is especially at these times that we need our support system (plus daily meditation) to regain perspective. We can be aware of the backward step, seek support from our relationship network, turn the corner, and proceed forward again.

Effective Leaders Accept Responsibility

It is easier to move from failure to success than from excuses to success.
John C. Maxwell

One theme from several of Maxwell's books is that an effective leader, and in fact an effective person, is someone who takes responsibility for him—or herself and the performance of his or her business unit and organization. This goes beyond self-managing and handling setbacks by focusing on the affirmative steps you take to lead. A 360-degree leader must be able to *take* responsibility while simultaneously having the ability to *give* responsibility to others.[165]

When Harry Truman was President of the United States, he famously kept a sign on his desk that said: "The Buck Stops Here." He knew that no matter who had primary responsibility for something within his administration, and no matter how many people down the chain of command might seek to avoid responsibility for any outcome, he as President would take responsibility for the result. Leaders can delegate many tasks, but the one thing they can never relinquish is ultimate responsibility.

In one of his other seminal books, *Sometimes You Win—Sometimes You Learn: Life's Great Lessons Are Learned From Our Losses,* Maxwell cites five self-destructive consequences that occur when we fail to take responsibility: [166]

1. *We develop a victim mentality.* The line is often blurred between feeling normal upset over failure or setback, and developing a victim mentality. Too often, we fail to see just how severely debilitating this victim mentality can be. When we attribute our feelings of distress solely to external forces, we fail to improve ourselves. We may not be in control of what happens around us, but we *are* in control of how we react. The victim mentality can quickly spiral into giving up control of our lives as we cease to self-manage and let outside forces dictate what we can and can't do. This loss of perspective can be regained through meditation.

2. *We have an unrealistic perspective of how life works.* An unrealistic perspective on life has us perceiving ourselves and our accomplishments, and others and their accomplishments, differently from how others perceive them. As leaders, we are responsible for looking through a lens of open-mindedness and trying to see situations and people as they actually are. In other words, by being more mindful, which can be practiced and improved through mindfulness meditations, we can better recognize things as they actually are.

3. *We constantly engage in "blamestorming."* I particularly like Maxwell's term "blamestorming," defined as the "creative process used for finding an appropriate scapegoat."[167] When something goes wrong, we usually are not eager to take responsibility. An effective leader can refrain from blamestorming and take responsibility for a problem instead of pointing fingers. Blamestorming can spread very quickly; once ingrained in an organization's culture, it becomes very difficult to eliminate. When I hear myself blaming others, I find lovingkindness meditation that includes those in the story to be a more beneficial solution.

4. *We give away the choice to control our lives.* Who is responsible for what happens in your life? Are you someone who takes personal responsibility, or do you feel that your life is outside your

control and that your ability to change is largely determined by the views of other people? Taking responsibility for your life is a choice. That doesn't mean that you can control every outcome, but you can control your reaction to any outcome. This is very similar to the choice to meditate regularly to learn to control our minds instead of letting our habits control us.

5. *We eliminate any possibility of growth for success.* Failures are inevitable, but excuses are optional. Maxwell claims that while all of these five consequences are critical, eliminating the possibility of growth is the most detrimental. Growth is eliminated when making excuses replaces taking responsibility. He equates excuses to "exits along the road of success that lead us nowhere."[168] If you keep veering off the road to success by making excuses and blaming others, there is absolutely no way you will ever make it to a successful destination. Maxwell recommends continuing to strive to achieve your goals, understanding that there will be setbacks and mistakes along the way, and taking responsibility for both the mistakes and the remedies. Personal and organizational growth will then result from the failures. This growth mindset is what we practice by dedicating ourselves to a regular meditation practice. By observing and accepting "what is," we move forward from one present moment to the next learning from the past, doing the best we can in the present and not worrying as much about the future.

Accepting responsibility means making difficult decisions. Making difficult decisions means you won't always make the right one and decisions will not always be popular, particularly in the short run and particularly among those adversely affected. Brené Brown in her book *Daring Greatly*, defines a leader as "anyone who holds her—or himself accountable for finding potential in people and processes."[169] She reiterates that the term leader has nothing to do with position, status or numbers of direct reports. In the long run, those who accept responsibility make difficult decisions, and hold themselves accountable, prove to be the leaders in an organization who develop the greatest influence.

Meditation can provide you with the confidence to take responsibility. By learning to see things closer to how they really are and learning to live more in the present moment rather than limited by the past by taking on a victim mentality or blamestorming, we observe our thoughts, become more aware of opportunities and can take responsibility for our lives, which facilitates the possibility for growth for success. Mediation thus becomes our antidote to adopting any of Maxwell's noted self-destructive tendencies.

Effective Leaders Have Influence

Leadership is not about titles, positions or flowcharts.
It is about one life influencing another.
John C. Maxwell

For Maxwell, leadership is ultimately about influence. In every organization, there are people of influence well beyond any bestowed title who can accomplish what they want, when they want it, while others face the proverbial "red tape" and find it difficult to get their good ideas implemented.

In *Becoming a Person of Influence*,[170] Maxwell and his co-author Jim Dorman describe the qualities of influence using INFLUENCE as an acronym:

Integrity—builds relationships on trust

Nurturing—cares about people as individuals

Faith—believes in people

Listening—values what others have to say

Understanding—sees from their point of view

Enlarging—helps others become bigger

Navigating—assists others through difficulty

Connecting—initiates positive relationships

Empowering—gives them the power to lead

Maxwell describes a 360-degree leader as someone people want to follow rather than someone who wants to attain a position that will make people follow.[171] The above traits do not just appear magically when someone is promoted; conversely, leaders of influence are often promoted because they already exhibit these traits.

If you are a middle manager, you may often find it easier to stay in your own narrow primary role. It is more difficult, but potentially more rewarding (both to yourself and your organization), to expand your influence to all those organizational areas where you can add value. Maxwell reminds us that we can lift people up or take people down. You can use your influence to lift up your boss, making her load lighter and making her more successful—or you can make it heavier. You rarely win when your boss fails. Instead, when your boss succeeds, you, your group and the organization as a whole are more likely to succeed. Being part of a successful group (whether that means profitable or recognized as well-run and effective) leads to influence for that group and its leaders and group members.

Meditation Is the Way

For many of us, beginning to self-manage means that we need to address our stress level. For me, 15 years ago, stress and my reactions to stress were holding me back. This manifested physically in back spasms, emotionally in being impatient and short-tempered, mentally in setting comfortable boundaries that I didn't try very hard to exceed, and strategically in limiting my potential by focusing on daily tasks without much attention to long-term goals.

One of the first useful ways to cope with stress is to question the use of the word "stress." It may be too imprecise to act on effectively. One important step in beginning to manage stress is to break the stress down into separate components, which often have different causes and different solutions.

For example, you might be feeling anxious about a project at work, annoyed with a colleague who isn't pulling his weight, hurt that your spouse isn't listening to you, or inadequate when juggling competing priorities. If you don't distinguish between these different forms of distress, you may just lump them together under the term "stress." This isn't helpful when it comes to dealing with them. Seeking to be more aware and precise in your observations about the cause of your stress can facilitate your ability to choose the right meditation or other technique for you to "de-stress" at a given moment.

The whole metaphor of stress comes from engineering. A load is put on a structure, and that structure experiences stress. The structure is passive. It can't respond any other way but by being stressed. You are not a building or a bridge. You are not a machine. When you experience anxiety, your particular response can become habitual. Sometimes you need professional or pharmaceutical intervention, and sometimes meditation can do the trick or supplement professional guidance.

Daily meditation is the support that I needed to hold up my structure. Simply deciding to dedicate yourself to a daily meditation practice is an act of personal responsibility. While there can be some variety in your meditation, most people find that 10 minutes of daily meditation defined by some regular habits works best. You may decide to meditate at the same time of day, in the same room, or in the same position to train your body and mind that when these things are occurring, it is meditation time.

The good news is that, if you are not good at coping with stress, you can learn meditative coping behaviors so that you can live in a more balanced way. This isn't a case of just "pulling yourself together." That may work for some, but the "will" doesn't work without the "way." Meditation is the "way."

Once you begin daily practice, you can identify the type and source of your stress, and you can choose the most appropriate meditation technique to address the source of that stress, whether that is physical, emotional, mental, spiritual, or some combination. I needed them all.

With your daily practice in place, when setbacks inevitably occur, you will have the meditation tools to deal with that setback. You will be able to step back, regain perspective and take responsibility for yourself and your actions. You can access your wisdom within and influence the outcome in a more effective manner than with a stressed and cluttered outlook.

Meditations for Breaking Down the Barriers to Influence

i. Ujayi Breathing

It is almost impossible to be stressed while engaging in Ujayi (pronounced oo-jai) breathing. This deep breathing is very calming and provides the body and mind with extra oxygen. Your breath will be audible to you and Ujayi breathing is sometimes referred to as oceanic breath or Darth Vader breath due to the sound that reverberates inside you while practicing this breathing technique.

Take a deep inhalation through your nose with your mouth closed.

Pause

With your mouth remaining closed, exhale through your nose constricting your throat muscles. You will hear a soft hissing sound or a soft "HA" sound.

This sound is made by the air rather than your vocal cords. Some people consider it similar to an out breath that would fog up a mirror but with your mouth closed.

Repeat

Keep your focus on your breath or that sound. Continue for 50 breaths or approximately 10 minutes.

Come back to your Ujayi breathing any time your body needs an energetic lift or your mind needs a momentary clearing.

ii. Putting Yourself in Others' Shoes Meditation

This mental mindfulness meditation is a variation of the emotional mindfulness meditation that we practiced in Chapter VII. However, in the emotional mindfulness meditation, we focused on your own emotion and emotional reaction during the situation. Here we consider the holistic perspective of another person. This meditation enables you to step back, consider others' views and to accept responsibility that you can change the outcome the next time a similar situation arises. Attempting to put yourself in another's shoes will increase your awareness, your attunement to others impacted by the situation and your influence.

Keep in mind that you won't really know the other person's story or all relevant facts about the other person. As we become more aware of the other person for who he or she is, we may begin to understand more of his or her relevant characteristics. However, you won't likely know if the other person was yelled at just prior to his encounter with you, her mother is gravely ill, or he is the type of person who only does a certain thing a certain "right" way. As noted, through these exercises, you may become more aware of these relevant facts.

Close your eyes. Relax and center yourself.

Replay 1. Think of one event that happened during the past week that involved another person and perhaps didn't go as well as you would have liked. Once you have identified the event, heighten your awareness and focus on the details as you relive it in your mind.

Replay 2. Repeat the same event but put yourself in the other person's shoes (if more than one other person, try each person separately). Try to really think what the other person might have been thinking rather than what you would be thinking if you were the other person. Consider what the other person might have been feeling based on what you know of his or her personality characteristics and background (to the extent that you know it).

Replay 3. Replay the event one more time from this new perspective, from your own point of view but with greater awareness of the other person's point of view. How might the situation play out differently? Are you potentially able to exercise greater influence with greater consideration of the other person? How can you act differently the next time a similar situation arises?

This is a great exercise to practice daily before you go to sleep. Choose one event from the day that didn't seem to go as well as you would have liked or one goal that doesn't seem to be getting accomplished. Run it through this meditation practice and see if you gain additional insight. As you practice, notice whether the other person in this exercise becomes more like the actual other person rather than yourself in the other person's shoes.

iii. I Did It Meditation

There is a difference between making mistakes and failing and covering up mistakes and tucking away our failures. By not acknowledging our mistakes and failures (or that it is ok to make mistakes and/or fail at something), we invite those failures to come back later to haunt us and repeat, whether by action or just by chipping away at our self-confidence and self-worth. We harmfully turn inevitable setbacks into a reduction of self-worth instead of a growth opportunity. By being mindful of our mistakes and failures we can handle them and let them go, and thereby eliminating any negative influence they may have rather than the positive growth of lessons learned. By being mindful of both our failures and our successes, we acknowledge our self-worth and build resilience for the future setbacks that will inevitably come our way.

Consciously acknowledge that making a mistake or experiencing an outcome failure does not make you a failure. You are okay. You are experiencing personal growth. Keep in your awareness that vulnerability is not a weakness but one of the deepest strengths of a leader. Change occurs within vulnerability. Without risk there is no change. Without change, there is no growth. Use your meditation to take the stigma out of mistakes and acknowledge that mistakes are part of growth.

Focus on your breath. You don't have to change your breath. You don't have to change at all.

Focus on an event or outcome or relationship that continues to bother you.

Relive the facts leading up to that outcome.

If your mind starts to rationalize with excuses, let those excuses go.

What lesson did you learn? How can you grow from the experience?

Relax your body and focus again on your breath. Consider a message of responsibility and self-forgiveness:

> I made a mistake (on inhale)
>
> It is okay (on exhale)
>
> I accept responsibility (on inhale)
>
> I am okay (on exhale)
>
> Everyone makes mistakes (on inhale)
>
> All is okay (on exhale)

Repeat as needed, focusing on the same mistake or outcome failure — one per session. Repeat the message of release until you feel the burden lifted. Sometimes, intention meditations are aspirational. All may not yet be okay, but with time and return to balance, it will be.

In doing so, you will learn to separate the outcome from yourself. Regardless of outcome, taking risk is not just okay, it is commendable. It is necessary to be an effective leader.

iv. TGIM Meditation

For many, starting the work week on Monday morning (and anxiety that begins sometime on Sunday) is the most stressful time of the week. Part of relieving stress is taking responsibility that you are partially causing that stress. You are inadvertently creating your own barrier.

Maxwell wrote another book entitled *Think On These Things: Meditations for Leaders*.[172] In a chapter entitled "T.G.I.M. (Thank Goodness It's Monday),"[173] Maxwell questions why we are so elated to say "T.G.I.F." come Friday, but groan in agony when Monday rolls around. That's when he began saying "T.G.I.M." instead of falling victim to the Monday blues. Basically, if we think Mondays are going to be horrible, they will be!

Maxwell took responsibility to change his "Sunday night blues" by creating his own happiness on Mondays by becoming cognizant of why it's such a great day. For him, Mondays:

- Mark the beginning of a journey towards the end of the week, and often the journey is just as fulfilling as the destination.
- Can be perceived as a blank slate in which "last week's sorrow can become this week's joy."
- Provides an opportunity to set goals and get priorities in order.
- Are the exciting opening action of the week!
- Are a chance to appreciate the beauty in life.
- Offer an opportunity to add value and bring joy to others.

Maxwell took a day so widely disliked by American society and transformed that misery into happiness. Take ownership for your feelings; only *you* have the ability to make yourself feel unhappy or stressed. A positive approach will often end up with positive results; the same goes for the converse.

Try this practice on Sunday evening or Monday morning. Don't work through the details, and don't "stress out" . . . just repeat to yourself: "T.G.I.M."

TGIM

Pause five breaths. Notice any thoughts and let them flow by

TGIM

Pause five breaths. Notice any thoughts and let them flow by

Repeat 20-30 times or for approximately 10 minutes, leaving enough time during the pause to listen

Observe whether ideas flow into your mind that are different (and better) than if you had simply sat down to make a task list for the week.

v. Integrating the Lesson and the Meditation Technique—Mindful Meeting Participation to Maximize Influence

A key place where decisions are influenced in any organization setting is the business meeting. This may be a board of directors or board of trustees meeting, a project group meeting, a management meeting, or a business negotiation with a third party. In every such meeting there is an agenda or other organizational framework and then people talk. If you don't talk at all, you don't get heard and don't have influence. If you talk too much, at some point, you will not be heard, will annoy others, and will not have influence.

While different situations require different levels of personal participation, in most effective meetings the fundamental conversation framework is the same. Widespread vocal participation, sharing of diverse ideas, and listening by others to those ideas, will achieve the best outcome and the most buy-in for that outcome. In any meeting, process matters, and a meeting led by a 360° leader will more likely be an effective one.

How can you practice effective meeting participation? Try the following exercise (you don't even have to tell anyone you are doing it).

1. Go into a meeting of any type with a goal range of how many times you will speak. For example, not less than two times or more than three times plan to speak.

2. Every time you are about to speak think first whether what you are about to say is worth one of those three talking opportunities. If so, go ahead.

3. Listen with close attention in the present moment to what others have to say rather than go into rebuttal mode (rebuttal is a speaking choice).

4. If the meeting is moving toward the end and you have not made a contribution, make sure to get in a comment.

5. Consciously determine your maximum influence range (speaking the optimal amount to maximize your influence in the meeting) and seek to stay within your maximum influence range consistently. Over time, you will find your influence grows, and people will care more about what you have to say.

Sometimes as a teaching tool, when leading my practice area meetings, I will announce the rule to the group — for the next hour I would like to hear from everyone at least once but not more than three times — think before you speak and allow everyone's ideas to be heard. You will be amazed how appreciated that is by the group, both by those who often don't speak much and those who do (the frequent speakers generally have a harder time with this exercise).

Building the Pillar of Perspective

Effectiveness in business is based in large part on how we process and utilize information. Meditation provides a moment of calm within the chaos so that whatever is most important can rise to the surface. When what is generally in the background arises in awareness, we can observe and later process these insights. Meditation provides access to our wisdom within, and can increase balance and equanimity so you can more successfully process that wisdom with context and implement that wisdom, thereby increasing your influence at work, at home and in your community.

Stress has become such a roadblock for many of us. It can impact our actions, our reactions, and our health and well-being. Meditation practice provides a break from the events that trigger stress, as well as greater perspective to avoid the same events retriggering the stress response.

From a less stressed and more balanced mindset, with the most important information having risen into our consciousness, we are able to improve our decision-making and increase our positive influence within the organization and the world at large.

Once the three pillars of Awareness, Connection and Perspective have been strengthened, you are in a position to grow. There is less fear of moving forward beyond your comfort zone and of accepting change. It is with an open mind that you will be able to strengthen the fourth pillar of Potential.

BUILDING THE PILLAR OF POTENTIAL

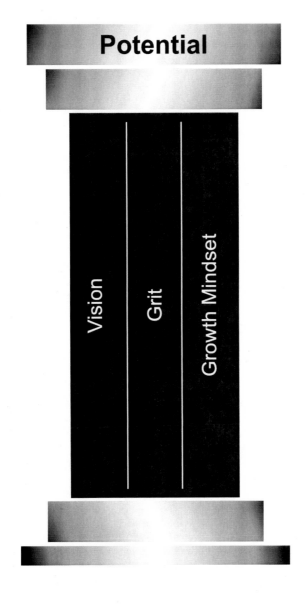

XIV. VISION—HOW MEDITATION CAN UNLOCK YOUR UNTAPPED POTENTIAL

Good business leaders create a vision, articulate the vision, passionately own the vision, and relentlessly drive it to completion.

Jack Welsh, retired CEO of GE

You may become more aware through practicing meditation regularly that you can make a difference. Your meditation practice positively impacts your physical stress level, emotional state and thought process. Your thoughts and emotions influence your actions. What you do can and does have impact, not only directly, but also indirectly, when those you influence take it a step further and influence others. Suddenly, your meditation practice is not just making you more effective, but making others around you more effective. Your impact on others in the organization can make your entire organization more effective. Your organization can make the world a better place because you are there. Might that be one of your life motivations or definitions of success? Maybe you realize that both you and your organization can have greater potential than you have been fulfilling.

We can do so much more than our mind lets us know we can do. As noted in the previous chapter, there is nothing wrong with failure or making mistakes, but many of us focus more on our mistakes than our successes. We judge ourselves harshly instead of with compassion for trying our personal best. As managers, we focus more on addressing our short-term output requirements and challenges (the crisis of the day) than our opportunities.

Vision is what separates effective leaders from effective managers and implementers. Sometimes it is a grand vision like Steve Jobs creating personal computing and integrated mobile devices, or Arianna Huffington identifying that online news could surpass traditional media. Sometimes it is vision of how to develop a relationship or how to win a basketball game. You can't achieve your potential if you don't envision it first. Creating vision involves more than your day-to-day thinking. It involves your gut instinct, following your heart and opening your mind for something new.

In the opening of his book, *The Other 90%:How to Unlock Your Vast Untapped Potential for Leadership and Life,* Robert K. Cooper shares words of wisdom from his grandfather. " . . .[A]ll of us are mostly unused potential. It's up to you to become the most curious person you know and to keep asking yourself, What is *my* best? Keep finding more of it every day to give to the world. If you do that, I promise that more of the best than you can ever imagine—and in many ways beyond money—will come back to you."[174] Robert's grandfather further encourages his grandson to do this by looking inside himself, by testing new possibilities, and by searching for what matters most. Cooper notes that few of us ever do that for ourselves. Instead, we hold our breath. We look away. We get by or go along. We defend what we have been. We say, "I've been living my life wrong and now it's too late to make it right."

Cooper uses his grandfather's challenge to develop four keystones for unlocking our untapped potential for leadership:

- Trust—Building and sustaining exceptional relationships
- Energy—Increasing calm effectiveness under pressure
- Farsightedness—Creating the future
- Nerve—Exceeding expectations

Cooper offers two simple contemplative questions to help us overcome our natural resistance to growth or change and achieve our potential. He suggests that we ask ourselves regularly:

What's the most exceptional thing I have done this week?

What's the most exceptional thing I will do next week?[175]

I started practicing this exercise each Sunday evening and Wednesday evening. On Sunday, I would reflect on the week that passed and consider the week ahead. On Wednesday, I would check my progress; if I hadn't yet accomplished anything exceptional I would refocus and still have time to implement something exceptional before the end of the week. I suddenly found the time and strength to work toward many more of my goals—whether they involved building a key relationship, making it through a critical situation, creating a plan for the future, or simply following through on my prior intentions—in other words, to fully realize my potential.

During one of the yoga classes I attended, yoga leader Lisa Greenberg Gonzalez mentioned: "There are two types of people: those who see opportunity and those who see barriers." It is similar to the old adage of seeing the cup as "half full" or "half empty." To do exceptional things, you have to envision the opportunity and not let the inevitable barriers hold you back.

I recall meeting with the founder of Bai Beverage when he was just starting out and selling locally in New Jersey. He had previously owned a high-end coffee shop in Princeton. On a buying trip to find unique coffee blends, he noticed that the coffee plant grew a berry fruit (who knew?) and that the coffee berry was discarded as the coffee beans were harvested. It is naturally flavorful with natural caffeine but tart and bitter alone. He developed blends and flavors and mixed with sugars and sugar substitutes until Bai5 was born, a naturally caffeinated five calorie beverage that tastes good (now available in dozens of flavors). In our first conversation, he noted that Bai Beverage would eventually be a billion dollar sales beverage business. He saw the opportunity. I started talking about manufacture and supply logistics issues, the need to build his team and regulatory restrictions that could impact claims on his packaging.

He responded these are among the many barriers he will overcome. He did, and eventually sold Bai Beverage for a reported $1.7 billion to Dr. Pepper Snapple.

I have the opportunity to work with many successful entrepreneurs and often hear about their visions to meet the potential of the opportunity they face. I recall the vision of Jeff Ginsberg, Alex Gellman and Marc Ganzi in the 1990s to build cell towers on rooftops, allowing commercial building owners to "monetize" their rooftop and to permit cell phones to work effectively in locations where free standing cell towers were too expensive or took too long to build due to land cost, permitting requirements and/or community objections; Mark Galant's vision to bring foreign exchange trading to the masses when it was then limited to a few big banks; Flint Lane's vision to create an online portal to receive all of your bills (whether sent to you via paper or electronically) and then a subsequent vision to allow businesses to send bills and receive payments more quickly electronically (with the cost savings being pure profit for the business owner); and literally hundreds of other innovative opportunities, not all of which proved successful; and Greg Mayes' vision to find a treatment for epileptic seizures that impact his child. These entrepreneurs didn't just think of these ideas. I have observed that the successful ones knew that devoting all of themselves for a portion of their lives was something they felt obligated to do, was worth doing, and was an opportunity for which the potential benefit of success overcame the time, cost, and likelihood of failure. They envisioned the world with their product or service to be a better and more efficient place and that vision created a resolve to pursue that business with all of their resources. They saw opportunity.

Better understanding how we process information can assist us in recognizing which thoughts can become meaningful ideas, some of which will become incorporated into our personal life vision. Cooper sets forth

262

a theory that the brain, the heart and the intestinal tract are connected neurologically. While we think in the brain, we can gain wisdom equally from the brain, the heart and the gut. All three sources of information (instinct, feelings and thoughts) enter our consciousness. This realization allows us to utilize more of our capability and thus expand our opportunity to accomplish exceptional things. Cooper describes this three-part theory as follows:[176]

The Brain in the Gut. Have you ever noticed something pop into your consciousness seemingly out of nowhere — different from your normal thought process? This is often called a "gut feeling". You may notice anticipation, excitement or fear as butterflies in your stomach. You may notice that your instinct, rather than your mind, will often more accurately help you answer the following: *How important is this new person to me? Is this situation a threat? Am I heading in the right or wrong direction?* The gut (known scientifically as the enteric nervous system)[177] reacts to situations quickly and independently of the brain, but its impulses are connected to the brain for interpretation. Whether or not you acknowledge your gut reactions, Cooper espouses that instinct is shaping everything you—and the people around you—do. In my experience, while my mind will often make mistakes, my gut is rarely wrong.

The Brain in the Heart. After the enteric nervous system's first response, it's the heart's turn to ponder the situation. Cooper highlights scientific studies conducted in the 1990s, in what was then the emerging field of neurocardiology, that indicate that a complex network of nerve cells and neurotransmitters make the heart "brain" as large as many of the key areas of the brain in our head and imbue it with "computational abilities."[178] Just as the gut acts independently from, but is connected to, the brain, the heart is independent yet connected through the flow of blood and the hormonal system to the rest of the body. Cooper posits that the heart is where our emotions lie, and for that reason, it is your heart and not your head that plays a dominant role in your passion and drive you to excel. This may be why someone with passion and compassion is said to "have heart." The heart is open to new opportunities to meet new people, to grow, and to learn. It establishes a "reading" of what others feel and monitors our own feelings. As a result, creativity and bravery often come from the heart. It is no wonder that when workers do not feel that their work is appreciated, they do not put their "heart" into their work. Cooper, citing a study by the Center for Creative Leadership, notes that the very best leaders are those who care about people and their organization.[179] When business leaders skip the brain in the heart in making decisions, those decisions may be less likely to lead to the best overall results.

The Brain in the Head. The third stop for nerve impulses is the part of the brain known as the medulla. This is where our reason lies. The brain receives nerve impulses from the gut and the heart and then uses reason to process their meaning, sometimes getting it right and sometimes getting it wrong. While the gut is rarely wrong, the brain sometimes incorrectly interprets the meaning. The brain contains and processes our historic knowledge and memory, and the brain manages the mind, which processes our conscious thoughts.

Try to be more aware of where your decision-making comes from as future choices arise. If we go back to the concept of "self" as a witness, we can become more aware of whether ideas are coming from our gut, heart or mind and then consciously use all three resources in our decision-making. Opening the heart and gut through meditation allows the wisdom to flow — the mind can then process that wisdom. This seems, intuitively and analytically, to be a better way to make decisions.

The value of accessing and relying on intuition is backed up by my personal experience since I began a regular meditation practice. When an insight comes from the background to the foreground during meditation, and I follow it, I experience positive results. This leads to greater confidence following vision derived from that wisdom rather than giving in to fear and other barriers to change.

As I was approaching my 50th birthday, my gut was repeatedly telling me to share what I learned in meditation. I could significantly help others overcome their natural obstacles to meditation, the language used, the settings taught and the fear that it wouldn't work, as I had overcome these obstacles myself. My heart was providing me with conflicting messages of excitement and joy at the possibilities, as well as with fear and self-doubt. Who am I to seek to teach others? What if I fail? What if people laugh at me? My brain was planning strategy: teach a meditation course at local community center, take meditation teacher training course, write a book, and ultimately help create an organization to make this bigger than myself and promote all those promoting meditation in different ways. My head also asked, where will I find the time? What if my law firm management objects? What if clients think I'm nuts? Will this hurt or help my professional practice? At every step, I faced a battle: my heart and head sent conflicting messages, while my gut kept pushing me forward.

What seems like my life's opportunity, where everything I have learned to date converges, is Meditation4Leadership, a recently formed organization to promote the concepts espoused in this book. The book was flowing out of me so I wanted to write it down, but I always knew there were limitations to just reading about meditation. It is an experience rather than a set of rules to be followed. I enjoy teaching, but I wanted to reach more than the 20-30 participants in the groups I was leading near my home. The impulse was strong and "felt right"—I had to do this, but I couldn't do it alone.

I also didn't know whom to partner with. I asked a few well-known meditation teachers and they declined. I reached out to a few leadership professors at colleges with leading business leadership programs, and they also passed. Ultimately, I looked inside my heart to where I felt connections, not initially sure what the interest or roles might be. I first discussed the idea with my wife, Stefanie knowing she would offer a lot of value. I discussed the idea with my yoga teachers, Alex Schimmel and Lisa Greenberg Gonzalez, who were inspiring me during virtually every class, and they were on board enthusiastically to spread yoga and meditation in any setting. I then discussed the idea with Marilyn Hailperin, an experienced non-profit leader with whom I always had a connection, who would recall conversations we had years ago that impacted her life. Without even an "ask," Marilyn in our first conversation said this is how she wanted to devote a portion of the rest of her life.

I then discussed the idea with Lisa Berg Jacobs. I had known and respected her father (former business partner of Wayne Kimmel, mentioned in Chapter IX and Steven Krein, whose story is still to come in Chapter XVI). I only had a few conversations with Lisa over the years, but she had taken one of my meditation seminars and had recently been transitioning from small business entrepreneur to full-time yoga teacher. That conversation felt right as we shared ideas. At the end of the conversation, I gave Lisa my then-current draft of this book. She read it in 24 hours and was hooked (no one had ever read it that fast).

Although it took a few months, I knew I wanted to try to get Scott Rosen involved. Scott is a successful entrepreneur who is a recruiter for human resources managers, author of two books on leadership and human resources management, and, about ten years ago, had founded a yoga and spiritual retreat studio in southern New Jersey. We had breakfast annually, sharing our journeys. Although he had also taken one of my meditation seminars and we had co-led a discussion series called "Story Share" at our synagogue, my mind didn't think he would have the time or be sufficiently interested. I was thrilled when he was "in" during our initial discussion and shared that he also long felt we had the opportunity to do something great together. These are people with whom I had always felt a connection, where there was always mutual respect. My gut got me going in the right direction; my mind never could have put these pieces together. Meditation4Leadership was born through heart connections.

From there, my mind did have to take over as Stefanie, Alex, Marilyn, Lisa, Scott and I shared ideas, discussed how we each thought we could add complementary value, and then determined how to refine our mission and create unique, signature programming. I was committed to this being a group effort and, we are all very proud that our meditation4leadership.org web site and initial programming are in fact the amalgamation of the best from each of us and a few others who have since joined the leadership group. We may have created it from our gut and come together from our heart, but ultimately we had to use our analytical thought process to confidently bring together what at times seemed like mutually exclusive approaches and styles in order to function as a team. We are seeking to pursue this opportunity without too much attachment to near-term results, but we are hoping to positively impact a lot of people and organizations over the long term. We continue to add to the team using instinct, connections and strategy.

One of the lessons from meditation is that each breath is a new moment. Each new moment is an opportunity. We sometimes get locked into a mindset that we can't effect change and therefore continue to repeat historic actions and thought patterns. This significantly limits our ability to achieve our potential. If you instead can alter that mindset to acknowledge your ability to be in the present moment, less restricted by the regrets from the past or fear of what may happen in the future, you can choose to take a new and different action in the present moment. You can choose to breathe instead of just breathing reflexively. You can choose to grow instead of just living reflexively. You can choose potential over stagnation. You can create your future.

I am choosing to lead with vision. I am choosing potential. I am choosing to leap into the Meditation4Leadership opportunity (while still maintaining my legal practice). I am choosing to share the value I have obtained from meditation with others. I want to make a positive difference in the world. While I'm not sure on what scale I can do so, the positive feedback from the initial course takers and book readers on the impact on their lives already demonstrates that this effort was not a waste of time. What is your potential? What is your future?

The Difference Between Your Mind and Your Brain

Most of the time, we use the terms brain and mind interchangeably. However, the distinction is key to understanding meditation.

The brain is physical. It is located in our head within our skull and we can touch it (not that most of us want to). It is composed of nerve cells and blood vessels that create a functioning organ. The brain coordinates movement and is the center of cognition.

The mind is more amorphous. It is a mental state. It exists but is not tangible. The mind generally refers to one's capacity to understand and process thoughts, feelings and sensory perceptions and to act as the warehouse for our memories. One of the Meditation4Leadership directors, serial entrepreneur Tom Drury, uses the analogy of a dog whistle. The dog whistle itself is like the brain and the sound is like the mind. We can't hear it but we know the sound waves physically exist.

Philosophers have debated whether the brain or the mind is in control. Does the mind control the brain (and us generally), or does the brain control the mind? That is a question for a different day. Either way, it is worth being aware of the difference.

Using this framework, I prefer to think of Cooper's theories not as the "brain in the head," "brain in the heart," and "brain in the gut," but as the "mind from your head," "mind from your heart," and "mind from your gut." There is only one brain, and it is in your head. However, your mind, and its resulting wisdom, may come from a combination of all three: your head (thoughts), heart (feelings), and gut (intuition). You need to use all three to maximize your potential.

The Difference Between Your Mind and Your Thoughts

Carrying this line of analysis further, if your mind is your consciousness, what does it contain? In clinical psychology, the mind generally includes autobiographical memory, personal identity, action control, introspection, and thought control.[180]

A single thought is a subcomponent or byproduct of the mind. A thought chain is a process that runs through the mind. My favorite analogy is that of the ocean. Like thoughts, waves in the ocean are impermanent — waves form and return to the ocean. Similarly, your thoughts form and dissipate back into the vastness of your mind.

Therefore, you are not your thoughts and your mind is different from your thoughts. It is possible to think of your mind as the sum of all of your thoughts, feelings and intuitions, current and past—but that leaves out the process in which those thoughts, feelings and intuitions are created and how they are observed.

For now, the key recognition is that when we are unaware of the difference between our mind and our thoughts, we blindly follow our thoughts without the benefit of our inner wisdom, often to adverse consequences.

The Difference Between Observing Thoughts Versus Thinking

The reason the distinction among your brain, your mind and your thoughts is important is that a key aspect of meditation is your ability to observe what passes in front of you (including thoughts, feelings and instinct) during the silence of your meditation practice.

This brings us to the following question: Who is the "you" that is doing the observing? Again, for answers, we could delve into the complexity of philosophy and religion beyond the scope of this book. For purposes of better understanding meditation, I suggest that the "you" is your consciousness that observes your thoughts. You are the witness. Your "self" is your consciousness. Perhaps the "you" that is your consciousness is a spirit that lives on beyond this world. The body (including your brain) is a vessel for physical existence, the mind is your software processing the brain's hardware into thoughts, and awareness of the output of your mind is your consciousness during this lifetime. As one of my teachers, James Van Prague, said during a weekend retreat: "Maybe we are spiritual beings living a physical existence, and not the other way around."

For now, we simply acknowledge the question and the possibilities. You may choose to ponder these questions further as you advance in your meditation practice. Maybe you—and society—will one day reach greater clarity on these issues than we have currently, which will bring our actions and thoughts into greater perspective.

What is important for us right now is to recognize the difference between active thinking and observing thoughts. It is hard to describe this difference in words, but you will experience the difference. Understanding of the process of meditation will dramatically increase your appreciation of the value of being in a meditative state of consciousness versus your active mind consciousness.

During a meditative state of consciousness, you are the observer, not the thinker. You observe with awareness what appears—whether that is light or shapes or colors or thoughts or feelings or physical sensations. It is your meditative state of consciousness where the wisdom appears. It is in your capacity as the observer (not as an active thinker) to identify from where the wisdom comes to you, whether it is from your brain, heart, gut or somewhere else. It is when you return to your active conscious mind that you determine what actions to take or not take with the benefit of that wisdom.

Observing also provides the opportunity to decrease suffering. When you believe all of your thoughts (including the story your mind tells you around your observations), you suffer. When you can differentiate the observations and question the truth of the story without judgment, you can observe more purely and release some of that mind-created suffering.

Meditation as a Technique to Unlock Your Untapped Potential

Accessing greater wisdom through meditation is an effective way to discover your untapped potential and lead yourself and others toward achieving that potential.

Let's go back to Robert Cooper's chapter entitled "No One Has to Lose for You to Win," where he describes his theory of successful leadership.[181] Create "win-win" situations using the four keystones (trust, energy, far-sightedness and nerve) with those who report to you as well as customers and the organization as a whole. When you act altruistically in the best interest of the organization, you win the trust of other members of the organization. When you continually demonstrate calm under pressure, people have confidence in you. When you clearly articulate the organization's vision, employees have direction. When you challenge workers to exceed expectations, they often do so. This leads to higher morale, a functional work environment and a win-win situation for workers and their leaders.

In another section of his book, Cooper asks: "Who Are You When No One Else is Looking?"[182] Sometimes, contemplative guided or focused meditations can help us to break beyond the habits of our daily lives and thinking patterns to access our true, authentic selves—the "self" when no one else is looking. This is the "self" that acts as the witness during meditation.

This book includes meditation techniques that focus on body, emotions, mind and spirit to provide greater knowledge of your "self" and greater personal equanimity or comfort with your "self," while acknowledging that there are no perfectly balanced people or people who act perfectly. Even the gurus stray in their personal lives from their place of balance; one often hears stories of illicit activities from gurus who have lost their perspective and equanimity, at least for a period of time. Striving to achieve potential and achieving perfection are two different concepts. By using meditation to envision what is possible, you become aware of your opportunities and use that awareness to create win-win situations. You can reach toward satisfying your untapped potential.

Start by envisioning positive outcomes. I heard Shaquille O'Neil on TV tell stories of how before a game, Phil Jackson would have the team envision how the victory might unfold and what each team member's role in that victory might look like. Although the details of real life didn't usually turn out the same as the vision, this technique boosted confidence and reduced anxiety during the key final game minutes. Victory had been envisioned multiple ways; now it was just time to implement.

A successful serial entrepreneur who I spoke with recounted a similar story to me as a key to his success. Starting at Wharton, he would go to a center where he would peacefully lie in a tank and envision his successful future. Periodically, he would repeat this activity with respect to his then-current enterprise. He did achieve that vision and did reach his potential (and maybe this meditation technique facilitated that outcome), although the details may have differed a bit from his vision.

Part of becoming exceptional can be envisioning being exceptional. Part of becoming exceptional can be using meditation as a technique to increase your awareness of what is and what is possible. It takes practice. Dan Harris observed in his book, *10% Happier,* "Meditation is simply exercise for your brain."[183] That resonates with me, although I would likely modify that to "Meditation is simply exercise for your mind."

Observation Meditations

The following meditation practices may help you to further practice being a witness, shed barriers, keep possible opportunities in your awareness, and serve as the key to unlock and become aware of your untapped potential.

i. Open Awareness Meditation

The objective of an open awareness meditative practice is to open the mind into a panoramic awareness of whatever is happening without a specific focus. Often this awareness is compared to the spacious sky or vast ocean. The capacity to be present and witness whatever arises without controlling the intention or outcome is developed through this practice. What is beyond and able to be witnessed is seemingly limitless potential.

Close your eyes or lower your gaze.

Try to become aware of awareness itself—become aware of that which is aware. Witness your own consciousness.

Notice that most of our attention is on things that arise in this consciousness. Objects, feelings, thoughts, sensations. It doesn't matter if thoughts and feelings are there or not there. It doesn't change the consciousness itself—what is usually in the background.

Allow everything to be as it is right now.

Allow yourself to rest the part of yourself that needs to know everything. It is okay to not know everything. It is okay to not know anything.

Be aware of that part of yourself that is not in need of change. Let go of any idea of understanding. Let go of any idea of perfection. Let it all go, maybe floating by on a cloud or just dissipating. Witness what is left.

As we remain in meditation, no issue is happening or not happening; just let it be, exactly the way it is. No need to change anything at all. No problems at all. No judgment.

If the thoughts, feelings and intuitions stop coming, observe. Witness all around and remain for a while in peace.

When you are done, bring your consciousness back to the present moment. Would you like to go back and visit this place of open awareness again?

ii. Light Visualization Meditation

Light is an often-used metaphor in spiritual practice. It literally brings us out of the dark. A focus on the light can also be metaphorically illuminating.

Close your eyes. Begin to focus on your breath—the inhale, the pause, the exhale, the pause.

Take a few deep breaths, sending the breath up into your head. Clear some space in your head with your breath.

Bring your mind to a standstill by visualizing a clean and pure light image as an object of meditation. It may simply be light within the darkness, or it may look like the sun, or it may be a pattern of light or the flicker of a candle.

Visualize the image of the light floating gently of its own accord around your mind. Witness it gently and relaxingly. Retain your focus on the light.

Feel yourself getting lighter, maybe floating a bit. To the extent you feel tightness in your body, try to let it release and float away as well.

Be open and allow whatever escapes to escape, alleviating what you carry around.

Send your breath to your heart area.

Feel the area around your heart. Visualize the image of the light beaming from your heart, beaming through the barriers that have built up around it. Observe whether the light continues to grow, to spread. Take a few deep breaths into your heart area.

Keep your focus on the light.

Send your deepest breath into your stomach area. Witness if there are blockages between your gut and your head. These stop you from following your intuition. Let the breath open the pathway and light to flow down. Witness in silence as you continue your deep breathing.

When you are ready, refocus on your breath. The inhale, the pause, the exhale, the pause.

Open your eyes when you are ready and notice how the light outside compares to the light inside.

iii. Envision Your Potential

Be aware of your present state—physical, emotional, mentaland spiritual.

Describe for yourself where you are in your life's work today.

No judgment, just awareness.

Flash back to high school, then college, then graduate school.

Recall prior jobs.

Consider how you got to where you are.

Consider where you are in your personal life.

Who were some of the key relationships along the way?

What have you learned at your current job and who are your key relationships?

Are you satisfied that you are on the right path to achieving your life's work?

Allow yourself to answer yes or no, as an observation. Without thinking or analyzing, envision your future; let it unfold however it does or doesn't unfold through your mind. Be a witness.

Pause.

What will be your legacy?

Open your eyes. You can now analyze any thoughts or insights you may have had.

iv. Integrating the Lesson and the Meditation Technique— *What is My Best Meditation*

Close your eyes.

Focus on your breath. You don't need to change your breath.

Ask yourself: What is my best?

Pause

Say aloud the first thing that comes into your mind.

Ask again: What is my best?

Answer again.

Ask yourself: What is the best thing that I did over the last week?

Then, ask yourself: What is the best thing that I did for someone else last week?

Then, ask yourself: What is the best thing that I can do next week?

Then, ask yourself: What is the best thing that I can do for someone else next week?

Come back into consciousness; focus on your breath and slowly return.

Consider trying this practice once a week. Cooper recommends asking these questions weekly, on Friday night or Sunday night or Monday morning each week at the same approximate time. Maybe on Wednesday, you might think, "I haven't done anything great yet this week; I'd better do so." That wouldn't be so bad.

XV. GRIT—YOU LIVE WHAT YOU PRACTICE

Success is how high you bounce when you hit bottom.

George S. Patton, United States Army General

While I have known many entrepreneurs who succeeded, I have known many more who have failed and some, who had not quite failed, but were unable to achieve the organization's potential. Sometimes it took the entrepreneur selling the business or having others lead the organization to reach its potential. I also noticed in my non-profit volunteering that many organizations with great vision and nice, well-meaning people leading them fail to reach their potential.

My big "ah ha" moment came from a comment during a yoga class (and the meditation in shavasana that followed). The instructor, Alex Schimmel, is one of my all-time favorites because of his focus in class on postures that push me to my limit physically and that require focus to remember and perform. Alex also leaves me with something to think about for the rest of the day. On this day, as we were struggling through a particularly difficult sequence of postures, he said something like, "Grit is more important than skill, talent or IQ. We are practicing grit."

I instantly realized that this is my observation as well. There is an intangible quality that I observe in effective leaders that underlies all the other qualities, and the best word I heard to describe it is "grit".

What is grit? Neither Google nor Webster's Dictionary provided a satisfactory definition (which tended to focus on sand and "toughness"). I needed to create my own working definition. Brainstorming different combinations of words helped me develop the following formula:

Grit = Passion + Effort + Perseverance + Resilience

Angela Duckworth, a psychology professor at University of Pennsylvania, has been transformative on the topic of grit. Professor Duckworth published her book *GRIT: The Power of Passion and Perseverance*[184] in 2016.

Professor Duckworth developed a Grit Scale that asks ten questions that encompass the elements of how she defines grit.[185] She applied this Grit Scale to a variety of groups, including incoming cadets at West Point, contestants in a national spelling bee, and athletes on a team. In each case, a person's Grit Scale score was a better predictor of success than skill testing or IQ testing.

In their book *Grit to Great: How Perseverance, Passion and Pluck Take You from Ordinary to Extraordinary*[186], Linda Thaler and Robin Koval reference Professor Duckworth's research and apply it to daily life. They define grit as a combination of guts, resilience, initiative, and tenacity.

Thaler and Koval describe grit as being at least as important (or, they argue, even more important) than talent and intelligence when it comes to being successful. Thaler and Koval describe talent as "nothing more than a great masterpiece unpainted, a sonata unwritten, a scientific breakthrough undiscovered, an invention unrealized."[187] Talent alone is overrated. Achievement in any field requires some talent, but more important, a huge amount of effort and some intangible quality (or qualities) that seem to separate out the great from the merely average. This, in essence, is grit.

Passion

It is quite simple. A leader with passion is more likely to be followed than a leader who says the same words and does the same things without it. People want to be inspired.

There are leaders whose passion is reflected in their inspirational speeches and actions—leaders such as Vince Lombardi (winning), Martin Luther King (freedom), and Steve Jobs (innovation). When these leaders spoke, people listened, were called to action, and followed the leader.

It is certainly easier to lead with passion in an organization focused on a cause about which people are already passionate. For example, a friend of mine, Lori Braunstein, formed and led Sustainable Cherry Hill, an effort to address environmentally damaging consumption in our hometown, and to educate and engage the community to address sustainability. This organization prompted the town to institute a broader recycling program, make township buildings more energy efficient, and communicate to its residents the steps each of us can take every day to make our world more sustainable. All of the organization's volunteers shared this leader's passion. However, when she started, most of the town did not. Part of being an effective leader of this organization was communicating the content regarding sustainability and communicating the message with passion. This is what inspired others to participate in the effort and become advocates for the message.

For many organizations, however, the product or service we sell does not invoke passion. We make widgets or sell insurance or provide mundane services (like legal services). However, we may feel passion for the people involved: passion for serving the customer, passion for satisfying the needs of employees, and passion for creating and nurturing a community. The difference can be very powerful. Customers stick with products and service providers that they feel good using—either because of the product or service itself, or how they perceive the brand. Employees stay longer, work harder, and are more effective in their jobs if they care about the organization and the people there. High employee turnover is rarely good for any organization.

Not all leaders need to make big speeches to communicate and demonstrate their passion. Rather, the value of passion can be effectively achieved by setting and communicating a vision or organizational mission, nurturing the culture of the organization, and plugging away at that mission within the culture.

For example, I don't think I have ever heard the CEO of Whole Foods speak (or even know who the CEO of Whole Foods is) but as noted in Chapter VIII, I do know that Whole Foods is a healthier grocery store with passion for health, wellness and social responsibility, including organic farming. This is clearly communicated to and by its employees and displays the differentiating passion of this organization.

Some leaders are inspirational writers, speakers or activists. Some leaders demonstrate their passion by being the first one in the office in the morning and the last one to leave in the evening. Some leaders demonstrate their passion through communicating goals and showing pride in goal achievement. It is not about the leader taking credit for an achievement, but sharing the achievement with the team. Some leaders, like both the former and current Chair of my law firm, seem to live their lives with passion and integrity; this is conveyed in every message they send (verbal and nonverbal). Those are the leaders whom people want to follow.

Effort

Duckworth examined the correlation between talent and achievement. What she theorized is:

Talent x Effort = Skill

Skill x Effort = Achievement

According to Duckworth, talent is how quickly your skills improve when you invest effort. Achievement is what happens when you take your acquired skills and use them. Thus, effort counts twice.[188]

During our learning phase, we use our natural talents to develop core skills. Although the most effective people continue to learn and develop their skills throughout their careers, in our youth we spend more of our time on skill development. We have all seen people with natural talent who do not make a full effort, as well as those who seem to have average talent and work twice as hard. In school, either tactic can work to get an "A". Similarly, in high school or even college, athletes can thrive with natural talent alone and hard workers can compete. However, once you get to the big leagues, you need a high level of both talent and effort to develop the skills necessary to compete successfully as a professional athlete.

Once you reach a higher level in your career, whether in business or as a professional athlete, everyone at that level has the skills to compete. It is what you achieve with those skills (developed as a result of both talent and hard work) that determines how effective and successful you will be.

What Duckworth's theory suggests is that when you consider individuals in identical circumstances, what each achieves does depend in part on talent (how fast you can improve your skill), but it depends doubly on effort because effort builds skills and greater effort turns those skills into achievement.

For some skills, achievement comes easily. For me, this skill is math. I have natural talent, and with a modicum of effort, I can develop math skills (or at least I could in my youth; this talent appears to be waning as I struggle to assist my daughter with high school math homework). For other skills, such as developing relationships, I have much less innate talent, so it took a much greater effort for me to develop that skill. Kindness and gratitude meditation practices were important to my effort to develop attunement and grow relationship building skills. Developing the relationship-building skills alone does not actually create relationships. I have to make an even greater effort to maintain and hone my relationship-building effort so that I achieve and perpetuate successful relationships.

In describing grit, Thaler and Kovel note that initiative and tenacity are two major components.[189] Initiative is the will to get started. Leaders are often judged by their initiative. One doesn't succeed without getting started, and most leaders are self-starters. Tenacity is the ability to stay focused on a goal through adversity, with elements of persistence and resilience. Both initiative and tenacity require effort. Effort is the one prong over which we have complete control. You can't fully control your talent, the obstacles you will face, or the ultimate result. What you can control is your effort, and effort counts twice.

Many successful entrepreneurs demonstrate what seems to me (and the average person) to be unbelievable effort. Mark Galant successfully grew Gain Capital from start-up through IPO by working 14-16 hours a day, seven days a week. He was almost always in the office at midnight (although also rarely in before 10:00 a.m.). He has the talent to develop proprietary foreign exchange dealing algorithms, the skill as a trader, and the vision to create a platform to allow anyone, rather than just large financial institutions, to trade currencies, but the trait that struck me was his drive and continued effort to propel the organization to success. I see countless similar examples of entrepreneurs displaying seemingly constant extraordinary effort.

Perseverance

"If at first you don't succeed, try, try again." Most of us probably remember that saying from childhood.

Perseverance is not the same as effort. Perseverance is a steadfastness in doing something despite difficulty or delay in achieving success. It builds on effort ... but is more than effort. The individual with perseverance approaches achievement as a marathon rather than a sprint. Perseverance is continuing on a course of action and course correcting around obstacles.

I have observed many emerging companies that were seemingly down to their last dollar and on the verge of bankruptcy and dissolution on their quest for success. Some entrepreneurs gave up and found a steady "day job." Others pushed through, stalled what seemed to others like inevitable failure, and pulled the proverbial "rabbit out of a hat" when the big customer order came in or a venture capital investor finally shared their vision.

I recently heard Mark Alles, the CEO of Celgene, tell the inspiring story of a failed clinical trial of the company's initial core drug product before scientists realized an ancillary patient benefit from the trial results, repurposed the drug, and developed it into a multi-billion dollar pharmaceutical product. The setback could have bankrupted this company, which now is one of the highest market cap biotech companies in the world, with products helping millions of patients. Alles noted how the company and its management persevered through the setback and wouldn't give up. He also noted how success often doesn't come in the way it was originally planned; a good company is agile and able to pivot to survive. Months later, Mark was considering a $75 billion offer to acquire Celgene.

Virtually all development stage companies go through similar struggles, at times excited by groundbreaking opportunities and at times frustrated by barriers seemingly too big or too numerous to overcome. A serial successful biotech CEO recently told me that his main job as CEO is cheerleader to keep the team's spirits up so the entire organization can continue to persevere on its road to, hopefully, success.

Interestingly, Duckworth points out that people with grit do not rely on positive feedback to spur them on and keep them motivated. Rather, they are more internally motivated and summon their perseverance from inner confidence that they are on the right path. It is for this reason that people with grit are often described as having strong character. Character is something you can continue to develop over time. Character is shaped by your experiences, your reaction to those experiences, and others' reaction to your reaction. Character can be developed regardless of job title, income, or education.

That is my observation as well. Effective leaders display more than passion and effort; they have strong character that facilitates not just their personal perseverance but leads their entire organization to persevere through the inevitable ups and downs of business and life in general.

Resilience

While perseverance is steadfastness in doing something despite difficulty, it is not sufficient to define grit. Grit includes resilience—one's reaction to failure along the way. Perseverance describes action, while resiliency describes mental reaction. Both are equally important components of grit. Resilience does not come from steady success, but from reaction to failure. Often those who demonstrate the most grit have overcome significant personal obstacles. We never know what obstacles we will face during our lives, and everyone faces different ones. Life is not linear. Sandberg uses an interesting analogy describing business advancements as no longer being a corporate ladder but a jungle gym where we climb from point to point, sometimes up but sometimes sideways, to get to a different path. [190] The key is how we react to the obstacles, and how resilient we can become.

SUCCESS

| What people think it looks like | What it really looks like |

This graphic[191] illustrates our path to success. Resilience is the willingness to stay on the path despite the detours.

Steve Jobs, in his commencement speech at Stanford University, noted that getting fired from Apple was the best thing that could have ever happened to him (although I am sure it didn't seem like it at the time). The heaviness of being successful was replaced with the lightness of being a beginner again, less sure about everything. It freed Jobs to fail again before entering the most economically successful period of his life. After his first stint at Apple, Jobs went on to found NeXT Computers, which failed. He could have given up—he had earned plenty of money and he could have bought an island and retired. Instead, he returned as CEO of Apple, with the same creativity and passion for innovation, but with more humility and a realization that he needed to communicate and build some consensus rather than ordering everyone around and trying to control every detail. Only during Jobs' second stint as Apple CEO did Apple become one of the greatest companies in the world.

After observing grit in effective leaders, I began to wonder what creates grit. Although some people seem to have more grit than others do naturally, Professor Duckworth considers that you can learn grit and teach it to your children.[192]

Professor Duckworth cites the work of Mike Feinberg and David Levin, who she describes as two "gritty" *Teach for America* teachers who developed what is known as KIPP (Knowledge is Power Program) for schools, which seeks to teach the core attributes of grit to children around the world.

In the same way that Dale Carnegie noted that it is not just what you say but how you say it that can make a difference, Feinberg and Levin recognized that the language that we use as teachers, parents and mentors could either undermine or promote the growth mindset and grit. Duckworth offers the following examples:[193]

Undermines Grit	Promotes Grit
"You're a natural! I love that."	"You're a learner! I love that."
"Well, at least you tried."	"That didn't work. Let's talk about how you approached it and what might work better."
"Great job! You are so talented."	"Great job! What's one thing that could have been better?"
"This is hard. Don't feel bad if you can't do it."	"This is hard. Don't feel bad if you can't do it yet."
"Maybe this just isn't your strength. Don't worry—you have other things to contribute."	"I have high standards. I'm holding you to them because I know we can reach them together."

When I first read the comments on the left side, they seemed like nice supportive statements that I might make—and have made. However, comparing these comments to those on the right side reveals how people who promote grit can promote greater achievement.

Thaler and Koval also conclude that grit can be learned—sometimes voluntarily and sometimes just through life's circumstances.[194]

Grit is promoted not just in our teaching, but in our doing. My wife and I both have grit (although we didn't have the name for it until recently). Duckworth cites author and activist James Baldwin, who said, "Children have never been very good at listening to their elders, but they have never failed to imitate them."[195] Maybe that is why our children exhibit grit. Still, now that I am more aware of it, I can see that tweaking my language can further promote grit in our kids and in the work place.

We often follow the bad habits of our fellow workers, as well as the best practices. It is also very difficult to change habits that have become ingrained in the culture of an organization. As leaders, we can't instruct those in our organization to exhibit grit or take a "grit course"; rather, we have to model it, reward those who exhibit grit (instead of blaming for failure), and change our language to promote passion, effort, perseverance and resiliency over time as part of organizational culture.

One of my favorite and most successful entrepreneurs, Bill Green, recently wrote a book called *All In: 101 Real-life Business Lessons for Emerging Entrepreneurs.*[196] His book starts: "I know people like you. You've got 'that look' in your eye. It's a look of fierce determination. While all your friends are out having brunch, playing Pokéman GO, or doing yoga in their spare time, here you are reading a business book…you want to make things happen."[197] Bill didn't use the word "grit" but he demonstrates it and uses the words that constitute grit. The irony that he is contrasting grit and yoga, as I seek to articulate how yoga can build grit, is not lost on me.

Bill tells great stories of his middle-class youth living on the edge of prosperity. Bill held more jobs before he turned 18 than I will hold in my lifetime. His father was a hardware buyer for a large regional department store chain and Bill would go to work with him as a child and work for stickers (which he would resell to his school friends for a profit). I also used to go to work with my Dad on Saturday mornings in the clothing manufacturing company he owned. I would do whatever needed to be done (my favorite location was shipping), and I worked for baseball cards (a dime pack a day). .

Over time, Bill developed a knowledge and passion for hardware. Bill started selling excess parts from a local supplier at flea markets, then opened a hardware store with his father. He got the idea to sell to apartment house owners on credit, and scaled the business nationally to get better supply pricing and replicate his business model in other markets. He eventually completed a private equity investment and IPO and acquired fifteen companies from 1996 to 2001 At the right time, Bill cashed out and transitioned management to someone who could scale further by moving into other industry areas. The business was ultimately sold to Home Depot for $1.8 billion.

Bill has passion. In his chapter *Turn Your Passion into Your Trade*[198], Bill notes: "If you can make your passion your business, you will have a fulfilling career and always love what you do. The happiest people I know do what they love." I feel that way as well. It wasn't that Bill innately loved hardware. It was one of the few things he knew a lot about, so he got to know more, the special parts, how each works, where it comes from, how it's made, the people who make and sell them, and the people who buy them and why. Over time, he became passionate about hardware. People often ask me why I like being a lawyer, since so many lawyers seem so miserable. I often respond that I love solving puzzles. Each transaction is a puzzle with a lot of moving pieces. The more complex the transaction (regulated industry, proprietary technology, doing business globally), the more complex the puzzle. I love solving complex puzzles. I witnessed how Bill's passion was infectious. You want to follow Bill. You want to be part of his team. You want to help him succeed.

No one outworks Bill. His effort was 24/7. I loved the story in his book about his three childhood paper routes.[199] Bill didn't get through college, but he unquestionably is smart and talented. Bill applied that effort along with the intelligence and talent he was born with; he experienced life and learned from those experiences; he read business books and listened to tapes from master salesmen; he developed skills. He then took those skills, surrounded himself with others who combined skill and enthusiasm, and achieved success beyond anything he would have imagined.

Bill also demonstrates the steadfastness over time that constitutes perseverance. Many of his 101 lessons are different ways of describing perseverance. A memoir is a great way to witness perseverance and the ability to adapt both personally and professionally. I realized reading Bill's book that there is a subtle difference between those who persevere simply by doing the same thing for a long period of time and those who continue to adapt and grow over time to overcome obstacles. I also noted that Bill performs triathlons, the physical demonstration of the perseverance that exhibits in everything he does in his life.

Bill's career was not without obstacles. In fact, in a chapter titled *Make Lemonade out of Lemons Life Deals*, Bill describes how his hardware career launched out of his father's job loss when Bill was 17. First, Bill had to make some money at flea markets to help the family, and his father, Marty, spent time teaching him all about hardware and business. I have always thought fondly of the fact that he named the company Wilmar (a combination of William and Marty).[200] In Bill's first acquisition, he tried to rebrand the business "Wilmar" and implement Wilmar business process improvements right away. That model resulted in lost customers and lost local key personnel, but he learned from his mistake. Thereafter, Wilmar transitioned the brand name and introduced efficiencies, including superior technology, over time in a seamless way to the customer and with sensitivity to acquired personnel of the benefits by explaining the value created from use of the national business processes.. Being resilient in the face of setback is different from being persistent, but both qualities are inherent in those with grit. Bill's grit is a key contributor to the effectiveness of the organizations he leads.

It is only thinking about this in retrospect that I realize that my grit characteristics were instilled during my childhood and grew during the course of my lifetime, in part, through yoga and meditation. Grit can be learned. I realize that when I feel passion for something and devote myself to make the effort, I can be resilient and persevere. I can be successful, lead others effectively as a team pursuing a goal, all of which facilitates achieving my personal and organization's potential, whether that is at work, in the community or at home. I also now realize the greatest facilitator of growth for me was the practice of yoga.

Yoga to Develop Grit

There are multiple styles of yoga. When writing this book, I initially focused on the more gentle styles of yoga, which seem at first more meditative. It wasn't until I started practicing different yoga styles, including "power yoga," that I realized the truth of what yoga teacher Alex Schimmel often says: "We live our life as we practice on the mat." Yoga is an ideal meditative practice to develop grit because it pushes you to your physical limits on that day at that time in that posture. If you look around the room, everyone is doing the posture a bit differently, bending farther or doing a variation of the posture. At the same time, it is a mindful push to your perceived limit. Simultaneously, you don't want to hurt yourself.

Grit is knowing the difference, pushing past your previously perceived limit, but not so far that you break. That is when the growth comes.

i. Yin Yoga

Yin yoga is a slow-paced style of yoga with poses, or asanas, that are held for long periods of time—five minutes or more per pose is typical. The teaching of yin yoga in the Western world, beginning in the late 1970s, was initiated by martial arts expert and Taoist yoga teacher Paulie Zink and was spread by developers Paul Grilley and Sarah Powers.[201] Physically, yin yoga poses apply moderate stress to the connective tissues of the body—the tendons, fascia, and ligaments—with the aim of increasing circulation in the joints and improving flexibility. Mentally, yin yoga can be a torturous effort after the first couple of minutes holding a pose. Interestingly, the torture is created primarily by your mind, which just wants you to move instead of staying still.

In one class, as we were holding our pose, Alex quoted Ralph Waldo Emerson, who said: "A hero is no braver than an ordinary man, but he is brave five minutes longer"—and it all clicked. We were practicing holding longer than our minds wanted us to hold. We were practicing and building courage and grit.

Ironically, weeks later, when I started to research grit, I found that Thaler and Koval used a similar General Patton quote to describe the fact that grit begins with the courage to take on a tough challenge. Grit is about putting yourself out there and declaring your intention to triumph, even if success seems unlikely or the path to success seems more difficult than you can handle.

Yin yoga teaches us that you don't succeed if you don't try, and sometimes (often), it is not your body or external situations that are holding you back, but your mind telling you that you can't do it. "Don't even try."

"It is too hard." Overcoming that "give up" message from the mind on the yoga mat trains us to bypass that message from the mind in life, showing courage, and persevering a little longer.

ii. Bikram Yoga

While yin yoga is a gentle holding of poses, Bikram yoga is physically rigorous and a different way to teach and practice the development of grit.

Bikram yoga is a system of yoga that Bikram Choudhury developed from traditional hatha yoga postures and popularized beginning in the early 1970s. All Bikram yoga classes run for 90 minutes and consist of the same series of 26 postures. Bikram yoga is a hot yoga style practiced in a room heated to 40 °C (104 °F) with a humidity level of 40 percent. All official Bikram classes are taught by Bikram-certified teachers who have completed nine weeks of formal training. I have never met anyone who didn't suffer in their first Bikram class. This was actually the first yoga practice to which I was introduced. A close friend was doing it and encouraged her husband and me to give it a shot by challenging us, saying that we couldn't even make it through one class. I had been used to working out in a gym with a combination of cardio and weight lifting, and I did not at that time consider yoga to be exercise.

At that time of my life, my ego was always up for a challenge. However, Bikram yoga was "butt kicking" from an exercise point of view. Just walking into the 104 °F room and sitting there for a few minutes is difficult. The postures start out with breathing exercises stretching the body in the heat. The standing postures promote flexibility, strength and balance. The postures require a significant physical effort and focus and are sufficiently difficult so that if you are not paying full attention to the postures, you can literally fall on your face (if you don't first pass out from the heat). This promotes being in the present moment. As the standing series continues, you get tired both physically and mentally (your ego and your passion for completion is pitted against your ability to persevere and the call of your mind to quit). On some days, I couldn't make it all the way through and needed to take a break (by break, I mean a few sips of water before I was supposed to drink, lowering my arms in between set numbers when I was supposed to keep them raised, or maybe a minute break on the mat in child pose). It was always a tough battle in my mind until "take a break" would win. The satisfaction of making it through or reaching a new level in a posture generally overwhelmed the mental chatter telling me to quit. We went at 6:30 am three days a week for six months. Nothing better taught me the lessons of grit—the passion for completion, the significant effort to make it through, the persistence when my mind wanted to quit, and the resilience to bounce back after a break.

After six months, I turned 40. I had learned enough lessons from Bikram yoga. It was just too unpleasant. Ten years later, my middle daughter started practicing Bikram yoga. I have joined her for a few classes. As a parent, I could think of no better way of teaching her grit.

iii. Power Yoga or Ashtanga Yoga

Ashtanga yoga is a combination of yoga breathing and fast-paced yoga flow or "vinyasa" yoga. The Sanskrit word "vinyāsa" refers to a transition between two different positions, and describes the process of transition between each yoga posture with the breath. Ashtanga means eight limbs or branches, of which asana or physical yoga posture is merely one branch, and breath or pranayama is another. Power yoga is a generic term that may refer to any type of aerobically vigorous yoga practice that flows with the breath.

Following the "what we practice on the mat, we live in our life" philosophy, I want to live my life with passion and intensity, but I don't want to be living my life with the extreme intensity of a Bikram yoga class. I prefer the smooth flow of the vinyasa, which includes breath (the inhale, the brief pause, the exhale and the brief pause) along with every movement.

Power style yoga provides a combination of the vinyasa flow and an intensity that requires being present, practicing reaching your fullest expression of the poses, and working through the periods of discomfort. It is also healthy physical exercise.

Yoga teacher Alex Schimmel often begins his power yoga class with: "This is a breathing class with postures to accompany the breathing." That is part of the lesson of power yoga (and the practice that we take into life). When life is moving too fast and seems too hard, we can seemingly slow it down by focusing again on our breath and taking one thing at a time—one breath at a time, one movement at a time. We keep up the effort, we persevere through the experience, and we are resilient; we bounce back when we are not able to accomplish something or have to adjust. We try to do so without any negative self-judgment. In yoga class, we can personally adjust for an injury or other physical limitation and do what feels right for our body on that particular day at that particular time. We use our meditative focus on the breath to push us through, while developing grit.

Another lesson from yoga practice that I learned recently was when yoga teacher Lisa Greenberg Gonzalez asked us to try to do our Vinyasa routine backwards (in opposite order). It was so uncomfortable. She explained that it is okay to sometimes go backwards; we are more comfortable going forward linearly, but that is not how life always works. If we sometimes practice going backwards in yoga and push through the discomfort, it will help us persevere through life's setbacks, which may still be unwelcome and uncomfortable, but we will know we can do it.

iv. Integrating the Meditation Technique and the Leadership Principle—30 Day Exercise Challenge

Choose a challenging exercise practice. It doesn't have to relate to yoga and certainly doesn't have to be Bikram yoga. You don't have to approach this as you would training to run a marathon.

If you don't think yoga is your thing (although I believe yoga can be everyone's thing), consider jogging or bicycling or another challenging activity. If you have a physical limitation, take that into account in choosing your challenge.

Set a goal beyond your comfort zone.

Set an intention for a 30-day practice.

Know that it will be difficult, that your passion for self-improvement will be tested. You will have to exert more effort than you will want to some of the time. It will be necessary to persevere, to push through the natural instinct to quit when times get tough, and on some days you will likely fail to achieve your goal (or even to start), which will require resilience to try again the next day.

You will be practicing and developing grit.

By making the effort to develop grit through these practices, you will develop the skills for greater perseverance and resilience in your life, both at home and at work, and new ways to express your passion. You will also benefit from healthy exercise. What you practice in your meditation, you will come to live in your life.

XVI. THE TIPPING POINT—HOW A LITTLE MEDITATION AND A GROWTH MINDSET CAN MAKE A BIG DIFFERENCE

When you change the way you look at things,
the things you look at change.

—Wayne Dyer, self-help author

One of my favorite Broadway show titles is the 1980s musical "I Love You, You're Perfect, Now Change" about New York City couples growing over time from dating to old age. That title really sums up for me the final leadership lesson for this book. A willingness to change doesn't mean there is something "wrong" with us. You may be "perfect" the way you are; it is okay that you are who you are (perfect even with all your imperfections). It is also positive (and not inconsistent) to have a willingness for further growth and to imbue within the organizations in which you participate (and maybe love) a willingness to change even when the organization is doing well, to continue to grow and to continuously seek to realize potential. That is a growth mindset. Effective leaders have a growth mindset and are willing to implement effective change. Sometimes that change is a tweaking improvement and sometimes that change needs to be transformational in order to meet evolving market demands and opportunities.

A Harvard Business Review article *What Sets Successful CEOs Apart*[202] notes four key behaviors of successful CEOs. The one that struck me is "adapting proactively." Effective leaders don't just implement change for change's sake (which does sometimes seem to happen when there is a change of leadership). Rather, they spend a greater percentage of time thinking about the long-term, while keeping an eye on the short term and medium term with reliable results, in order to proactively implement over time the changes that will maximize overall performance.

Change is daunting. For most of us, change is one of our biggest aversions or fears. We might believe change is an admission that we were wrong before, or at least not doing things as well as we could have. Changing something in an organization is even more difficult, as the change is often met with group resistance. The leader of the change may be taking a personal and professional risk. Being aware of changes needed in your organizations as well as the barriers to those changes is critical to planning successful tactics to implement change effectively. You can't use the same solution or same style for every situation. However, if you work in an organization where people don't believe that the organization can change or be changed, the organization will not change. Over time, a static organization is unlikely to prosper. At the same time, too much change too fast, or the wrong changes, can disrupt short-term performance—and without reliable short-term performance, a leader may not be in his or her position for the long term.

As discussed in Chapter XIII, being aware of resistance to change, and avoiding the potential shame from making mistakes or a failed outcome, can open us up to a greater willingness to take thoughtful risks, adapt and grow. As discussed in Chapter XIV, developing vision and keeping our focus on the opportunities while being in tune with our gut and heart, as well as our mind, can provide us the insight that will facilitate reaching our long-term potential both personally and professionally without undue short-term sacrifice. As discussed in Chapter XV, passion, effort, perseverance and resilience, the qualities of grit, push effective leaders through the ups and downs, the mini-successes and mini-failures, that accompany the realization of potential. To be an effective leader, you need more than good intentions—you need to have a growth mindset, both personally and professionally. You need to be part of an organization where continued evolution is part of your organization's corporate culture.

One of the most insightful observations about change is from Malcolm Gladwell's book, *The Tipping Point: How Little Things Can Make a Big Difference.*[203] The observation that little things can make a big difference is not a new theory, but Gladwell's application of it to business is quite insightful. Gladwell's tipping point is that magic moment when an "idea or trend . . . tips and spreads like wildfire." It is but a series of little moments by many people happening at roughly the same time that creates the tipping point moment.

Gladwell notes that ideas, products, messages and behaviors can spread like viruses. Those that spread have three common characteristics:[204]

1. Contagiousness
2. Little causes have big effect
3. Change happens in a moment

Gladwell's book is a series of examples of his observations of tipping point products and behaviors along with analyses of the reasons. Fashion trends create a classic tipping point situation. A new style appears in Vogue or GQ; that fashion is photographed on a celebrity or other trend-setter online, on TV, or in popular magazines; other social influencers take notice; and stores add the fashion to their collections. People buy them and post photographs of themselves on Instagram and Facebook, and a new fashion success is born. Gladwell's "tipping point" examples range from new product offerings to communicable diseases to popularity of a children's television show. Once the idea, concept or product reaches the tipping point, it "tips" into widespread popularity.

We see this all the time in the workplace with the introduction of a new technology. Initially, no one wants to change, and many people ignore or try to ignore the new technology. It is disruptive. A few tech-friendly "early adopters" begin to use it, and they tell the rest of us of the benefits. More people adopt. At some point, no one wants to be left out or left behind, so others go ahead and try it. Pretty soon, everyone (or almost everyone) is using the new technology.

This can also work in reverse. We may have an opportunity to try something new. If early adopters are not satisfied and discuss the disadvantages, significant resistance to change develops. Memos from bosses may "instruct" implementation. Resistance feels justified as long as most people continue to resist. In these circumstances, change just won't happen.

This example may "date" me, but I remember when our law firm switched word processing programs from WordPerfect to Microsoft Word. For a while you could use both, but more of the world outside the legal market was using Microsoft Word and there were compatibility issues with clients and other law firms when converting documents. The resistance was intense, particularly among the administrative staff, who knew WordPerfect inside and out. Many had no experience with Microsoft Word. I recall the outrage over the footnoting feature — how much easier and better WordPerfect was. The "reveal" field for formatting documents was far superior in WordPerfect and not at the time incorporated into Microsoft Word. I didn't even know what a reveal field was, and I rarely used footnotes in a document, but I wanted to support my outraged secretary. I recall using WordPerfect while both were available to us until the last minute when, due to lack of consistent adoption, the IT group pulled our ability to create new WordPerfect documents. It was fortunate that they did. Although the change was hard, not using the same word processing program as our clients would have certainly cost us clients. Change was necessary.

Gladwell analogizes change in the workplace and the world to health epidemics. He describes the three rules of epidemics[205] and how we can deliberately start and control positive epidemics. Epidemics are a function of: (i) the people who transmit the infectious germs, (ii) the infectious germ itself, and (iii) the environment in which the infectious germ is operating.

For businesses wanting to spread a message, the people doing so matter. Gladwell indicates that to reach a tipping point, an idea needs people who are (i) connectors (bring key people together), (ii) mavens (thought leaders who adopt), and (iii) salespeople.[206] If the right people endorse your idea, concept or product, it has a shot.

In 2002, I met Steven Krein and Unity Stoakes. They were selling promotions.com to iVillage, and I was recommended as legal counsel by board member Ian Berg (partner of Wayne Kimmel from Chapter IX); this recommendation was supported by general counsel Bari Krein, with whom I had served on a panel at the Wharton School several years earlier. Several years later in 2007, Steven and Unity formed OrganizedWisdom. com, which obtained venture capital investment from Wayne and Ian's venture fund. OrganizedWisdom's mission was to organize for consumers the wealth of medical information available on the Internet so that patients could make informed decisions. Other sites such as WebMD, Health Control and Health A to Z grabbed this market more quickly, but Steven and Unity had seen the opportunity to reinvent how healthcare information is obtained, shared and used to improve patient outcome.

They pivoted in 2010 to form the StartUp Health movement to transform healthcare. In addition to Wayne, they recruited credible "mavens," to serve on the board. Steve, Unity and Wayne are masterful "connectors", but they needed a compelling vision and business model. The mission became to improve the health and well-being of everyone in the world by supporting a global army of entrepreneurial health transformers. Thinking big, talking big and following it up, they created an entrepreneurial ecosystem for digital health companies and other organizations. Word spread. StartUp Health onboarded ten companies in its first group, then raised funding to onboard close to 100 additional companies over the next couple of years; they now have onboarded over 250 health transformer companies. They attracted major corporations in the health field as sponsors to connect the entrepreneurs with potential strategic partners. They improved their added value substantive Academy, which provides valuable best-in-class guidance to the entrepreneurs and facilitates situations whereby the entrepreneurs can connect and learn from each other. Finally, they hired staff to further sell and implement the vision (and used their appreciative portfolio companies and StartUp Health Transformers™ to "spread the word"). StartUp Health passed its tipping point and, with its portfolio companies and partners, is literally improving the health and well-being of nearly everyone in the world.

In epidemics, the messenger matters because the messengers are what makes something spread. But the content (the infectious germ itself) matters as well. The quality of the idea—and how well it resonates with those who hear about it—affects whether the spread will be successful. An idea that adds value becomes "sticky" (some for a period of time and some seemingly permanently), while other ideas pass by our eyes and ears and are never seen or heard of again, much less spread. The "stickiness factor," as Gladwell calls it, is the quality that compels people to pay close attention to a product, concept or idea and then stick with it.[207]

The final prong of epidemics is the context or environment in which an idea spreads. I can't tell you how many times I have seen great entrepreneurs with a great idea and a great plan, but they are not at "the right place at the right time" and go bankrupt, only to watch some other company years later launch a similar idea and be successful. According to Gladwell, the context in the social or community environment must provide the right atmosphere for an idea to tip.[208]

As a parent, each Fall I tried to guess the fad toy of the upcoming holiday season so I could try to get the "must have" toy early and not disappoint my children. The toy companies jockey to get mind share and prime the toy-buying environment. Remember Cabbage Patch dolls, Koosh balls, and Tickle Me Elmo? The successful toy company creating the trend must pick the right toy for that year in the context of the environment.

Other attempts at new product introduction don't go so well. I recall when the Coca Cola Company tried to change its formula for the first time in close to 100 years. They sampled consumer groups blindfolded, who chose the sweeter version as better. The company took a huge risk to increase its cola market share over Pepsi and introduced "New Coke." The company must have thought the environment was right for change. However, the firestorm against the change was loud and definitive. The consumer didn't want to change a good thing. At least Coke quickly admitted its "mistake" and reintroduced the original formulation within three months, on its way to future increases in global Coke sales in part due to the publicity and raising of awareness of how much people prefer original Coke (even if not in blind taste tests).

Part of my motivation in writing and publishing this book is the belief that meditation is not a "New Coke." My intuition tells me that this may be the right time and environment for meditation practice to reach its tipping point. That requires those who have benefited from meditation to share their experience—the payback from meditating just 10 minutes a day. My observation is that enough influencers, who may include you, are now taking an interest in yoga and meditation practice. If it works for us, not just for personal wellness but as a performance enhancer, and we stay with it, it is sticky and it will be contagious as we live as we practice and "spread the word" regarding the benefits of meditation to others.

The step from vision of change to actual change is a very big step indeed. If meditation can help us improve ourselves, our relationships, our ability to facilitate the success of others and our organization; if it can develop our grit characteristics and our ability to create greater influence from a place of perspective and balance, why isn't everyone doing it? Why isn't everyone meditating every day?

For some, the answer may be simply lack of awareness of meditation. Others may be aware of the benefits of meditation, but for one reason or another just don't have a willingness to adopt the daily commitment at this time in their lives. Others may find Buddhist or other religious language off-putting or think of meditation as only as a potential fix for stress reduction. Simply following your intuition to choose the right technique and teaching resource for you at this time may be all you need to get started. You may only use meditative practice as a supplement when you feel a little off track and have difficulty staying in the present moment. You may use it when something inside is blocking intuition's path to your mind or your ability to connect from your heart to others. Meditation can be the tool to get you back on track when needed. You may be able to make meditation a habit and benefit from a daily practice. Stay aware of your experience both during and derived from your meditation practice. Can you tie the experiential benefit to any or all of the four foundational meditation pillars. Can you observe yourself being more effective in any of the 13 traits of effective leaders? Does your meditation practice facilitate a growth mindset and the desire and ability to grow your skill level with the other traits?

Once you try meditation and experience the benefits, convincing is no longer necessary. You can pursue your own preferred meditation technique, style and frequency. Maybe you will tell friends, family and social media of your success, and pretty soon more people are experiencing the benefits. Maybe we can together create a meditation epidemic.

For meditation practice to reach the tipping point, we need to:

1. Practice meditation daily
2. Follow our intuition
3. Spread the word

Meditate Daily

How does whether or not you meditate make a difference in the world? The world is big, and so much is out of our control that we often feel defeated, as if what we do doesn't make a difference. At the same time, there is only so much each of us can do; very few of us have an opportunity to impact more than a person or two at a time for more than a moment or two. That is the beauty of the tipping point concept. You only have to do your small part to make a meaningful impact.

What if you are making a little contribution to humanity by simply meditating daily? What if having a group of leaders engage in regular meditation will incrementally help your organization be more successful? A daily meditation practice begins to bring those key "little things that make a big difference" to the front of our minds. If we can just hang on to one insight a day, one relationship to solidify, one deep-seated anger to forgive, one action to take, one sight to behold, these little things add up to make a big difference.

I have heard that Mahesh Prasad Varma, who developed Transcendental Meditation (TM), also studied math and physics at Allahabad University. In 1957, he embarked on a world tour with the intention to spread TM. He was vocal about the idea that if enough people (to be precise, a number equaling the square root of 1 percent of the world's population) practiced TM, the positive energy would bring about world peace.

This is what Gladwell would later call a tipping point.

From the feedback I have received, what stops a lot of people from meditating is a belief they can't do it or may "fail." They may have an experience or two where the mind won and the chatter wouldn't stop. That happens for everyone, which is why meditation is called a "practice". Don't quit.

I find that about half the time, I don't come up with anything impactful during a meditation session, but the insights from the other half make daily meditation practice worth it. I have never come across anyone who "fails" at meditation—it is just a question of patience and practice (and letting go of judgment of result).

You may simply need to be using the right meditation technique for you at this time. Sometimes you may focus on your breath, seeking nothingness and seeing what fills the void. Sometimes you may set your intention to focus on your relationships and sometimes you may focus on who you are and what your life is all about. Sometimes you may set your intention to focus on an issue that you haven't been able to solve in your daily consciousness. Sometimes you may set your intention on something and something different pops up. You may only achieve quiet mind when you stop trying to do so. Commit yourself to sit and try not to judge the results. Untimely, by accessing your inner wisdom during meditation, you obtain the potential to lead a more fulfilling life, feel in sync with your self, and be more aware. We often don't know why we are in sync or out of sync with realizing our potential, but we do generally know the difference.

We all lead frenzied lives. Many things occur that we can't control. Most of us don't choose to have a frenzied life. However, we *can* choose to take 10 minutes a day to make our frenzied lives better and more effective. We can remind ourselves over and over that each breath is a new moment, and while we may not control all around us or the result, we do control our reaction and how much we attach to the result. We can then choose to have a willingness to change, and subsequently we can choose *what* to change. That is a growth moment.

Follow Your Intuition

A by-product of meditation that facilitates realization of potential is greater access to and awareness of your intuition. In his book *Blink*, Gladwell focuses on the role of intuition. Gladwell describes how the reading of a situation by our adaptive unconsciousness (intuition) can actually be much more accurate than our conscious perception of a situation. Gladwell notes that intuition assists us with the "little things,"[209] those moment-to-moment decisions that make an impact. Intuition also assists us with the "big things." When you learn to be more aware of the difference between your intuition and your thoughts, you learn from your personal experience that your intuition is correct; you begin to trust your intuition because your personal experience demonstrates it to be true. Your mind may try to insert fear and self-doubt, but you become more effective at everything you do when you are able to push through the fear and self-doubt to pursue the action (or inaction) that your intuition tells you is the correct choice.

With practice, we can bring wisdom and perspective to all aspects of our life and leadership by operating with a bit more reliance on intuition (the brain in our gut, as Cooper put it). Huffington references the work of psychologists Martin Seligman and Michael Kahana, who note that important decisions are best arrived at by intuition rather than by linear reasoning, although linear reasoning may help rationalize the value of that decision. They go on to describe intuition-based decision making as "(a) rapid, (b) not conscious, (c) used for decisions involving multiple dimensions, (d) based on vast stores of prior experience, (e) characteristic of experts, (f) not easily or accurately articulated afterwards, and (g) often made with high confidence."[210]

This intuition comes from deep inside, which is why we sometimes refer to it as a "feeling in my bones." Intuition, more than thought, is coming from your place of wisdom and perspective.

Gladwell describes in *Blink* how reading a situation using intuition can actually be much more accurate than carefully considered, logical, conscious, sequential reasoning. Gladwell relays a story of a Greek statue acquired by the J. Paul Getty Museum in Los Angeles.[211] After executing all of the traditional authentication tests over fourteen months, a team of scientists was ready to vouch for its authenticity. Thomas Hovering, former director of the Metropolitan Museum of Art, intuitively knew otherwise: after a few seconds of looking at the statue, he had an instant repulsion. He didn't know why, but he knew from his lifetime of experience to trust his instinct. They ordered more tests, and it turned out that Hovering's instinct was right. The statue was a fake.

We all have access to intuition if we listen to it and nourish it. We may not be able to identify a fake Greek statue, but we can use our intuition for what is important in our daily lives. Meditation is a tool to uncover, access, and remain aware of that intuition, and to make sure its wisdom doesn't stay buried. Once you let intuitive information into your conscious mind and become aware of it, you are not required to follow it. However, you may, over time, choose to do so more frequently. After analyzing your intuition with your conscious mind and experiencing success when you follow it, you are likely to find that your intuition can be your best guide to change and resulting growth.

An engineer in one of my Leadership and Meditation classes indicated that he had been working on a project for weeks and just kept getting stuck. One day, during the meditation we were practicing in class, the entire solution just "popped" into the front of his mind. It had not been his intention to focus on that problem during the meditation, but that is just what happens. I hear similar stories repeatedly from people who experience similar breakthroughs in business or personal issues. I experience this phenomenon myself.

Meditation techniques create the opportunity to learn how to pull more from your gut and heart creating greater awareness of your intuition. What we practice in meditation, we can incorporate into our life.

So why do we often ignore or shut out that inner voice and our intuition in our lives instead of nurturing it? If we do so in the jungle or on a city street, it can literally be a matter of life and death. If we do so in our careers, it can be the difference between success and failure. It is often easier to keep doing the same thing we have been doing, even if that "sixth sense" is starting to whisper to us that something is wrong and needs to be changed. Try to pay attention when you hear that whisper. Try to come back to that intuitive feeling in your daily meditation and let it unfold. Then take whatever steps you are comfortable with and see if there are positive results that reinforce your faith in continuing down the path of change. Give your personal experience a chance to reinforce your trust in your intuition and to overcome any thoughts of self-doubt or feelings of fear that may be barriers. Cultivate a willingness to change and continue to grow. Having an open mind to personal and professional growth and taking the ten minutes a day to access your inner wisdom to know what to do are all you need to get there.

Spread the Word

The Internet has created new tipping points every day. At what point in the evolution of Facebook or Twitter or LinkedIn was there a sufficient number of users to make you want to join? Now, ideas spread quickly via social media. As you tell your friends and followers about these new ideas, they are shared by their friends and followers, spreading their reach in days or weeks or sometimes hours or minutes across the globe.

Today, ideas, products, messages, and behaviors can spread like viral epidemics do, but the tipping point concept is as old as humanity itself.

Several years ago, I heard in a speech that 2015 will be seen as the historic tipping point when access to content on mobile devices and tablets became more influential and spread information more quickly than on personal computers, TV or other forms of media. How can that knowledge alter how your organization will spread its most vital messages? Can a business continue to resist social media and thrive, short—or long-term, as a relevant organization? Technology has enabled an entirely new level of peer-to-peer communication about products and ideas and reputations.

This will certainly affect my legal practice. The introduction of Kickstarter and Crowdfunding sites may change the very essence of our emerging business legal support business model, because these sites match companies and capital on pre-arranged terms without the negotiation of legal documents. Artificial intelligence software may one day be used to prepare complex documents from simple term sheet commands. I have meditated on the question of whether or not I will continue to have a career as an emerging business lawyer if start-up businesses are not negotiating legal documents. My instinct is "yes", but my day-to-day activities may look different. With this awareness, I am able to recommend as a manager that my organization adopt knowledge management tools and adjust staffing and pricing models to be at the forefront of changing client demand, rather than left behind wondering what happened.

Spreading the word to achieve a tipping point is not a new concept and does not require technology (although it helps to speed the spread). For example, Gladwell notes that Paul Revere was able to galvanize the forces of resistance during the American Revolution in the 1770s because he knew the right people.[212] He knew the revolutionary leaders of the towns he rode through. In two hours, he covered 13 miles, but obviously couldn't talk to everyone in such a short period of time. Revere wasn't just the man with the biggest Rolodex in Boston. He was someone who had valuable content. People wanted to know precisely when the British were coming—and he knew whom to tell in each town who could then spread the word effectively and quickly. Revere had the right message at the right time. Without Facebook or the Internet or telephone lines or radio or television, colonists used bells ringing, drums beating and door knocking to spread the news like a virus until soon, everyone in town knew when the British were coming. As we all know, when the British soldiers marched into each town, revolutionary soldiers were armed and ready to ambush them.

This story teaches us that the little things each of us do, the role each of us play, can have big effects. When a small number of people start behaving differently and spread the word, that behavior can ripple outward until a "critical mass" of awareness (a tipping point) is reached, changing the world. It also teaches us that you can't do it alone. Paul Revere could not reach every door in one night. He needed to access the "connectors," have his message verified by the "mavens," and have the "salespeople" in town spread the word in order to be successful.

You can be more effective and make a positive impact on the world. In 10 minutes a day, you may find yourself intuitively wanting to spread the word of how meditation has benefitted you. As more people practice meditation, more people will be in tune with their intuition. Our intuition, when recognized and processed by our conscious mind, becomes our wisdom. Ultimately, if more of us meditate regularly, we as a society will reach a tipping point of people accessing and processing wisdom. We will stand strong on the Four pillars of Awareness, Connection, Perspective and Potential. We will display more of the 13 traits of effective leaders. We will make better decisions. We will lead the organizations in which we work and volunteer to become more effective.

Your daily meditation is key. Your daily meditation practice can create that difference.

Growth Mindset Meditation Practices

The following meditation practices can help you nurture your intuition and clear space so that the wisdom within can be released.

i. Every Moment is a New Moment Meditation

Every moment is a new moment in the universe. Every breath is a new beginning. There are literally billions of people evolving and interacting with one another so that nothing is ever the same one moment to the next. To some extent, this can seem daunting; we could consider our actions to be pointless if all actions are only momentary and fleeting. On the other hand, this presents an opportunity, as we really are not bound by our own history and are free to choose our next thought and next action in each brand new moment. We have the ability to change if we have the willingness to change.

Close your eyes or lower your gaze to a focal point in the room.

Focus on your breath, the inhale, the pause, the exhale, the pause, knowing that each breath is a new moment.

Consider this moment to be starting fresh.

Consider this moment one of infinite possibility and ability to think and act however you choose, even if different from your past tendencies.

Take deep breaths and during the pauses observe what fills the void, then take another deep breath.

Continue for approximately 10 minutes.

When you are done, make a written note of any item or items for later follow-up.

ii. Special Trait Meditation

Sometimes the wisdom comes to us simply by stepping back and looking at our self and our lives from a different perspective.

Close your eyes or lower your gaze on a focal point in the room.

Focus on your breath, the inhale, the pause, the exhale, the pause.

Repeat five times with focus, the inhale, the pause, the exhale, the pause.

Ask yourself: Why am I here?

Why are you in this room right now doing this meditation? Why did you choose to read this book?

Ask yourself: What are my top personal attributes? What makes me special?

What are the first one, two, or three most special attributes that pop into your mind?

With your attributes, your special traits, the value you can add, is there something you can do to make a greater difference—a greater difference at home, a greater difference at work, a greater difference in fulfilling why you are here?

If you are doing all you can, that is fine. If not, what stops you from doing so?

What can you do to fulfill your potential? What is the first thing that pops into your mind? If nothing pops into your mind, repeat the question.

Return your focus to your breath.

When you are ready, return to consciousness.

iii. Just Be Meditation.

We are going to end meditation technique training with what some people may have begun this book believing was all meditation was about—just being with a silent mind.

Be devoid of intention. No need to focus on nothingness, simply choose not to focus on anything. Whatever comes into your mind, let it gracefully pass on through.

Allow everything to be as it is.

Let go of your ideas and try to approach the next ten minutes from a place of radical not knowing, just observing.

Close your eyes and just be.

When you are ready, become aware again of your consciousness. Let the witness of your consciousness step back and begin to let your consciousness itself back in control of your mind. Does that seem different? Does that feel different to be back thinking versus just being?

Would you like to go back to your awareness again?

iv. Integrating the Leadership Principle and Meditation Practice—30 Day Meditation Practice

You can only change your life and better fulfill your purpose one moment at a time, one intention at a time, one day at a time and one meditation practice at a time.

Commit right now to a willingness to change.

It takes time and repetition to develop a habit. Devote yourself to 30 days straight of meditation practice at the same time in the same place for about the same length of time. If it helps you, set a timer or alarm to beep when you are supposed to be done. Try 10 minutes or whatever feels right.

Each day, you can simply focus on your breath or practice any of the meditation techniques described in this book. You can use the same technique every day or a variety based on what feels right in your gut that day.

After that, if you miss a day, you miss a day. If it doesn't work for you, it doesn't work for you. You won't know unless you give it a fair try. Thirty days is a fair try.

Building the Pillar of Potential

Meditation puts you in touch with your true authentic self—the "self" when no one else is looking. This "self" acts as a witness during meditation, whether that is observing mental pictures, thoughts, feelings, body discomfort, or something more abstract.

Meditation can help you become more aware of your strengths and the opportunities available to you. This facilitates putting yourself in a position for your strengths to shine, to take advantage of opportunities for growth and to become more effective. Meditation can also reinforce hard-to-describe intangible qualities that seem to characterize true leaders; passion, effort, perseverance and resiliency. Sitting regularly in meditation is hard to do. You must want to do it. You must actually do it. You must keep doing it when you don't want to. You must return to doing it when you cease, You must demonstrate grit.

Where your mind goes, your attention follows. As you utilize your grit traits to pursue your vision, you will encounter barriers and areas in yourself and your organization that require change. Willingness to change and continue with a growth mindset facilities your ability to add more value to others in your organization; the organizations in which you are active become more effective. The world becomes a better place. That is your potential.

CONCLUSION

If every 8-year-old in the world is taught meditation, we will eliminate violence from the world within one generation.

Dali Lama, spiritual leader

How do you progress from reading this book to evolving your own leadership style, making a greater impact in your organization and the world we live in, and becoming more effective?

Be more aware of your strengths and weaknesses. Put yourself in a role and a place where your strengths allow you to shine, and continue to work on the traits with which you are less comfortable. Add value to others whenever you can. Make and grow your relationships. Keep your actions and reactions in perspective. Accept that no one is perfect. You will not be perfect. But . . . you can be more effective. Find moments of stillness within the chaos. You can be what you want to be. You can realize your potential.

During moments of stillness, I observed the Four Pillars from meditation that provide a foundation to become more effective:

Awareness

Connection

Perspective

Potential

Each of these pillars is expressed through leadership traits I have observed in effective leaders and espoused by well-regarded business leadership authors who have influenced me. Each of these traits, and thus the pillars themselves, can be built and reinforced through daily meditation practice. As Goleman and Davidson conclude through scientific study, meditation actually changes the brain both structurally and functionally resulting in altered traits.[213] Future studies will be needed to fine tune the analysis and apply it to the Four Pillars and 13 leadership traits I have observed through my meditation practice.

Can you see the practical benefits of change through meditation? Can you see the potential for personal and organizational performance enhancement? Can you see how changing your perspective or lens by letting go of your barriers can improve your relationships with your spouse, children, work colleagues, customers and others? Can you see how reducing your stress level can increase your patience with others and your physical and mental health? Can you see how living more in the moment is the key to having more meaningful moments? Are you now more aware? For me, meditation didn't just make me "10% happier," as Dan Harris would say, but 100% more effective.

There are tangible steps that you and your organization can take to realize these practical benefits:

Center yourself as you start your day each morning.

Take a daily lunch break.

Practice different meditation techniques with awareness of what you need each time.

Introduce meditation practice to others.

Set up a wellness room at the office where anyone can take a balancing break when needed.

Return your focus to the opportunities.

Pause when you need to do so.

Listen to your inner wisdom.

Spend more time in the present moment.

We are each different, with different attributes, different purposes, in different positions with different organizations. The wisdom to know what those leadership solutions and traits are for you at this time in your current position is different for everyone and can only come from within you. Meditation assists you in accessing that wisdom.

Eckhart Tolle notes: "The transformation of human consciousness is not long a luxury...but a necessity if humankind is not to destroy itself. At the present time, the dysfunction of the old consciousness and the rising of the new are both accelerating. Paradoxically, things are getting worse and better at the same time, although the worse is more apparent because it makes more "noise."...It is in the inner stillness that we will save and transform the world."[214]

Meditation is a practice. It is not a practice to become perfect, but a practice that can help each of us grow and be more effective. It is a practice of techniques that can facilitate growth of each of the Four Pillars and development of each of the 13 Leadership Traits. It is a practice that is not isolated to your meditation time; what you practice in meditation, you extend to your life.

Different meditations help us practice being more aware physically, emotionally, intellectually, and spiritually. Some of these meditations are based on "doing something" to bring us into greater awareness of what we are doing, and some are based simply on "being" and observing for a while. What do you need at this time? As you practice meditation daily, extend your insights from meditation to live what you practice. Be more aware. Be more focused. Express more gratitude. Be more balanced. Exercise your influence wisely.

We create our own limits. As leaders, those personal limits limit the potential of our organizations. Your potential is beyond those limits. The potential of your organization is beyond those limits. Your life doesn't just happen to you, it comes from you and lives within you. Meditation teaches you to recognize your potential, and how to use your intuition and wisdom to achieve it. When you observe your life and your thoughts, feelings and actions without judgment, you will obtain a more clear perspective and have greater ability to positively impact the outcome.

Organizations are only as effective as the people leading them—not just at the top, but throughout the organization. Leadership effectiveness, both personal and organizational, starts with awareness of how things are and doesn't happen until there is a willingness to change. Organizations don't evolve unless leaders get buy-in from all levels of the organization. This requires vision, communication and focus.

The world itself is changing; technology is continuing to accelerate the pace of those changes, including how we obtain and process information. The Industrial Age gave rise to mass amounts of printed information that evolved into radio and television information, which was pushed to us by the creators of that information. We transitioned during the late 20th century to the Information Age, where information became available digitally from a variety of sources; now, there are vast amounts of additional information available for us to pull off the Internet. Factual knowledge and data analytics have become more easily available to everyone, and this is changing how we work and how we live. Can meditation be the next evolutionary step in how we process information and access wisdom?

Yoga teacher Alex Schimmel told the following story (while we were holding forearm plank, both to distract and enlighten us). Three brothers approach a wall. The first climbs the wall slowly and looks over it. He looks back at the others and shouts, "This is amazing!"; he jumps over the wall and disappears. The second brother climbs a bit faster and looks over the wall. He looks back at his third brother, reassures him that this is awesome, climbs over the wall and disappears. The third brother climbs to the top of the wall, looks over in awe and pauses. He climbs back down, walks back to town and tells the others about the greatness on the other side of the wall. He brings others from his community back to the wall so each is aware of it and can climb it when ready.

Perhaps meditation by more leaders of our commercial, political, religious, cultural and family organizations will lead us from the Information Age to the Enlightened Age. Through meditation, we develop traits and skills that allow us to become the leaders for that new age, an age where people understand that there is something greater than themselves. We will all climb the wall to access the wisdom to understand that our lives are interconnected; we as a human race are in this together. We will understand the impact of our actions on others and the need for sustainability of our physical world. We will awaken to the realization that we are connected as a species, and thus take into account in all our business and personal decisions the impact of each decision on the greater whole. We will understand that altruism is not against human nature, but rather, that if we are all connected, helping others is really helping ourselves. It is each of our responsibilities to make the world a better place — there is no one else to do so. As Maxwell might say, this will be a world in which we are all 360-degree leaders. That would be a nice world to turn over to our future generations of leaders.

This is our will—meditation is our way.

ENDNOTES

1 Wikipedia referencing Castells, M. "The Information Age" (Cambridge, Mass., Oxford 1999).

2 Darren S. Good, Christopher J. Liddy, Theresa M. Glamb, Joyce E. Gono, Kirk Warren Brown, Michele K. Duffy, Ruth A. Baer, Judson A. Brewer and Sara W. Lazer, *Contemplating Mindfulness at Work: An Integrative Review* (Journal of Management, 2015).

3 Britta K. Hölzel, James Carmody & Sara W. Lazar, "Mindfulness practice leads to increases in regional brain gray matter density", *Psychiatry Research—Neuroimaging*, Volume 191, Issue 1 (2011): pp. 36-43.

4 Gotink RA, Chu P, Busschbach JJ, Benson H, Fricchione GL, Hunink MG. *PLoS One*. 2015 Apr 16;10(4):e0124344.

5 Matthieu Ricard, Antonine Lutz, and Richard J. Davidson, "Mind of the Meditator," *Scientific American*, (November 2014): 40-43.

6 Strauss C, Cavanagh K, Oliver A, Pettman D. Mindfulness-based interventions for people diagnosed with a current episode of an anxiety or depressive disorder: a meta-analysis of randomized controlled trials. *PLoS One*. 2014 Apr 24;9(4):e96110.

7 Zou L. Yeung A. Li C. Wei BX, Chen KW Kinser PA, Chan JSM, Ren Z, *Effects of Meditative Movements on Major Depressive Disorder: A Systematic Review and Meta-Analysis of Randomized Controled Trials* (J Clin Med. 2018 Aug 1; 7(8).

8 Rod, K. Observing the Effects of Mindfulness-Based Meditation on Anxiety and Depression in Chronic Pain Patients. *Psychiatria Danubina*. 2015 Sep;27 Suppl 1:209-11.

9 Khoury B, Sharma M, Rush SE, Fournier C. Mindfulness-based stress reduction for healthy individuals: A meta-analysis. *Journal of Psychosomatic Research*. 2015 Jun;78(6):519-28.

10 de Fátima Rosas Marchiori M, Kozasa EH, Miranda RD, Monezi Andrade AL, Perrotti TC, Leite JR. Decrease in blood pressure and improved psychological aspects through meditation training in hypertensive older adults: A randomized control study. *Geriatrics and Gerontology International*. 2015 Oct;15(10):1158-64.

11 Bai Z, Chang J, Chen C, Li P, Yang K, Chi I. Investigating the effect of transcendental meditation on blood pressure: a systematic review and meta-analysis. *Journal of Human Hypertension.* 2015 Nov;29(11):653-62.

12 Aggarwal M., Bozkurt B., Panjrath G., et al; American College of Cardiology's Nutrition and Lifestyle Committee of the Prevention of Cardiovascular Disease Council. Lifestyle Modifications for Preventing and Treating Heart Failurs. J Am Coll Cardiol. 2018 Nov 6; 72(19): 2391-2405.

13 Martires J, Zeidler M. The value of mindfulness meditation in the treatment of insomnia. *Current Opinions in Pulmonary Medicine.* 2015 Nov;21(6):547-52.

14 Khalsa DS. Stress, Meditation, and Alzheimer's Disease Prevention: Where The Evidence Stands. *Journal of Alzheimers Disease.* 2015 Aug 28;48(1):1-12.

15 Banth S, Ardebil MD. Effectiveness of mindfulness meditation on pain and quality of life of patients with chronic low back pain. *International Journal of Yoga.* 2015 Jul-Dec;8(2):128-33. doi: 10.4103/0973-6131.158476.

16 Cramer H, Rabsilber S, Lauche R, Kümmel S, Dobos G. Yoga and meditation for menopausal symptoms in breast cancer survivors-A randomized controlled trial. *Cancer.* 2015 Mar 4. doi: 10.1002/cncr.29330. [Epub ahead of print]

17 Castellar JI, Fernandes CA, Tosta CE. Beneficial Effects of Pranic Meditation on the Mental Health and Quality of Life of Breast Cancer Survivors. Integr Cancer Ther. 2014 Jun 5;13(4):341-350.

18 Chafos V, Economou P. Beyond borderline personality disorder: the mindful brain. *Social Work.* 2014 Oct;59(4):297-302.

19 Chadwick P. Mindfulness for psychosis. *British Journal of Psychiatry.* 2014;204:333-4.

20 Khoury B, Lecomte T, Gaudiano BA, Paquin K. Mindfulness interventions for psychosis: a meta-analysis. *Schizophrenia Research.* 2013 Oct;150(1):176-84.

21 Chiesa A, Serretti A. Are mindfulness-based interventions effective for substance use disorders? A systematic review of the evidence. *Substance Use and Misuse.* 2014 Apr;49(5):492-512.

22 Godfrey KM, Gallo LC, Afari N. Mindfulness-based interventions for binge eating: a systematic review and meta-analysis. *Journal of Behavioral Medicine.* 2015 Apr;38(2):348-62.

23 Grace Buillok Phd, *Meditators Have Younger Brains*. Mindful. March 7, 2017.

24 Ibid.

25 Herron RE. *Changes in physician costs among high-cost Transcendental Meditation practitioners compared to high-cost nonpractitioners over 5 years*. Am J Health Promote. 2011; 26-56-60.

26 Britta K. Hölzel, James Carmody & Sara W. Lazar, "Mindfulness practice leads to increases in regional brain gray matter density", *Psychiatry Research—Neuroimaging*, Volume 191, Issue 1 (2011): pp. 36-43.

27 Studies performed by Sara Lazar and Britta Hölzes at MGH Psychiatric Neuroimaging Research Program.

28 Attributed to guru Sri K Pattabhi Jois.

29 *Healing Back Pain, the Mind Body Connection*, John E. Sorno, M.D. (NY, Warner Books, 1991).

30 John Roach, *Friday the 13th Superstitions Rotted in Bible and More*, (National Geographic, May 4, 2011)

31 Daniel Goleman and Richard J. Davidson, *Altered Traits: Science Reveals How Meditation Changes Your Mind, Brain, and Body* (New York, Penquin Random House, LLC, 2017) at p. 6.

32 Ginka Toegel & Jean-Louis Baroux. "How to Become a Better Leader." MIT Sloan Management Review, (March 20, 2012).

33 Ibid.

34 Jim Collins, *Good To Great: Why Some Companies Make the Leap...and Others Don't* (New York, Harper Collins Publishers, Inc.), p.20.

35 Collins, *Good to Great*, pp. 17-40.

36 Collins, , *Good to Great*, p. 35.

37 Collins, , *Good to Great*, p. 63.

38 Sheryl Sandberg, *Lean In, Women, Work And The Will to Lead* (Alfred Knoff, New York 2017)

39 Id at p. 149.

40 Id at p. 41.

41 Selana Rezvani, *The Next General of Future Leaders: What You Need to Lead but Won't Learn in Business School* (Praeger, Colorado 2010).

42 Id at p. 15.

43 Id at p. 16.

44 Collins, pp. 16-20.

45 Raymond M. Kethledge and Michael S. Erwin, *Lead Yourself First, Inspiring Leadership Through Solitude* (New York: Bloomsberg 2017), forward by Jim Collins

46 Robert Wright, *Why Buddhism is True, The Science and Philosophy of Meditation and Enlightenment* (Simon & Schuster, New York, 2017)

47 See www.umassmed.edu/cfm.

48 See Time Magazine Special Edition, *Mindfulness—The New Science of Health and Happiness* (2017)

49 Eckhart Tolle, *The Power of Now, A Guide to Spiritual Enlightenment* ([Novata], California New World Library, 1999)

50 John Kabat-Zinn, Wisdom 2.0 Conference, 2018.

51 Goleman and Davidson, *Altered Traits*, p. 37

52 Thomas J. Peters & Robert H. Waterman, Jr., *In Search of Excellence: Lessons from America's Best-Run Companies* (New York, Harper & Row, 1982)

53 Peters, *In Search of Excellence*, pp.13-16.

54 Ibid.

55 Walter Isaascson, *Steve Jobs* (New York: Simon and Schuster, 2011), p 49.

56 Isaacson, *Steve Jobs*, p. 45.

57 Isaacson, *Steve Jobs,* p. 46.

58 Isaacson, *Steve Jobs,* p.47.

59 Isaacson, *Steve Jobs,* p. 49.

60 Isaacson, *Steve Jobs,* p. 121.

61 Isaacson, *Steve Jobs,* p. 123.

62 Walter Isaacson, "The Real Leadership Lessons of Steve Jobs", *Harvard Business Review,* Volume 90, Number 4, (April 2012): pp. 92-102 [*OR* hbr. org/2012/04/the-real-leadership-lessons-of-steve-jobs/ar/1].

63 forbes.org/2012/04/02/10/leadership-tips-from-steve-jobs-/#386a84f25a02.

64 Grant, Adam, Originals: How Non-Conformists Move the World (Viking, 2016).

65 Grant, *Originals,* at p. 3.

66 Time Magazine Special Edition, *Mindfulness—The New Science of Health and Happiness,* p. 76

67 Wikipedia, "Yoga".

68 Erich Shiffman, *Yoga: The Spirit and Practice of Moving Into Stillness* (NY, Pocket Books, 1996).

69 Ibid.

70 Stephen Cope, *The Wisdom of Yoga: A Seeker's Guide to Extraordinary Living* (NY, Bartam Books, 2006)

71 Cope at p. xiv.'

72 Dale Carnegie, *How To Win Friends and Influence People* (New York: Gallery Books, 1981), p.193.

73 Carnegie, *How to Win Friends,* p. 236.

74 Carnegie, *How to Win Friends,* p. 82.

75 Sheryl Sandberg and Adam Grant, "Option B Facing Adversity, Building Resilience and Finding Joy" (Alfred A. Knopf, New York 2017).

76 Jill Bolte Taylor, *My Stroke of Insight, a Brain Scientist's Personal Journey* (New York: Penguin Publishing, 2008)

77 Deborah Tannen. Ph.D., *You Just Don't Understand* (New York: Balentine Books, 1990).

78 Brené Brown, Ph.D., L.M.S.W., *The Gifts of Imperfection: Let Go of Who You Think You're Supposed to Be and Embrace Who You Are* (Hazelden, 2010).

79 Daniel H. Pink, *Drive: The Surprising Truth About What Motivates Us* (New York: Riverhead Books, 2009), pp. 28-33.

80 Pink, *Drive*, p. 9.

81 Deloitte Touche Tohmatsu Fifth Annual Millenial Survey (Fall of 2015).

82 Pink, *Drive*, p. 170.

83 Pink, *Drive*, pp. 77-81.

84 Pink, *Drive*, pp. 170-173.

85 Oprah Winfrey Show, final episode.

86 Daniel H. Pink, *To Sell Is Human: The Surprising Truth About Moving Others* (New York: Riverhead Books, 2012), p. 3.

87 Pink, *To Sell is Human*, p. 21.

88 Pink, *To Sell Is Human*, p.21.

89 Pink, *To Sell is Human*, pp. 67-154.

90 Pink, *To Sell is Human*. p. 70

91 Id at p. 73

92 Id at p. 75

93 Tindell, Kip with Keegan, Paul and Shilling, Casey, *Uncontainable: How Pas-*

sion, Commitment and Conscious Capitalism Build a Business Where Everyone Thrives (New York: Grand Central Publishing, 2014).

94 Tindell, *Uncontainable*, p. 53.

95 Tindell, *Uncontainable*, p. 190.

96 Deloitte Touche Tohmatsu Limited Fifth Annual Millennial Survey of 7700 millennials from 29 countries in Fall of 2015.

97 Ibid.

98 Ibid.

99 Bell, George, *8 Differences between Gen Z and Millenials,* Huffington Pose (Nov. 6, 2017).

100 Ibid.

101 Kramer, Adam "Experimental Evidence of Massive-Scale Emotional Contagion Through Social Networks." Proceedings of the National Academy of Sciences of the United states of America (17 June 2014).

102 Keith Ferrazzi and Tahl Raz, *Never Eat Alone: And Other Secrets To Success, One Relationship At A Time* (New York: Crown Publishing Group, 2014), p. xiv.

103 Ferrazzi and Raz, p. 30-34.

104 Wayne Kimmel "Six Degrees of Wayne Kimmel" (Wayne Kimmel 2016).

105 Kimmel, *Six Degrees of Wayne Kimmel,* p. 56.

106 Richard Davidson, *The Emotional Life of Your Brain* (New York: Penguin Group, 2013).

107 Oprah Winfrey Network, "Soul to Soul with Legendary NBA Coach Phil Jackson," YouTube video (02:18), posted (June 2013). https://youtu.be/UMhyn-hFDgU8.

108 Phil Jackson and Hugh Delehanty, *Eleven Rings: The Soul of Success* (New York: Penguin Books, 2014), pp 7-8.

109 Jackson and Delehanty, *Eleven Rings,* p. 79.

110 Jackson and Delehanty, *Eleven Rings,* p. 85.

111 Jackson and Delehanty, *Eleven Rings,* pp. 18-19.

112 Jackson and Delehanty, pp. 11-23.

113 Four Noble Truths (Buddhism).

114 https://www.buddhanet.net/e-learning/history/b3schthe.htm

115 https://www.buddhanet.net/e-learning/history/b3schmah.htm

116 https://www.buddhanet.net/e-learning/history/b3schvaj.htm

117 https://www.buddhanet.net/e-learning/history/b3schjap.htm

118 Wikipedia.

119 Mother Theresa, Something Beautiful for God, p. 48.

120   Stephen R. Covey, *The 7 Habits of Highly Effective People: Powerful Lessons In Personal Change* (New York: Simon & Schuster, 2004).

121 Covey, 7 Habits , p. 55.

122 Stephen R. Covey, *The 7 Habits of Highly Effective People: Personal Workbook* (New York: Simon & Schuster, 2003), p. 13.

123 Ibid.

124 Covey, *The 7 Habits Personal Workbook,* p. 14.

125 Ibid.

126 Ibid.

127 Stephen R. Covey, *The 7 Habits of Highly Effective People: Powerful Lessons In Personal Change* (New York: Simon & Schuster, 2004), p. 251.

128 Covey, *The 7 Habits Personal Workbook,* p. 14.

129 Ibid.

130 Stephen Covey, "*The 8th Habit: from Effectiveness to Greatness.*" (New York: Simon & Schuster, p. 3-5).

131 Covey, *8th Habit*, p. 39

132 Covey, *8th Habit*, p. 46

133 Covey, *8th Habit*, p. 50.

134 Wikipedia, Vipassana

135 David Newman, *The Timebound Traveler* (UK, Non-duality Press 2014).

136 David Newman, *The Timebound Traveler*, p. 110.

137 Eckhart Tolle, *Stillness Speaks* (Novato California: New World Library, 2003), p. 1

138 Don Millmand, *The Life you Were Born to Live, A Guide to Finding Your Life Purpose* (California: Kramer Book 1993).

139 Ainslie MacLeod, *The Instruction: Living the Life your Soul Intended* (Colorado: Sounds True, Inc. 2007).

140 David Newman, *The Timebound Traveler*, p. 110.

141 Arianna Huffington, *Thrive: The Third Metric To Redefining Success And Creating A Life Of Well-Being, Wisdom, And Wonder* (New York: Harmony Books, 2015), pp. 2-3.

142 Huffington, *Thrive*, p. 3.

143 Huffington, *Thrive*, p. 1.

144 Huffington, *Thrive*, pp. 38-53.

145 Huffington, *Thrive*, pp. 38-39.

146 Huffington, *Thrive*, p. 39.

147 Huffington, p. *Thrive*, 40.

148 Ibid.

149 Huffington, Thrive, p. 41.

150 Dan Harris, *10% Happier—How I Tamed the Voice in My Head, Reduced Stress Without Losing My Edge, and Found Self-Help That Actually Works—A True Story* (New York: Harper Collins, 2014) pp 1,2.

151 Ibid at pp. 151-156.

152 Huffington, *Thrive*, p. 8.

153 *Live Like You are Dying* written by Tim Nichols and Craig Wiseman (2004).

154 Huffington, *Thrive*, p. 137.

155 Huffington, *Thrive*, p. 137.

156 Huffington, *Thrive*, pp. 228.

157 John C. Maxwell, *The 360 Degree Leader: Developing Influence from Anywhere in the Organization* (Nashville: Thomas Nelson, 2011).

158 Maxwell, *The 360 Degree Leader*, p. 113.

159 Maxwell, *The 360 Degree Leader*, p. 81.

160 Maxwell, *The 360 Degree Leader*, p. 81.

161 Maxwell, *The 360 Degree Leader*, p. 84.

162 Maxwell, *The 360 Degree Leader*, p. 85.

163 Maxwell, *The 360 degree Leader*, p. 21.

164 Maxwell, *The 360 degree Leader*, p. 139.

165 Maxwell, *The 360 Degree Leader*, p. 2.

166 John C. Maxwell, *Sometimes You Win—Sometimes You Learn: Life's Greatest Lessons Are Gained From Our Losses* (New York: Center Street, 2013), 58-64.

167 Maxwell, *Sometimes You Win—Sometimes You Learn*, p.61.

168 Maxwell, *Sometimes You Win—Sometimes You Learn*, p.64

169 Brene Brown, *Daring Greatly, How the Courage to be Vulnerable Transforms the Way We Life, Love, Parent and Lead* (New York: Penguin Group/USA Inc., 2012).

170 John C. Maxwell, Jim Dorman, *Becoming a Person of Influence: How to Positively Impact the Lives of Others* (Nashville Thomas Nelson, 1997).

171 Maxwell, *The 360 Degree Leader*, p. 7.

172 John C. Maxwell, *Think on These Things: Meditation for Leaders* (Kansas City: Beacon Hill, 1979).

173 Maxwell, *Think on These Things*, chapter 28.

174 Robert K. Cooper, *The Other 90%: How To Unlock Your Vast Untapped Potential For Leadership And Life* (New York: Three Rivers Press, 2001), pp. xiv-xv.

175 Cooper, *The Other 90%*, p.8.

176 Cooper, *The Other 90%*, pp. 15-19.

177 Young, Emma, "*Gut Instincts: The Secrets of Your Second Brain.*" New Scientist, 12 December 2012).

178 D. Childre and B. Cryer, *From Chaos to Coherence* (Boston: Butterworth Heinnemann, 1999); J.A. Armour, "Anatomy and Function of the Intrathoracic Neirons Regulatin the Heart", *Reflex Control of the Circulation*, ed. I.H. Zucker and J.P. Gilmore (Boca Raton: CRC Press, 1991); M. Cantin and J. Genest, "The Heart as an Endocrine Gland", *Clinical and Investigative Medicine, Vol. 9, Issue 4 (1986)*" pp. 319-327.

179 Cooper, *The Other 90%*, p. 18.

180 Dr. Paul King, US Berkely Redwood Center for Theoretical Neuroscience.

181 Cooper, *The Other 90%*, p. 26.

182 Cooper, *The Other 90%*, p.39

183 Cooper, *The Other 90%*, p.39

184 Angela Duckworth, *Grit: The Power of Passion and Perseverance* (New York: Schribner, 2016).

185 Angela Duckworth, *Grit*, p.55.

186 Linda Kaplan Thaler & Robin Koval, *Grit to Great*, (New York: Crown Publishing Group, 2015).

187 Linda Kaplan Thaler & Robin Koval, *Grit to Great*, p. 29.

188 Duckworth, *Grit: The Power of Passion and Perseverance*, pp. 42-44.

189 Thaler & Koval, *Grit to Great*, p. 24-25.

190 Sandberg, *Lean In*, p. 53.

191 Demetri Martin, *This is a Book* (New York: Grand Central Publishing, Hatchette Book Group, 2011), p. 130.

192 Duckworth, *Grit: The Power of Passion and Perseverance*, p. 181

193 Duckworth, *Grit: The Power of Passion and Perseverance*, p. 182.

194 Thaler and Koval, *Grit to Great*, p. 72

195 James Baldwin, *Nobody Knows My Name* (New York: Vintage Books 1993), p. 61-62

196 Bill Green, *All In: 101 Real-Life Business Lessons for Emerging Entrepreneurs* (Virginia: Köehler Books, 2017).

197 Bill Green, *All In*, p. 1.

198 Green, *All In*, p. 37.

199 Green, *All In*, p. 40.

200 Green, *All In*, pp. 53, 60 and 67.

201 Yin yoga", Wikipedia, Date Last modified (March 12, 2016), Date Retrieved (August 8, 2016), < https://en.wikipedia.org/wiki/Yin_yoga>.

202 Elena Lytkina Botelho, Kim Rosenkoetter Powell, Stephen Kincaid and Dina Wang, *What Sets Successful CEOs Apart* (Harvard Busines Review, May-June 2017).

203 LN Malcolm Gladwell, *The Tipping Point: How Little Thnks Can Make a Big Difference* (New York: Little Brown & Company Hatchette Books, 2000).

204 Gladwell, *Tipping Point*, p. 9.

205 Gladwell, *Tipping Point*, p. 15.

206 Gladwell, *Tipping Point*, p. 30

207 Gladwell, *Tipping Point*, p. 89.

208 Gladwell, *Tipping Point*, p. 182.

209 Gladwell, *Blink*, p. 8.

210 Martin Seligman and Michael Kahana, *Upacking Intuition: A Conjecture* (University of Pennsylvania).

211 Gladwell, *Blink*, p. 3

212 Gladwell, *Tipping Point*, p. 56.

213 Goleman and Davidson, *Altered Traits*, pp. 46 and 290.

214 Eckhart Tolle, *Stillness Speaks* (Novato California: New World Library, 2003), Introduction.

Acknowledgments

I am grateful to so many people for contributing to the content and production of this book and promotion of the benefits of meditation.

My special thanks to my wonderful wife and soul mate, Stefanie Levine Cohen. At this point in our lives, it is impossible to separate my own original thoughts from hers. We are connected in all respects. I would also like to thank my daughters, Jessica, Maddie and Lizzie, who are wise beyond their years and provide inspiration for our future.

This book would not have been possible without editing and production assistance from Stefanie, my valuable professional assistant, Chris Fenimore, dear friend and stellar editor Debbie Neveleff, summer intern Natalia Queenan, citation checking by Marilyn Hailperin and Eliana Trommer and author support services from Lyn Adelstein and BookBaby.

I have learned so much about meditation and communicating the benefits of meditation from the Meditation4Leadership leadership team of Lisa Berg Jacobs, Alex Schimmel, Lisa Greenberg Gonzalez, Tom Drury, Marilyn Hailperin, Scott Rosen, Stefanie Levine Cohen and Elizabeth Mell, our sage meetings with Awake at Work pioneer, Michael Carroll and the many yoga and meditation teachers with whom I have had the privilege to practice.

I have learned so much about leadership from the hundreds of entrepreneurs and business leaders with whom I have been fortunate to work, including the following mentioned or referred to in this book: Al Altomari, Jeff Becker, Ian Berg, Lori Braunstein, Aaron Davenport, Tom Drury, Mark Galant, Jeff Ginsberg, Steve Goodman, Jamshid Keynejad, Bari Krein, Steven Krein, Wayne Kimmel, Greg Mayes, Jami Wintz McKeon, Matt Miller, Fran Milone, Jack Norris, Barry Siadat, Unity Stokes and Scott Zucker. There are many others who are equally inspirational but where noting their individual strengths or positive impression on me was not necessary to make a point in this book.

I also want to thank my early readers who provided valuable input and encouragement to continue the journey including: Ferial Abbas, Rabbi Richard Address, Amanda Bruno, Rhonda Clarke, Michele Coffey, Fred and Anita Cohen, Alan Cohn, Charlie Engros, Carol Hupping Fisher, Ron Fenska, Rick Forman, Natalie Franzblau, Marilyn Hailperin, Gwen and Michael Levy, Margie and Malcolm Levine, Elizabeth Mell and Reena Meltzer.

This is an ongoing process. I would love to hear your feedback, particularly your personal stories of how meditation has made you more effective. I can be reached at steven.cohen@meditation4leadership.org.

ABOUT MEDITATION4LEADERSHIP

Meditation4Leadership, Inc. is a not-for-profit business focused on promoting the widespread adoption of the discipline of meditation as an approach to enhancing leadership skill. The company targets business, not-for-profit and community leaders, with the goal of both communicating the broad-based benefits of a daily meditation practice, and teaching the methodologies required to develop such a practice.

The company's work is based on *Leading From Within: A Guide to Maximizing Your Effectiveness Through Meditation.* The book includes an informative analysis of core leadership traits as espoused by some of the country's best known business leaders. This analysis identifies and groups 13 key leadership traits into four cornerstone "Pillars" for effective leadership. The book then describes in detail how specific meditation practices serve to improve, strengthen and enliven the Pillars, leading to significantly enhanced leadership skills.

The company offers a variety of programs including lectures, workshop series, one-on-one coaching and multi-day retreats designed to introduce and train participants in the development of sustainable and results-oriented meditation practices.

Meditation4Leadership also supports and promotes other organizations spreading the value derived from meditation and yoga practice.

For more information regarding Meditation4Leadership, please contact Lisa Jacobs, President, at lisajacobs@meditation4leadership.org or visit our website at www.meditation4leadership.org.